HAUNTED MINNESOTA

by Hugh E. Bishop

Lake Superior Port Cities Inc.

First Edition: June 2006

LAKE SUPERIOR PORT CITIES INC.
P.O. Box 16417
Duluth, Minnesota 55816-0417 USA
888-BIG LAKE (888-244-5253)
www.lakesuperior.com

Publishers of *Lake Superior Magazine* and *Lake Superior Travel Guide*

5 4 3 2 1

Library of Congress Cataloging-in-Publication Data

Bishop, Hugh E., 1940-
    Haunted Minnesota / by Hugh E. Bishop. – 1st ed.
        p. cm.
    Includes bibliographical references and index.
    ISBN 0-942235-71-1
    1. Ghosts – Minnesota. 2. Haunted places – Minnesota. I. Title.

BF1472.U6B566 2006
133.109776 – dc22   2006040987

Printed in the United States of America

Editors: Paul L. Hayden, Konnie LeMay
Book Design: Mathew Pawlak
Cover Design & Illustrations: Joy Morgan Dey
Printer: Sheridan Books, Chelsea, Michigan

Dedication

For Liz, a most enduring good spirit.

A Few Minnesota Cities –
Haunted and Otherwise

Roseau
International Falls
Crookston
Red Lake
Babbitt
Grand Marais
Chisholm • Eveleth
Bemidji
Hibbing
Hoyt Lakes
Schroeder
Cohasset • Coleraine Brimson
Silver Bay
Grand Rapids
Two Harbors
Moorhead
Cloquet
Duluth
McGregor
Brainerd
Moose Lake
Fergus Falls
Little Falls
Alexandria
Hinckley
Sauk Rapids
Milaca
Collegeville
Dalbro
Paynesville
St. Cloud
Mississippi River
Wilmar
Minneapolis
St. Paul
Stillwater
Hutchinson
Hastings
Marshall
Chaska
Red Wing
New Ulm
Northfield
Faribault
Winona
Mankato
Brewster
Rochester
Fairmont
Austin
Luverne
Albert Lea

Table of Contents

Introduction

Greetings from the world of the weird and eerie in Minnesota! Our fair state is blessed, or some might say cursed, with an abundance of stories of unusual, supernatural or paranormal occurrences and presences. Be it tales of malevolent spirits, little gray men from somewhere else, giant bipeds of indeterminate intent or gentle ghosties that seem determined to do someone good, Minnesota can't be topped.

Collected in these pages are some of the more interesting or bizarre stories that I discovered from a number of sources. With a plethora of tales out there, I've exercised an author's privilege in which of those many tales to include here. Basically, I winnowed out those I found to be completely far-fetched or poorly supported by multiple sightings or by paranormal investigations. Those that have been included in earlier books carried more weight than those coming from a single, unsubstantiated source.

Some of the stories reported here come from personal interviews (mainly by telephone) that I was able to conduct with the folks who experienced the events themselves. Others are contained in earlier volumes that I used for research. I will warn researchers to beware of Website reports that cannot be substantiated in other sources. One of the first Websites I came across by Googling "Minnesota ghosts" was www.shadowlands.net. With 20 pages of short entries in the Minnesota link, I thought I'd discovered the mother lode of ghostly lore. Unfortunately, that enthusiasm was suddenly dashed when, within a few entries, an unattributed entry for the town of Aurora raised my immediate skepticism, since I have personal knowledge about the location that did not support the Website entry.

East Mesabi High School in Aurora, Minnesota, is reported on that Website to be haunted by spirits of three or more students killed in a horrific 1977 fire. Since I lived in that school district from 1975 to 1983 while employed at the former Erie Mining Company in nearby Hoyt Lakes, I can categorically state that there was no such fire at East Mesabi in that time frame (or any other that I can find). Indeed, as a freelance reporter working for the local newspaper, I spent many hours in the building during evening meetings, recording school board actions and, while some of *those* actions were a little scary, there was never any sense of supernatural or paranormal activity in the building, and I never heard such a tale from anyone I ever talked to in that area.

Thus, a warning to those surfing the net for their ration of ghostly tales. Do not take reports from a single Internet source at face value, since the above instance is one that obviously sprung from someone's overheated imagination rather than from the great beyond. It is also unfortunately true that this falsehood is proliferating on the Internet, as other paranormal Websites copy and paste the Shadowlands tales and post them on their own sites without substantiating the veracity of those stories. The Web is a reasonable starting point to discover what tales are "out there," but, if you're looking for genuine tales of paranormal or supernatural occurrences, it's worth a bit of additional searching to discover new or corroborating material edifying the story.

As much as possible, I checked postings by paranormal research groups like Minnesota Paranormal Study Group or the several regional Minnesota Paranormal Investigation Groups for reports on their investigations of a story. I was sometimes disappointed to find that they are not as useful as one would think in researching paranormal activities. Gina Teel's 2001 *Ghost Stories of Minnesota* also fulfilled a substantiating role for a number of these tales. Footnoting cites where tales from her volume are paraphrased. Otherwise, I simply cross-checked to ensure that her version corroborated the facts as I discovered them.

A disappointment that a serious researcher will encounter with most books of the paranormal is lack of footnoting and indexing to provide quick references for particular information being sought. I have scrupulously footnoted and indexed the information contained in this volume, but because previous writers failed to do so, I can only cite the source I used, rather than the earliest sources from which some of these stories are drawn. I had to comb through a lot of unused material to select these tales and I believe that their sources are worth noting and documenting and give them greater validity. I would encourage future tellers of such tales to likewise take the time and effort to similarly document their sources.

While the stories related here are barely the tip of the iceberg as far as reports of supernatural presences in Minnesota, I have selected them because each seems to me to carry a certain weight of credibility. In some cases, that weight comes from the fact that solid, sensible people are reporting on strange occurrences they have experienced. Often, these tales are recounted in a number of credible sources. In a few instances, the stories gain credibility because a number of similar reports were forthcoming over a long period by more than one observer. I have also often given greater credibility to reports by people who are willing to be identified, because it's one thing to tell a story anonymously, but quite another to put your name on it for all to identify.

Many intriguing stories have not been included here simply because they are too vague or too recent to readily identify their basis. Such a recent tale was told on Minnesota Public Radio in 2000, involving the possible haunting of Minneapolis' Foshay Tower. Security guard Julie Canny reported having a strong sense of a ghostly presence. In fact, she claimed to have actually glimpsed the specter, describing the sighting thusly: "There was one night when I was working on a floor and I turned around, and it was like a shadow of a man and he darted around the corner. That was about the best manifestation I ever saw."

Mort Levy, the operator of the museum on the top floor of the Foshay, is a historian and guide. He claims to be skeptical of reports of hauntings. He does admit that people love to tell stories and there are unusual incidents that might spur such stories – like the sole elevator to the 30th floor making an unscheduled stop along the way, the doors opening with no one there. "When that happens, I jokingly tell people that Wilbur Foshay's ghost must want to get on."[1]

Whether Julie Canny's observance of a shadowy Foshay figure will manifest itself to others will determine if this possible haunting gains validity or not. That is for the future to tell.

Meanwhile, I have confidence in the stories I tell here because I have confidence that the sources used are as reliable as I could find. As much as possible, I present the information with very little embellishment, since embroidering facts puts a writer in jeopardy of warping those facts or simply getting them wrong.

I hope you have fun with this book, since that is the "spirit" in which I worked on it and put it together. If I've accomplished an interesting read for you, both of us should feel happy at this result.

Happy reading and – oh brrrrr. Is that a passing cold spot we feel?

Hugh E. Bishop
May 2006

CHAPTER 1

Earliest Forces
of This Land

From the earliest times in Minnesota, spiritual forces were known and recognized by the native people who long preceded the arrival of non-native people. For example, a very early group of inhabitants are known as the "mound builders" and it's believed that the ritual burial of their dead brethren in large mounds was connected in some unknown way to the religion that they practiced.

Considerably after the mound builders, the Ojibway succeeded in driving the Sioux (Lakota/Dakota) out of the northern reaches of Minnesota by about 1700. Having migrated from the east over a period of several hundred years and occupying all of the northern reaches of the state by the time the earliest French explorers arrived, the Ojibway practiced a rather elaborate religion, but one of their strongest beliefs was that their forested lands were inhabited by an evil, ghostly white 15-foot-tall spirit they called the windigo. Feeding only on the flesh of unfortunate people who encountered it, the windigo's appetite for human flesh could never be sated because, as it ate, it grew larger and its appetite increased apace. The Ojibway also applied the same name to anyone who was known or suspected to have eaten human flesh, either as a result of insanity or to avoid starvation.[1] Likely as a result of their preoccupation with the windigo, Ojibway lore contains a number of tales of human windigo cannibalism into the mid-1800s and there is at least one story of a spiritual windigo being sighted by Native Americans in the Roseau area as late as the 1920s. The sighting of that windigo always presaged a local death.

Meanwhile, the Siouan people who inhabited the southern half of Minnesota told of a war they fought against a tribe of giants that attempted to move into Sioux territory. The giants are believed to have been the remnant population of an eastern tribe called the Alliigwe, who were driven westward out of Pennsylvania and Ohio by the Lenni Lenape people, the ancestors of the Ojibway and a number of other northern and eastern tribal groups. Sioux lore states that the giants were of fearsome stature, but were discovered to be cowardly in battle and were soundly defeated by the Sioux.

Lest we give too little credence to these prehistoric tales, we should remember that most stories that are passed down orally from generation to generation are usually learned and passed down word for word, tending to remain faithful to the original telling. I explore both the windigo and Alliigwe legends a bit more in Chapter 5 of this volume.

Both the Sioux and Ojibway religions, though quite different, are strongly spiritual, but they do converge in reverence for nature and the importance it plays in their everyday existence. At least among early Ojibway, a talisman from nature was often among their most revered possessions. Pieces of native copper, in particular, were believed to be particularly powerful and might be passed down for generations – or might be left with the deceased to accompany the spirit to their paradise.

By the late 1600s, French fur traders were moving into Minnesota, making contact first with the Ojibway, but shortly with the Sioux as well. With the voyageurs came the black-robed Jesuit missionaries, who piously and tenaciously sought to convert the "pagans" they encountered in the wilderness to Christianity. At least nominally among the Ojibway, their early efforts did bear fruit and substantial numbers of Ojibway "Christians" were baptized by the missionaries. The Sioux were a different story.

But the timing of the sightings of the Roseau windigo in the 1920s seem to raise at least some question about just how deeply the Ojibway adoption of Christianity might have been. The native people in that border country were in sporadic contact with white missionaries for nearly 200 years by that point, yet their belief in the windigo's evil existence remained strong enough that they related sightings well into the 20th century and noted the evil that such sightings presaged. It may more likely be true that the Ojibway as with other native people simply added the "white man's" religion to their own.

The influence of the Jesuits in North America waned after the French were defeated by the English in the French and Indian War of the late 1750s, but was also undermined by dissension within the Church in Europe and the rising tide of Protestantism. Without the support and protection of France's monarch, mission efforts by the Jesuits declined and Protestant missionaries eventually moved into the area to try and make up for their late entry in the field. By the mid-1800s, a number of Protestant mission societies and church groups were placing dedicated missionaries in the Upper Midwest, but non-Jesuit American Catholic missionaries like Father Frederic Baraga were also extremely active in attempting to build on the earlier groundwork with tribal people that the Jesuits accomplished.

By the mid-1800s, too, the tidal wave of non-Indian settlers was under way, in some cases spurred on by missionaries like Father Francis X. Pierz, who almost singlehandedly promoted Stearns County in central Minnesota to the German Catholic immigrant farmers that predominated in settling that area.

The recently arriving Minnesotans soon discovered, however, that there were forces in this land that required grave consideration and jeopardized their efforts to settle in this land – severe winter cold, devastating tornados in summer warmth and howling blizzards in winter cold, hailstorms of monumental destructive capability, floods covering entire townships, forest fires that roared over them with terrifying speed and ruination, not to mention crop failures from drought and swarms of voracious locusts that darkened the sky and ate the wood of farm buildings if other forage was not available.

For those of us who live in the great state of Minnesota today, we need only ponder the relatively recent immobilizing effect wrought by the Halloween blizzard of 1991 to recognize that such natural forces have a dramatic effect on all who live here. While the Halloween blizzard took few lives, history records thousands of Minnesotans who have lost their lives in tornados, blizzards, forest fires, floods, epidemics and other natural disasters. Two of the worst natural disasters may illustrate how devastating such events are.

On April 14, 1886, a giant funnel cloud formed southwest of St. Cloud, roaring through the heart of that city and racing northeasterly across the Mississippi River to also shatter Sauk Rapids. It then raced onward to the north and east through the villages of Buckman and Pierz, before spending its force at Sullivan Lake just west of Lake Mille Lacs. In its wake, 72 victims either lay dead or would shortly die of injuries from the twister. An additional

213 injuries, many life threatening, are also recorded. Perhaps most poignant from a human standpoint, 11 members of a wedding party were killed when the rural home of Charles Schultz was destroyed about four miles south of the village of Rice. Included was the bridegroom, Henry Friday.

The tornado destroyed a total of 109 businesses and homes, valued at $290,000 of 1886 currency. Entire sections of the two major cities were razed by the funnel and the power of the twister is illustrated by the fact that a safe weighing a ton was apparently picked up and carried across a street in Sauk Rapids, leaving no trace or track between where it started and where it was dropped. An oak log 14-feet long and a foot in diameter was picked up in the St. Cloud railyard and dropped near the Rice Station, about a dozen miles away. Destruction marked nearly the entire 60-mile path of the storm. It remains the single worst tornado in the state's history.[2]

As my second example of nature's fury unleashed, we again turn to the latter 1880s when, on January 12, 1888, a monster blizzard blanketed most of the state in deep snow and drifts that seemed to reach to the skies. A blizzard is defined as a storm delivering heavy snowfall driven by high winds and accompanied by frigid temperatures. Every Minnesotan recognizes a blizzard as an extremely dangerous storm that quickly kills anyone unprepared for the elements. The term was first used to describe these storms by the Esterville, Iowa, *Vindicator* newspaper to describe an 1870 storm. It was originally a boxing term to describe a volley of punches.

As with numerous reports of other historic blizzards, the day of the 1888 storm dawned as a pleasant and mild winter day. The kids were off to school and adults happily busied themselves with outdoor tasks that had been delayed by severe cold the previous several weeks.

Suddenly, shortly after noon, an extreme wave of cold blew in on fierce winds that also delivered blinding snow. The temperature quickly dropped to minus 37 degrees F. and the winds continued to rage with whirling snow.

Teachers, realizing that worse was yet to come, released students to walk home from the many one-room schoolhouses – a major blunder, since many of those youngsters perished in the blizzard's furies. Indeed, the storm has come to be called "the children's blizzard" for the many pupils who died.

Raging through the afternoon, into the night and the following day, the storm was unremitting to anyone caught in an exposed situation. Farmers attempting to tend their livestock became disoriented by the wind-driven snow and were lost, some perishing within sight of their homes.

The final death toll of the blizzard was 200 souls, and this storm remains the deadliest in Minnesota history and among the worst recorded anywhere.[3]

While these two examples of deadly natural forces gives us an idea of what nature is capable of wreaking, I'd be remiss if I didn't also point to two monster forest fires that have come to be named for the two largest cities they devastated, the Hinckley and Cloquet fires. Their combined total of an estimated 800 to more than 1,000 deaths ranks them as the deadliest disasters in Minnesota history. That death toll could have been considerably higher but for heroic actions by many people who were either only briefly honored or whose deeds went unidentified in the immediate aftermath of the fires.

Considering that natural disasters have caused the deaths of thousands of Minnesotans, what explains the curious fact that there are few stories of hauntings by those who lost their lives in such devastating calamities? Indeed, I only discovered a couple of ghostly tales from natural disasters. The first dates from an 1873 blizzard that killed 70 people and remains one of the worst ever recorded in the state.

January 7, 1873, dawned as a lovely winter day, unusually mild and pleasant, according to Ruth D. Hein's *More Ghostly Tales from Minnesota.*

Farmer John Weston left his Nobles County homestead in southwestern Minnesota to get a load of wood in the Graham Lakes area in the northeastern corner of the county. The nice weather gave no clue of what he would encounter once the wood was loaded and he prodded his oxen for home.

Around noon, a white wall descended on the area from the northwest, whipped by high winds as the temperature plummeted. Despite the blinding storm, the farmer managed to find his property and drove the ox team and sled across the land searching for the warmth and security of home. Unfortunately, despite circling twice, he missed the house and turned more northerly, back toward the direction from which he'd come. Finding no refuge from the storm's fury and frigid temperatures, he unhitched and abandoned his oxen – who wandered aimlessly before the yoke turned on their necks and strangled the animals.

Walking southward with the northwesterly winds, Weston plodded 12 miles toward Hersey (Brewster today) before deepening snow in tall grass tripped him and he fell face downward. Exhausted, he had little chance of survival under these conditions, and he succumbed to the brutal storm in a short while.

The storm raged on for three days before word of the missing farmer could be spread. Search parties found his sled loaded with wood, the dead oxen, but no sign of John Weston. It would be three long winter months before his remains were located – and thereby hangs the ghostly portion of this drama, as first reported by A.P. Miller in the *Worthington Advance* newspaper of January 13, 1881.

According to that report, Weston's good friend and neighbor, D.J. Cosper, was a member of that first unsuccessful search party, but the spiritual aspect of this story occurred late in the day after that first search effort. Cosper was doing evening chores and was headed to the well to get water for his horses. Suddenly, he spotted John Weston coming toward him on the path, but thought nothing of it at that moment. Everything seemed normal, as Weston cordially greeted him.

Cosper's response was reported to be, "Why, Weston, I thought you were frozen to death!"

Weston is said to have answered, "I am, and you'll find my body a mile-and-a-half northwest of Hersey."

He disappeared and, after a moment, Cosper went on with his evening routine, realizing that he had seen the ghost of his friend. He openly told the story to others, who believed him.

But the ghost of John Weston was not simply satisfied to reveal the place of his death. His wife, Mary, revealed that on the second night of the storm she heard a knock on the door, but ignored it at first. A second rapping got her attention and she shouted, "What do you want?"

In her own words, she told the story thusly: "Someone said, 'Did you know that John was frozen to death?'

"The voice sounded like my brother's. Our son heard it too and said from his bed, 'Mother, did Uncle say Pa was frozen to death?'"

Mary went to the door, but no one was there, and there were no tracks in the snow to indicate that anyone at all had been in that area of the house. Like Cosper, she also told her story to others, who deduced that John Weston had returned in spirit to let his wife know of his death, using the voice of his brother-in-law to avoid frightening his family.

When the snow melted in April, a search was conducted in the vicinity where the specter had indicated his body lay, and John Weston's remains were found exactly where he had told his friend Cosper they would be – a mile-and-a-half northwest of Hersey.[4]

6

The only other story I discovered derives from a natural disaster that occurred after the October 13, 1918, forest fire overwhelmed the Moose Lake area and ferociously devoured everything in its path. It was told to Gina Teel by Moose Lake area historian Walt Lower.

According to Lower, the Lund family lived on a farm outside of Moose Lake and as the fire approached they made preparations to protect their property. Two of their children, a boy and girl ran past them, saying they were going to Moose Lake, where the lake's water would protect them. But the fire was moving faster than the children could run and they were never seen again. The flames apparently consumed their bodies in the wooded area where they were believed to have perished, because no remains were ever recovered.

As the years passed, the surviving Lunds passed on and the farm was purchased by new owners. Those folks had not yet heard the story of the dead children when they told Walt Lower their story, but said that they believed they are not alone on the farm and that they often felt the presence of other people. They also said that they hear strange sounds at night and at times something seems to be trying to open locked doors.[5]

Since the ghostly activities reported by the current owners do not identify any specific source of the haunting, might we infer that they are the lost Lund children still trying to rejoin their family circle? Or, conversely, might the noises and ghostly presences be the efforts of one or both of their parental spirits attempting to locate and embrace the spiritual remains of their long dead children?

However that may be, our earlier question remains. With thousands of lives ended in naturally induced tragedies in Minnesota, why do I find so few ghostly tales from those tragedies? Wouldn't the circumstances of some of those deaths have given rise to more than just this handful of disquieted spirits wandering the unhappy locale of their demise?

As the ensuing chapters document, Minnesota is amply endowed with ghostly presences deriving from a wide range of manmade causes. Do the few hauntings reported from natural causes mean that the uneasy spirits from such circumstances are somehow neutralized or negated by the nature of their dying? Or were the deaths of their worldly beings so logical that they simply passed into the light without question? Perhaps hauntings are the result of more "unnatural" acts, with natural occurrences having less effect on the future potential of a haunting spirit.

As with nearly all paranormal encounters, the more we seek rational answers, the more likely we are to face additional questions – questions that simply elude our earthly understanding. What is the nature of the supernatural? Can a ghost exert enough energy to truly endanger human life? Is the "light" that is frequently alluded to in ghostly lore indeed a portal to paradise? How might we judge the good or evil nature of a haunting?

As you move into the rest of this volume, you may keep these and other questions in mind, and may find clues to better understand the supernatural world in this haunted Minnesota.

CHAPTER 2

Haunts of Public Places

If we can believe the evidence of ghostly encounters that is presented, it seems that a goodly number of specters prefer to make themselves known in public places like theaters, museums, bustling businesses and government buildings. Theaters and museums seem especially prone to house ghostly presences that either return or simply refuse to leave their former digs, with seemingly any older building housing one or the other operation claiming its share of ghosts.

For example, in far southwestern Rock County, the Palace Theater in Luverne is said to be home to the spirits of Herman and Maude Jochims. Herman had the theater built in 1915 at a cost of $50,000, opening the beautiful building in September of that year. A year or two later, Maude came on the scene as the pianist for the silent movies that were shown at that time. In addition to the movies, the theater hosted operatic and dramatic productions, a variety of traveling shows and would later be converted for talkies.

In 1919, Herman and Maude were married. Maude eventually became organist for the theater when a pipe organ was installed, faithfully producing the music that set the mood for whatever was happening on the screen.

Eventually both Herman and Maude passed away, but were not content to pass on. Apparently, if numerous stories by actors, patrons and workers at the theater are to be believed, Herman likes to watch over things from his favorite vantage point on the balcony. Maude, meanwhile, appears to return to her former perch at the organ in the orchestra pit.

   Nothing of a malicious nature has been ascribed to either of the apparitions, although there have been reports of objects mysteriously being moved, broken or lost. One actor reported that a prop he was to pluck from a coffee table during a live performance simply vanished. It had been there the night before and at every rehearsal before that.

   It's speculated that the ghostly couple hopes to keep some control over what happens in the building they occupied for so long. Maude apparently on occasion can be heard playing the organ and Herman seems to enjoy sitting in his balcony seat listening to the music she makes. But Herman isn't the only one hearing that spectral music, for restoration work in the 1990s silenced the organ, yet janitors heard the sound of its music in the theater. Workers closing the building late at night have also heard snatches of music as they tend to their late-night chores.

A night janitor is reported to have heard classical music as he finished closing up the building, noting that there also seemed to be someone or something turning out lights ahead of him. "I get out of here as fast as I can when I'm alone at night. Nobody hangs around here long after the lights go down," he told Ruth D. Hein for her 1999 book, *More Ghostly Tales from Minnesota*.[1]

The old Guthrie Theater in Minneapolis was without question the premiere stage operation in Minnesota, founded by Sir Tyrone Guthrie, whose desire was to establish a new kind of theater to encourage the production of great works of literature and cultivate actors' talents away from the more commercial environment of Broadway. The Guthrie Theater first opened its doors on May 7, 1963, with a production of "Hamlet," with George Grizzard playing the lead. The classic was directed by Tyrone Guthrie himself. Immediately, the theater gained world acclaim for its thrust stage, two-thirds of which was surrounded by the audience, and for other innovative theatrical devices built into it.

The Guthrie was also reported by many different sources to have been haunted for a number of years by the ghost of an usher who committed suicide while employed at the establishment.

Said to be a loner and somewhat of a misfit, Richard Miller attended classes at the University of Minnesota and eked out his living from meager wages at the Guthrie. Loneliness and despair apparently deepened, until Miller finally walked into a Sears store on Saturday, February 5, 1967, purchased a pistol and ammunition and went back to his car in the store parking lot. Here, he put the gun to his head and shot himself, dying instantly. His body would be discovered the following Monday, still dressed in his Guthrie usher's uniform. No one had apparently missed him after his death.

Within just a few weeks of his death, theater patrons in his formerly assigned section complained to management about the distraction of an usher constantly walking back and forth during the shows. Describing the miscreant, their stories identified Miller exactly, including a large mole on the phantom's cheek. The apparition was said to follow patrons with his eyes or by moving its head, but did not speak or make a sound.

The ghost of Richard Miller is thought to have been banished by a 1994 exorcism performed at the theater. If so, the ghost of the lonely, tragic young man with nowhere else to go apparently found one.[2]

A proud, new $125 million three-stage Guthrie Theater was scheduled for completion in June 2006 to replace the original.

Owned by the Walker Art Center, the original building was to be razed to make way for a Walker Center sculpture garden, but efforts were under way by preservationists to save the original structure as this was being written. That effort might cause some of us to ask, "Where is the spirit of Richard Miller, when his help might be useful?"

Not to be outdone by its crosstown rival, St. Paul's historic Fitzgerald Theater, which has been home to Garrison Keillor's "Prairie Home Companion" on public radio, is said also to be home to a variety of spectors, the most active of whom is called Ben and who made his presence known when the theater was being renovated in 1985. He continues to plague performers and workers with unexplained cold spots, dusty and empty muscatel wine bottles and a shadowy presence in shadowy recesses of the building.

The Fitzgerald hauntings are nearly as ubiquitous on the Internet as the Guthrie wraith, and both are also recorded in Gina Teel's 2001 *Ghost Stories of Minnesota*.[3]

While the identity of the ghost of the Guthrie was well established, the one said to inhabit the Hibbing High School Auditorium is much more nebulous.

Built in 1922, the auditorium is an exuberant expression of the use of mining taxes in furthering local institutions during that period. Ornate, spectacular in many respects and sporting crystal chandeliers crafted by a small shop in southern Europe that are said to be worth millions of dollars, the auditorium was refurbished to its original glory in the late 1970s.

But for generations of users and patrons, there has been the persistent legend that the auditorium is also graced by something that seems to prefer seat J47. Commonly, the ghost is attributed to stage director Bill Ratican, who was hired away from Broadway in the 1920s and worked at the facility until the 1960s. Legend tells that he died from a chandelier falling on him or by falling from the stage into the orchestra pit. Both legends are untrue, as are most others attributing deaths in the auditorium. The only confirmed death there is recorded as a handicapped girl during the 1970s, and no ghost story identifies such an apparition – just the persistent story of the aging gentleman who haunts the backstage dressing rooms or is seated in the infamous J47.

The Northern Minnesota Paranormal Investigation Group has investigated the haunting and reports finding substantial evidence of several entities there, depending both on stories by credible witnesses and on video, photography and use of taped electronic voice phenomena (EVP) equipment to record sounds that aren't audible to normal hearing.

Nonetheless, one cannot but wonder who or what it is that is haunting this beautiful facility. Perhaps just the spirits of folks who found extreme pleasure in the auditorium and want to continue that pleasure long after they could otherwise cross over into the great light beyond.[4]

While there is no whisper of anything evil in the reports connected with the Hibbing Auditorium ghosts, it is a matter of fact that high school sophomore theater lover Michael "Mickey" Kelly was killed in a tragic two-car collision on icy roads in January 2005. At grief meetings for students after his death, a fellow thespian shared the story of his and Mickey's "run in" with a ghost in one of the dressing rooms during rehearsals for a school theater production.[5]

While I could go on almost endlessly telling of haunted theaters, I need to move on and discuss apparitions in other types of public spaces.

Museums are the other category of public facility that seem to draw inordinate numbers of hauntings. This likely stems from the fact that many are housed in buildings that are historic in their own right and therefore have existed for long periods in which former inhabitants would become comfortable – perhaps too comfortable from the standpoint of those who must endure their presence in the present.

The Pipestone County Museum in southwestern Minnesota, for example, is located in the old city hall, but includes space that also apparently served in earlier history as a doctor's office. In the museum itself, a number of museum workers and patrons have seen a small blonde girl flitting about in a blue 19th century dress and white apron. In addition, employees and guests have reported loud noises like heavy footsteps and stomping upstairs when no one was there. There are also reports that a number of people have heard the long deceased doctor working in his office, which is located upstairs off a library. Papers shuffle, a chair squeaks and there are sounds quite consistent with offices, even though no one is ever there.[6]

In south Central Minnesota, the Le Sueur County Museum is likewise reported to be haunted, as a number of employees have said they hear voices talking but find no one around when they go to investigate the mysterious conversations. Museum artifacts also seem to have a life of their own, as an antique typewriter started typing by itself and in another instance an ancient record player started playing a song from a long gone repertoire with no one near it.

13

Three employees working after hours on the second floor at the museum heard the small service bell ring downstairs. They were surprised because they knew the building was secured at closing, so all three trooped downstairs not knowing what to expect. Nothing or no one was there and the bell stood starkly alone where it normally would be. Nothing was near it and there was no evidence of anything that could have made it ring.

In another unexplainable incident, two employees were working on the ground floor when they heard a loud crash in the basement. They went down to investigate the cause of the noise. There is a bathroom in the basement that is never used, and after checking around, they concluded that the crash had been the toilet seat being slammed down, since they agreed that it was normally left up and they found it to be down after that crash. But who, or what, would have caused it to crash down? And who, or what, was demanding service by ringing that little bell? And what sort of force would activate an antique typewriter or an old record player?[7]

Judging from the toilet seat incident, we might conclude that the unseen presence is feminine, since nearly every man in America knows how women complain when toilet seats are left in the up position. There is little else in these infrequent manifestations, however, that gives any clue to who the ghost might have been. Museum staff can but wonder, too, what goings-on occur in the building during the five months when the museum is closed and their ghost has free run of the house.

Although staff until recently refused to talk about it, the elegant Glensheen Historic Estate in Duluth is another museum property that has been identified as the haunt of at least one spiritual resident. Identified only recently by an employee as a lady in a blue dress, the observer's report came to the author secondhand from a member of her family, since the museum staff member was under some restraints about revealing her perception at the time.

Certainly, the brutal events of late June 1977 were enough to create a troubled spirit, but do not in any way point to the identity of this specter.

On that fateful day in 1977, the feeble, 83-year-old Elisabeth Congdon was smothered in her bed upstairs at Glensheen. Her night nurse, Velma Pietala, was bludgeoned to death in a hallway outside Elisabeth's bedroom. Police and the district attorney came to the conclusion that Elisabeth's son-in-law, Roger Caldwell, had surreptitiously traveled to Duluth from Colorado to commit the crime, which would free up a handsome inheritance for his wife, Marjorie Congdon Caldwell.

Roger was arrested, convicted and served a year in jail before his conviction was overturned. Marjorie beat prosecution as an accomplice to murder. Marjorie would later be convicted for arson in another case and served about 10 years in prison. Roger would later confess to the murders, was sentenced to the time he'd already served and committed suicide in 1988.

Regardless of the notoriety of the murders and the subsequent legal proceedings, those events were never discussed by staff at Glensheen after it became a University of Minnesota-Duluth museum property. And certainly, no nonsense like a story of a ghost in the magnificent mansion would be condoned during public tours of the building. That no stories of ghosts come down from the era when the facility served as home to the Congdon family is not surprising, since patriarch Chester Congdon would not have been a man to abide such nonsense concerning the estate that he had constructed to showcase his wealth and prestige among the Duluth monied elite.

Thus, the mystery of who that lady in the blue dress might have been in her lifetime comes to us as just that – a mystery. Certainly, the first suspicion would be that it is the restless spirit of one of the murder victims, but our observer didn't report any perception of age or physical characteristics that would help establish the identity – just the presence of an ethereal lady in blue.

The Glensheen worker remains firm, however, in her assertion that she indeed encountered an apparitional being that could not have been any mortal person.[8]

As somewhat of an update to this story, the University has loosened its grip on what workers at the mansion may discuss with people on the tours, but that may or may not include talking about encounters with spiritual beings.

Just a short drive east of Glensheen Estate is another public structure that has been identified by at least four people as having a ghostly inhabitant. The Two Harbors Lighthouse, while one of the most historic sites in northeastern Minnesota, is not a museum but has become the property of the Lake County Historical Society, which has renovated the lightkeeper's quarters into a bed-and-breakfast inn. The light remains an active aid to navigation and many B&B guests are especially intrigued by the opportunity to stay in this historic operating lighthouse. (The guests are designated as keepers for the night.)

Built in 1892, eight years after the first Minnesota iron ore was shipped from the Vermilion Iron Range through Two Harbors, the station not only provides lighted guidance to mariners, but a fog horn could be heard for up to six to eight miles during the frequent fogs that Lake Superior generates along Minnesota's north shore. Today, the fog signal's volume is considerably lower and directionally pointed to the lake. During the century that it served strictly as a light station, nothing has been recorded of a haunting there, but shortly after the inn opened there were a number of tales of "something funny" there. Such stories seem to arise inevitably in association with lighthouses, so not much was made of the reports.

But it would be Jeanne Hatch's story that would seem to nail down the probability that the spirit of someone yet lingers in the historic structure. Not one given to wild flights of fantasy, Jeanne is a responsible member of the Minnesota Historical Society staff in St. Paul.

Jeanne, husband Mike and his parents, Arlene and Bill, reserved two of the three rooms for Friday and Saturday nights shortly after the B&B opened.

As they settled in comfortably Friday evening, everything seemed just right. The third couple were honeymooners, adding a bit more romance to the atmosphere. They all retired to their second floor guest rooms at a reasonable hour and the inn settled into peaceful quiet, with just the occasional splash of a wave against the lakeshore creating tranquility.

Sometime later, Jeanne was wakened by a din that seemed to originate from the kitchen area on the first floor. It sounded like pots and pans rattling, and she distinctly heard an unusual sound that she later identified as a knife scraping against the metal tabletop in the kitchen. Annoyed that the innkeeper was so inattentive to the comfort of the guests, she decided to take advantage of her wakefulness for a trip to the bathroom. There, she looked out the window and was surprised to find pitch blackness outside. Surely, it was nowhere near dawn and therefore much too early for all the racket that the innkeeper was making.

She returned to bed and glanced at the bedside clock, whose digital dial read 3:45 a.m. Flouncing down under the covers, she again reflected on the discourtesy of the employee before preparing to return to sleep. Suddenly the large Maglite flashlight sitting on the table at the foot of the bed flipped off the table and landed on the floor, startling her, but not enough to get her up again. Sweet sleep returned, despite the noise, and she woke refreshed at her usual time.

"When we went downstairs for breakfast, I mentioned the noise to the others and told the innkeeper that she had certainly gotten an early start. But she said that she arrived at her usual time, 7 a.m. I thought she was kidding, so I questioned her again. She had a funny look on her face. I said, 'Well someone was downstairs in the kitchen at 3:45 this morning.'

"I also noticed the enameled metal work table and knew that one of the sounds was a knife scrapping and cutting against the table. None of the others had heard the noise, which seemed strange because it was very loud and distinct.

"I asked the innkeeper if she knew anything about the strange noises I'd heard and she said she didn't, but that it wasn't her. I had a feeling that she may have been hesitant to say anything more, but she did tell us later that she was looking for another position, and I wondered if she had had some unpleasant experiences at the lighthouse."

But the culinary racket wasn't the end of Jeanne's story, for that afternoon she and Arlene were looking at cookbooks stored on a shelf in the kitchen. Arlene was wearing a pair of hoop earrings for pierced ears and one of those hoops suddenly jumped out of her ear as though someone had hurriedly jerked it. This seemed decidedly peculiar to them, because the earrings were fashioned in such a way that they couldn't simply come loose or fall out.

Later that evening as they were going up the stairs to their rooms, the other earring did the same thing, landing on the stairs. All four of them saw it happen and were taken aback – realizing that something unusual was going on. Someone or something obviously wanted the earrings and Arlene stated emphatically, after picking up the earring, "Fine then, just take them if you want them so badly."

But Jeanne says that isn't the end of the earring episode, for when Arlene packed the next day to check out, she couldn't find the earrings anywhere. After a careful search, she asked the innkeeper to keep an eye out for them after they left. When she arrived home, she suddenly discovered the earrings, but not in a place she would have packed them.

"Arlene and Bill didn't believe in ghosts before, but they do now and they still talk about it today, several years later," Jeanne told me.

Finally, after they checked out and were driving home, Mike told them about the mystery of the armoire door that wouldn't stay closed, even though he securely latched it several times. Jeanne also remembered latching the door closed as she went by on her way to the bathroom. While she was gone, Mike turned the key to actually lock it shut. Nonetheless, they found the door inexplicably open when they got up the next morning. Mike also confessed at breakfast the second morning that he was wakened by the same kitchen din that she'd heard. He had to go to the bathroom but decided to tough it out after experiencing the noise. He also checked the time and found it to be 3:45. After Mike's confession, the man on his honeymoon stated that he, too, woke about the same time, but did not hear any racket and went down the hall to the bathroom.

Jeanne says she and Mike deduced that, since they were the only ones to experience the noise, perhaps it occurs only in the room they occupied. She also says she wishes that Mike had wakened her that second night, but doubts that she would have had the courage to go downstairs to investigate. She also says she tried to talk Mike into going back to the inn to see if it would happen again, but says he absolutely refuses, convinced that something unnatural was happening while they stayed there.

In the case of a Two Harbors Lighthouse ghost, there seems to be scant reason for any troubled spirit to dwell there. Only one death of anyone is recorded during the history of the light and that occurred off the lighthouse property. Marjorie Covell, daughter of assistant lightkeeper Franklin Covell, succumbed in October 1924 to ptomaine poisoning, but her family lived in a private home in town. Covell was later advised to move his family into the assistant keeper's quarters on the lighthouse property, which he apparently did, but would only stay until December when he accepted a transfer to Split Rock as first assistant keeper.

The events that Jeanne reported do have the feel of a child's playful or mischievous spirit, like those involving Arlene's earrings, but the kitchen racket that she and Mike experienced would hardly seem the work of a child, so the origin of this Two Harbors ghost remains a mystery.[9]

Two Harbors Lighthouse B&B is not unique among inns said to be haunted. There are doubtless many B&Bs in historic buildings that can claim a spirit or two, but it's unlikely that any can better Thayer's Historic Bed 'n Breakfast in the resort town of Annandale on Highway 55 about 25 miles south of St. Cloud.

Built in 1895 as a railroad hotel, Thayer's takes its name from Gus and Caroline Thayer, who were longtime hosts at the 11-room establishment, which has been fully modernized and transformed by current owner Sharon Gammell into a luxurious B&B that has won many awards and recognitions for its antique laden decor, sumptuous dining, a wide assortment of theme dinners and – well – its host of ghosts.

Indeed, the atmosphere here is so "spirited" that Sharon, who has a 45-year history as a psychic medium, has identified not only the shades of old Gus and Caroline, but those of many of their friends and regular customers who regularly drop in for a visit, as well as three of her own deceased cats, her late husband and perhaps one or two specters that she hasn't yet recognized. None of the ghosts she has encountered bothers her especially, since all seem benign or even helpful. She credits the incredible service and comfort at her inn to the ghostly influence of Gus and Caroline, her esteemed predecessors, saying that the Thayers were well known for their hospitality and food. She also says Gus leaves pennies lying about for her guests to find.

But while the inn offers comfort, elegance and a haunting experience to its guests, Sharon also functions as a professional psychic, medium and life coach who is available seven days a week for readings by appointment either in person or by telephone. She does note, however, that weekend appointments are difficult, since she is often busy with weddings, theme dinners and other events for which she serves not only as hostess but lead chef and as a minister officiating at weddings on the property.[10]

B&B inns are not by any means the only hospitality establishments housing supernatural beings. Minnesota bars and eateries seem to be a particularly fertile area for spiritual encounters.

The most commonly reported restaurant that has been identified as haunted is Forepaugh's Restaurant in St. Paul, which also boasts a reputation as a fine French eatery in an elegant 19th century Victorian mansion. The aegis of this haunting reads like a great American tragedy.

Joseph L. Forepaugh was a leading businessman and pioneer in St. Paul, establishing J.L. Forepaugh & Company as the largest wholesale dry goods dealer in the Upper Midwest. By 1870, at age 36, he was firmly established in both the business and social community and decided to exercise his position by building a spacious, impressive home for his wife, Mary, and their two small daughters.

With the new home completed and occupying five city lots of prime real estate on Exchange Street, there was the need for a sizable staff of servants to maintain the home. In time, Forepaugh is said to have been smitten by one of the maids, whose name was Molly. His attentions were soon returned by the maid, and they are reputed to have had a torrid affair that caught the eye of Mrs. Forepaugh, who quickly and stridently ordered him to stop his philandering. Faced with the ramifications that his wife presented, he cut off the affair, but not before impregnating Molly, who did not take kindly to his abrupt abandonment of her.

Distraught, the unfortunate servant fashioned a noose, tied the other end of the rope to a light fixture, placed the noose around her neck and threw herself from a third floor window. Molly's suicide, likely coupled with a deepening paranoia about his business interests, seems to have started Forepaugh on a downward spiral into extreme depression. He shot himself to death on July 8, 1892. At the time of his death, he believed that his business interests were doing poorly, perhaps sagging under the weight of yet another of the cyclical depressions that plagued the economy in the late 1800s. In fact, his estate was valued at $500,000, a veritable fortune at that time.

The ghosts of both suicide victims are implicated in the Forepaugh Restaurant hauntings, with reports of Molly's spirit lingering near the third floor location where she died. Joseph Forepaugh's specter has been reported in the dining areas by a number of restaurant employees and patrons, who describe the spirit as a nice-looking man who walks through the dining room as though he owns it, then disappears.[11]

John Savage of the Minnesota Paranormal Investigative Group says his group's research and investigation at Forepaugh's indicate that the evidence of the hauntings is very credible, but says that further study may not be possible since new owners have taken over and do not choose to cooperate in further paranormal studies there.

Former restaurant owner James Crnkovich was less reticent to discuss the possibility of a haunting, recalling a special event when the servers wore 19th century period clothing as costumes. A waitress setting up for the dinner saw an unknown woman in the same type of clothing (though not a dress supplied by the costume company) walking down a nearby hallway. Suddenly as the server watched her, she simply disappeared. Staff members also tell of unusual events like lights turning on and off in the basement, cold chills, strange noises and, of course, the ghost of Molly.[12]

There are numerous references to this story and, as one might expect with numerous retellings, the sequence of events changes from one version to the next. In some, Molly commits suicide after learning of Joseph's suicide. In others, the sequence is the one recorded here.

A complicating factor for the entire haunting story is found on the Website for Forepaugh's Restaurant. In a synopsis of the history of the building, the site confirms most of the information reported above for the earliest days of the mansion.

The complication comes a couple of paragraphs further down, as the history notes, "In 1886, the house was sold to General John Henry Hammond, a retired Civil War veteran. Forepaugh and family were traveling to Europe 'for an indefinite time.' They returned in 1889 and built a second palatial home at 302 Summit Avenue, overlooking the city and his first home."[13]

There is no reason to doubt the veracity of this Website history, since the owners would have access to the abstract of ownership for the property from its very beginning. This historical tidbit does, however, raise some niggling questions about this well-documented haunting.

Remembering that Forepaugh's suicide is recorded on July 8, 1892, six years after he sold the mansion to General Hammond, it seems clear that if Molly committed suicide in that building, it was long before his death. That is the sequence that I use here, but how then do we explain the well-documented ghostly presence of Joseph Forepaugh at the restaurant, since he had long since disposed of his interest in the property and had built a new mansion in an even posher neighborhood? A further complicating question is why he would sell the property in the first place, since the family obviously planned on returning to St. Paul after their European tour.

And if he was as increasingly paranoid about his finances as he is reported to have been, why would he suddenly abandon his business to take a three-year grand tour of Europe?

Having pondered each of these quibbles, I've come to the conclusion that Mary Forepaugh played a dominating role in the events that ensued. As already stated, she demonstrated her strength of will by putting a swift halt to Joseph's dalliance with the pretty little maid. Molly's suicide under her roof probably tainted the home in Mary's eyes. It undoubtedly proved to be a source of extreme distress to her husband – distress that likely added to his business paranoia and depressive personality.

As an antidote for his increasing depression and to rid herself of the accursed house that constantly reminded her of her husband's duplicity, I believe Mary laid out the European trip, likely pointing out to him the positive cultural benefits of such an experience for their maturing daughters. At that time such a trip was also nearly compulsory for people of wealth who hoped to climb the social ladder. With the double whammy of his distress at losing Molly and the onus of his sexual indiscretion, Joseph was unlikely to disagree with the strong-willed Mary.

And so the house was sold and the Forepaughs sailed away on their grand adventure. My theory stretches a bit further, however, and I believe that Joseph did not get over his love for Molly nor his depression at his role in her suicide. His melancholia deepened during the time overseas, perhaps brightening now and then and giving Mary hope that she was prevailing against the ghost of Joseph's mistress.

By the time they returned to St. Paul in 1889, Joseph had had little influence for three years in the business that he founded and he may have been less than impressed with events there during his hiatus. He also had the expense of building that new mansion to worry about and his financial concerns magnified in his mind, coupled with his guilt and depression over the lost Molly.

Since the new home was started after they returned in 1889 and may have taken upward of a year to complete, it's unlikely that he spent any extended period in his new home before wandering away with a gun and taking his life. He would have had much less of a tie to this house than to his original mansion, and the spirit of Molly seems to have attached itself to that former home, so perhaps Joseph's spirit chose to linger in that building accompanied by the maid who he found irresistible in life – and, it seems, in death as well.

A few miles away from Forepaugh's swanky elegance, the basement of Benchwarmer Bob's Sports Cafe was said to be haunted by the ghost of a Native American. The owner and namesake of the facility is Bob Lurtsema, who persisted for quite a while on the Vikings football team as a second stringer and remains one of the more renowned of the ex-Vikings – not for any consistently brilliant play, but for the good humor he showed in his continuous role as the benchwarmer behind bigger stars of the time.

He freely admits that there was something unnatural in the restaurant and believes the origin of the spirit may be an Indian burial ground that occupied the location where the cafe is now. One version of the story is that the Burnsville Police Department K-9 dogs refused to go into the basement where the spirit or spiritual events were most commonly encountered. Lurtsema himself is quoted by Gina Teel in *Ghost Stories of Minnesota* as saying that one time, while he was discussing the haunting with some new customers who asked about it, the lights in the room dimmed and brightened a number of times, despite no one being near the lighting controls for the restaurant. On the advice of Native Americans, he feels he has made peace with the spirits by hanging a Native American dreamcatcher at the doorway to his establishment as testament of his recognition of the ghostly presence. Not mentioned was whether or not the K-9 unit of Burnsville Police Department shared his optimistic faith in the efficacy of the exorcism.[14]

In St. Cloud, the 1886 D.B. Searle Building houses a ghost of unknown origin. Now the site of the popular D.B. Searle's Food and Libations, through these many years the building has seen service variously as a funeral home, a communal sleeping parlor, a rehearsal hall for musicians, a Masonic Temple, a bank, a tailor's shop and, for a few years around 1917, the top two floors were leased to the manufacturer of the Pan Motor Car. Located on Fifth Avenue South in the downtown area, managers and servers have long told tales of strange goings-on there. While its longtime occupation by Colbert's Funeral Home might raise suspicions that would be the source of the haunting, no current evidence substantiates that suspicion, leaving the staff, and now us, to wonder just who or what it is that disturbs the peace at Searle's.

And the evidence of strange events pointing to a ghostly presence does mount up. It's not uncommon, as an example, for staff to find work they know was accomplished the night before to be undone when they open in the morning. Startled patrons have reported a strange draft of icy air rushing past them and occasionally a heavy stained-glass light shade inexplicably begins swinging wildly in the serving area, as though pushed by unseen hands. It's been a frequent occurrence to find chairs turned around from their normal placement and the elevator for no apparent reason goes up and down with no one in it.

As in several other stories of haunted eateries, the table candles also figure into the evidence, as a late evening server tells of having extinguished all the flames in the restaurant, yet turned to find the candles in one section rekindled.[15]

Back again in St. Paul, longtime rumors have circulated of a ghost purported to be the spirit of a legendary Prohibition gangster, Jack Peifer. Photos from the March 30, 2001, wedding of Kimberley and Joseph Arrigoni seem to prove that a male ghost does, indeed, haunt the Landmark Center in the downtown area.

The historic 1902 structure originally served as the Federal Court House and Post Office for the Upper Midwest. The decaying building was rescued from the wrecking ball in the 1970s by determined citizens who restored it to its former grandeur and re-opened it in 1978 in its present role as a cultural center for music, dance, theater, exhibitions, public forums and special events.

The news of the ghostly photograph was first carried in a bylined article August 16, 2001, *St. Paul Pioneer Press* by Don Boxmeyer, the paper's resident ghost chaser. It ran under the headline "Gangster Ghost Appeared in Wedding Photo." Boxmeyer stated that the photo showed a rather fuzzy, gray image of a guy who no one at the wedding knew or had ever seen.

Said to be looking over the shoulder of the 5-year-old ringbearer in a group picture of the wedding party taken on a balcony, the ghostly character wasn't even noticed by Kimberley or Joseph at first, but her niece, Jamie Ness, pointed him out to them, asking, "Who's that?"

Looking more closely, they had to admit that he was no one in either of their lists of acquaintances. Pointing out the fuzzy character to their wedding photographer, Steve Tompkins of C&S Photography in Chaska, they were told that an extra image such as one caused by a double-exposure would be unlikely and that a blur in the picture was also not likely, since no one was moving about when the image was snapped.

"I've been in the business since 1984 and I've never seen anything like it," Steve told Boxmeyer. "I think this is all very thrilling."

The photo also gave Landmark Center events coordinator Pam Sicard the thrill of vindication, for she had been telling whoever would listen that the building was haunted and had found precious little sympathy from supervisors or fellow employees. Saying she had long sensed his presence, especially on elevators and the building's third floor, she told Boxmeyer, "We've even had women guests here who go into the second floor bathroom and come out shivering, saying that they saw a man in there who disappeared. He's a little menacing and I've actually felt him touch me. I think he threw himself on my desk one day."

She named the ghost for Peifer after reading gangster-era literature that described him as a former carnival worker and bellhop who went on to become a banker and hospitality merchant for the mobsters who invaded St. Paul in the 1920s and 1930s. The bellhop connection proves interesting, since Boxmeyer ran down a newsletter article by St. Paul history buff and former Landmark tour guide Woodrow Keljik, who told the story of two men describing what they believed was a ghost in the glass-topped elevator that lifts disabled passengers from the sidewalk to the first-floor level.

According to Keljik, the men were looking down through the glass roof of the elevator and observed a fellow in a bellhop uniform operating the lift. When it arrived at their floor, however, the elevator was empty. The elevator had made no stops, but the bellhop had vanished, seemingly into thin air.

Boxmeyer quotes Keljik as telling him, "They were serious, and they were not making anything up."

The ghost's affection for elevators is also documented by Pam Sicard, who told Boxmeyer of elevator doors mysteriously opening and closing when no one called for the elevators. Sicard also said that she may have sent the ghost on its way to the beyond.

"I got mad at him one day and told him he doesn't have to open doors for me anymore and that he doesn't even belong here. I told him, 'I'm alive and you're dead, dammit. Go!'" Pam said. "I haven't heard from him since."

In life, Jack Peifer was a prominent, if questionable, presence during the Prohibition era in St. Paul. Peifer was fingered as the point man in the June 1933 kidnapping of brewery heir William Hamm Jr. by the infamous Barker-Karpis Gang, which specialized in armed robbery, extortion and high-ransom kidnappings. William Hamm Jr.'s abduction certainly fit into that latter category of crime.

By 1933, the Hamm's family place among St. Paul's elite was well established. The patriarch, Theodore, had taken possession of a small brewery in 1864 and his family would transform the brewery into the largest beer purveyor northwest of Chicago, growing Hamm's Brewing Company from 500 barrels a year in 1864 to more than 26,000 barrels in 1882. His son and his grandson would continue the aggressive expansion and build Hamm's Brewing Company into the beer powerhouse of the Upper Midwest. William Sr. started with the company as general manager in 1880, was appointed vice president-secretary of the company in 1891, then his father unofficially retired but retained the title of president. William Sr. inherited the presidency in 1903 and would hold that position until his death in 1931, when his son, William Jr., took over the rapidly expanding business and continued his predecessors' expansionist traits.

With the family fortune growing daily, William Hamm Jr. made an attractive potential kidnap victim, and Jack Peifer was well positioned in St. Paul to know it, supposedly vouchsafing that fact to the Barker-Karpis Gang when they went looking for someone they could abduct and hold for a substantial ransom.

On June 14, 1933, the gang, led by career gangsters Alvin Karpis and Freddy Barker, a son of the infamous Ma Barker, confronted the 39-year-old Hamm Jr. on the street at noon as he walked from the brewery toward his home on Greenbrier Avenue. At 6 feet 4 inches tall, he must have presented a formidable figure when the gangsters nabbed him from the street, stuffed him into a car and drove him to a hideout.

Demanding $100,000 from the Hamm family, the gang held Hamm for several days, then, a bit surprisingly given their otherwise violent record, released him after the ransom was paid. The relatively new forensic technique of fingerprinting had just emerged and the FBI was able to obtain fingerprint evidence from the ransom note that implicated the Barker-Karpis Gang. From that break, Jack Peifer's aiding and abetting of the crime was also uncovered.

Meanwhile, after his release by the gang, William Hamm Jr. returned to work as head of Hamm's Brewery and would maintain his presidency through 27 years of tremendous growth until he retired in 1960 and his family exited the business – just as television was turning the Hamm's Bear and his buddies into advertising icons with the catchy jingle celebrating their Minnesota location:

"From the land of sky blue waters,
From the land of pines, lofty balsams –
Hamm's, the beer refreshing
Hamm's, the beer refreshing."

In a 1936 trial that was held in the federal courthouse that is now the Landmark Center, Jack Peifer was tried and convicted for his complicity in the kidnapping. At the time, public outrage at the kidnapping and killing of Charles and Anne Lindbergh's infant son was high and the judge threw the book at Peifer. Sentenced to 30 years in prison at Fort Leavenworth, Kansas, Peifer was so shocked by the severity of the sentence that he committed suicide by ingesting potassium cyanide a day or so later in his cell. On this story rests Pam Sicard's identification of the ghost.

Pam's other observations about the spiritual presence in the Landmark Center are that it seemed to be especially agitated around the bars, where glasses mysteriously shattered and liquor was frequently spilled. On the other hand, the spirit did seem to like being around "girls, gin, parties and the third floor."

As for Kimberley and Joe Arrigoni's wedding photo, Kimberley says that "it gave me the willies at first," but that she's come to accept the strange image. Joe has shown the picture to friends and, when he explained the phantom image, "they got goosebumps," he said.

While Pam Sicard's identification of the ghost was based only on her own intuition, there was no ghostly sign to indicate otherwise. Her possible exorcism of the specter seems to have been efficacious, since no stories of the haunting seem to have surfaced since 2001.[16]

Another criminal ghost is said to inhabit the fifth floor of the Minneapolis City Hall. John Moshik was convicted in a fifth floor courtroom in March 1898 of murder during a robbery yielding $14 to the crook. Sentenced to death by hanging, within a few days he was taken from his cell, his hands and feet were securely bound, his mouth was taped shut, a noose was placed around Moshik's neck and the chair kicked out from beneath him.

The hanging was seriously botched, however. On the first try, the noose slipped out of place and had to be removed and again placed around his neck. Even then, it took many minutes for Moshik to die. Apparently outraged at not only the severity of sentence, but by the ineptitude of his execution, his spirit is said to still remain at the site of his death. Eerie footsteps have been heard on the fifth floor and his ghostly presence reported by everyone from janitors to lawyers, bailiffs and judges. And his ghost seems to be particularly bitter toward prosecuting attorneys and judges, for the courthouse has recorded a number of deaths or the onset of serious illnesses on the premises.

In the 1950s, the fifth floor was renovated and the courtroom where he was sentenced was removed, but this did not placate John Moshik's outraged spirit. His presence has been seen and heard on the floor right to the present, as have unexplained noises and strange, unexplainable shadows.[17]

In Northfield, Thorson Hall on the campus of venerable St. Olaf College is said to be haunted by the spirits of at least two young men, who have been observed and reported by a number of students through the years. Indeed, so common are the reportings that director of housing, Greg Kneser, began collecting the stories into a "ghost file" that was featured in an October 21, 2003, article in *St. Olaf News* by Jake Erickson.

According to the article, two sophomore women students first brought Kneser's attention to the ghostly presences, asking him to let them see the St. Olaf ghost file. He discovered that there was no such file, but after the girls told of their experiences he began to collect ghostly stories into his own "ghost file."

The two young women told Kneser that they first encountered a spiritual presence in their dorm room during a kick-off bonfire for the year. Glancing up at their window, they saw a figure wearing a red baseball cap standing there.

Feeling uneasy, they soon found other reasons for their discomfort. Noises and shadowy appearances unnerved them and their stereo began stopping and starting during certain songs. The spiritual presence apparently didn't care for Led Zeppelin's "D'yer Mak'er," which was always stopped when the students tried to play it. On the other hand, Pachabel's "Canon in D" appeared to be a favorite and would play whenever the CD was in the player, whether they started it or not.

One night, they saw two shadowy young men sitting at the end of their loft and on another occasion one of the women woke to find her roommate sobbing. At first the crying roommate refused to talk about what had upset her, but later calmed down and said that she had awakened to see two young men sitting on the floor playing cards.

After telling Kneser about these episodes of ghostly encounters, they felt somewhat easier about their haunting, and they made it through the rest of the year without any more scares.

But their story inspired Kneser's love of folklore and storytelling. He began collecting their story and others into his ghost file. In fact, he became dean of students and took to visiting first-year dorms each fall, telling some of the stories he has collected to the new St. Olaf students.[18]

Back in Minnesota's northland, the Cross River Heritage Center in Schroeder on Lake Superior's north shore is a relatively new operation, having been renovated from what was once the Cross River General Store and previously Lambs' General Store. Here, a very recent haunting is still taking shape and was first revealed in my earlier *Haunted Lake Superior* volume.

Completely remodeled both inside and out, the center opened in 2003, and it wasn't long before staffers began reporting weird goings-on to then director Amy Biren, who told me the story.

"I've never had anything ghostly happen to me," Amy said, "but a few times my computer has done weird things, and I've also had instances of doors being locked that I knew were unlocked shortly before."

She said there is little chance of doors being inadvertently locked. "Our locks are the type where you have to consciously make the effort to lock them. In one case, a group of quilters was working upstairs at the Center and one of them left the room. Upon returning, the door to the activity room was locked, preventing her from entering. No one had been near the door and everyone was surprised because that door had definitely been unlocked when she left the room."

Another woman told Amy that she was working late one day as the Center was being finished. She heard footsteps outside of the basement workroom she was in and, thinking it was the contractor coming back to finish up the building, the lady shouted, "Hello!" The footsteps halted, but a little later she heard them again and again called out a greeting. The footsteps again stopped, so the lady went to the door to speak with the contractor – only to find no one there and no sign that anyone had been there.

Amy said, "She's one of those people that I would say are very sensible and not likely to be nervous about such things, but she got her coat on and left as quickly as she could."

Amy said there seem to be two presences and that the staff had playfully named them Horace and Fannie after an early proprietor and his mother-in-law who lived above the store. She also postulated that the spirits may have been roused by the extensive remodeling the building underwent during its conversion into the museum.

"I've been told that spirits grow restless during renovations and we've certainly been involved in major work here that could cause any spirits to become interested or apprehensive about what was happening to the building."

Bill Jordan, the longtime former owner of the store, stated emphatically that he never experienced anything unusual during the many years he worked there. He certainly spent enough time after hours creating his extraordinary sausages to have experienced something, if it sought to make itself known to him. His testimony may add credibility to Amy's theory that the renovation raised the spirits of the Center.

In an update for this book, current Center director Marie Mueller says that she is more skeptical than Amy was about the presence of ghosts, but that she is convinced that there is something spiritual that occupies the building.

"In the morning when I first come in here, I quite often hear the elevator operate when no one else is here," Marie says. "I also think that Fannie has played tricks on me at times."

But it is the handprints on the wall of the room that Fannie once occupied that gives the most graphic evidence of a haunting, according to Marie.

As she tells the story, work was under way to return that room to the 1930s appearance of when it was occupied. As old wallpaper was being stripped preparatory to putting up new paper, a skeletal handprint or handprints suddenly appeared on one strip of the old wallpaper, as though some ghostly personage was attempting to save the ambience of the room.

Distinctive enough to be instantly recognized by the workers, the decision was made to preserve that small piece of the old paper, with its spectral handprints.

"It looked like Fannie might have been trying to stop us from removing the old paper. We did save that area of old paper and now point out the handprints to anyone who is interested or who asks about our ghosts," Marie says.[19]

A number of miles north of Schroeder, canoeists may be surprised to learn that there may be something spiritual that has nothing to do with the serenity, peace and fulfillment many of them feel in the Boundary Waters Canoe Area Wilderness (BWCAW).

As told to author Ruth D. Hein by Paul Minerich of Hibbing, the tale comes from Hein's 1999 *More Ghostly Tales from Minnesota*.

Paul said, "Four of us had decided to go fishing at Ima Lake in northern Lake County. It was a Thursday morning in May 1995 when we left Snowbank Lake early in the morning and we were all happy to be on our first BWCAW canoeing adventure of the year."

Four hours of paddling brought the fellows to their first portage to Disappointment Lake, a largish body of water that would take them to their destination via a couple of portages and paddles on smaller lakes. They wanted to reach the protection of the smaller lakes before the wind increased.

They'd barely left the shoreline of Disappointment Lake when Paul glanced to his left and saw something moving in the timber of the shore. Pale, misty and indistinct, it moved quickly in and out of the timber up the shoreline. He couldn't make out what it was, but called to the others to look at it. By the time they looked, whatever it was had vanished. Paul took a ribbing from the others.

They continued paddling, but Paul kept a lookout for whatever it was he had seen. The same misty mass appeared again. This time, he immediately called out to the others, and they, too, witnessed the amorphous "something" moving amongst the trees.

Paul told Hein, "This time, my partner saw it too. He asked what it was and had no clue. That bothered him a little because he was the one who always had answers for everything.

"This time the apparition was nearer the shoreline, and we could see it better. It appeared to be a large, loose mass like a huge white puffball of some kind, or maybe a billowy cloud hanging low over the shore. It made no sound – none that we could hear anyway. As we watched, it shifted direction a little, then moved farther along and was suddenly out of sight...."

Three of the men immediately spoke of the phenomenon, but the more skeptical fourth man kept to himself until later when they pulled up to shore in the area where they had seen "it."

He finally admitted, "I don't know what it was, and I don't see it now, so we can't examine it even if we wanted to, but it clearly, definitely, absolutely was there!"

As their trip progressed, they all admitted to a feeling of eeriness as they watched whatever that mysterious mass was. He can't speak for what the others thought of the misty apparition, but Paul has come to his own conclusion. He believes the mass is the spirit of an old Ojibway chieftain whose spirit yet lurks along the shoreline of Disappointment Lake and makes itself known to a few paddlers by assuming the form of a low hanging cloud or a strange patch of fog that wafts through the trees lining the shore.[20]

Although this author has lived in the Duluth area for more than 22 years and has never heard any stories of ghostly presences at the city's Historic Union Depot, John Savage of Minnesota Paranormal Investigation Group states that he recently visited the Depot and its many attractions, shooting photos of their visit there.

Historic Union Depot, better know as simply The Depot, is the former Union Railroad Depot. Built in 1892 in the French Norman architectural style by the Boston firm of Peabody, Stearns and Furber, by 1910 the Union Depot was serving seven different rail lines with up to 5,000 people passing through its doors daily, many of them foreign immigrants seeking a better life in the forests or iron ranges of northern Minnesota. In 1971, this beautiful landmark was listed on the National Register of Historic Places.

After it served its last train and underwent major renovations, the Union Depot reopened in 1973 as an area arts, history and culture center housing exhibits by four different museums. Its theater wing functions as a studio and administrative home to five performing arts organizations. As a focal point for the area, it is visited by hundreds of thousands of people each year.

"There is some really interesting evidence of possible hauntings at The Depot in the photos I took during our visit," John told me. "It's definitely on my list of places to investigate more closely in the future."[21]

That investigation is pending as this book goes to press. Having been an important part of life for the nearly 2 million passengers using The Depot each year, there is certainly history enough at the Historic Union Depot to support the presence of one or more spirits who may have simply chosen to remain in that building after their earthly remains were laid to rest.

No collection of Minnesota ghost stories can be printed that does not include the story of the haunting of St. Mary's University (formerly College) of Winona by the angry spirit of an insane priest. The version here focuses most heavily on the more "ghostly" aspects of the story, although there are other versions that are somewhat tamer – or gorier, depending on the source.

The story begins gently enough with 55-year-old Father Laurence M. Lesches requesting to be assigned a parish of his own. Bishop Patrick Heffron of the Diocese of Winona refused his request, accusing the priest of being emotionally unstable. The Bishop elaborated by telling Lesches that he was unfit for clerical life and would be better off working on a farm.

Displeased, Lesches brooded over what he perceived as the Bishop's mistreatment of him. Events came to a head on August 27, 1915, when Lesches ran up behind Heffron, who was kneeling before the altar in the chapel. Hearing Lesches' rapid approach, Heffron turned just in time to see a pistol pointed in his direction. Lesches pulled the trigger and two bullets found his target.

While Heffron writhed in pain on the chapel floor, the mad priest returned to his room, where police shortly found him, still in possession of the pistol.

Heffron survived his wounds and assisted police in their investigations. He and Lesches had known one another for 20 years, but had never been close. According to Bishop Heffron, the priest was unstable, arrogant, self-absorbed, hot-headed and had neither tact nor close friends.

It should also be noted that the Bishop himself was no paragon, even though he had nearly single-handedly raised the funds to establish St. Mary's College. Known as a perfectionist, he was well known for putting people in positions where they could only fail. He then took pleasure in pointing out to them their own incompetence. Indeed, he had been dismissed from his position with the St. Paul Cathedral because of his infamous mean streak, but became the king of all he surveyed at the college that he had founded. And, indeed, despite his failings, in his career the Bishop established 27 churches, helped establish the world-renowned St. Mary's Hospital in Rochester and raised funds to build parochial schools and a new dormitory at St. Mary's, which bears his name, Heffron Hall. He would die on November 23, 1927.

Likely partially because of Bishop Heffron's statements to the police, the first-degree assault charge against Lesches was dismissed by reason of insanity. The judge ordered the priest committed to the State Hospital for the Dangerously Insane at St. Peter, where he would languish under treatment for paranoia until 1931, at which time the doctors pronounced him to be in sound mental health. Still under guardianship of the Winona Diocese, he asked to be released from the state hospital, but the new Bishop refused his request. Again the priest was left to brood over his mistreatment by his superiors.

Unlike most ghostly hauntings, the vengeful spirit of Father Lesches is said to have become malignant even before his bodily remains were laid to rest, since a short while after the diocese refused to sign his release from St. Peter, one of the priests with whom Lesches did not get along was found dead in his own room at St. Mary's.

On May 15, 1931, the charred remains of Father Edward Lynch were discovered by a nun. Burned beyond recognition, the body was sprawled across the bed but, inexplicably, the sheets and mattress beneath the body showed no signs of scorching. His Bible was also burned, with the exception of one passage: "And the Lord shall come at the sound of the trumpets." This is apparently what set people to the belief that Fr. Lesches was implicated in the death, for he had been heard to shout the passage at Fr. Lynch numerous times during their heated arguments.

According to the official record, Lynch's death was ascribed to an electrical accident when he inadvertently touched a radiator as he shut off the lamp hanging from his headboard.

Unfortunately for that official record, the electric utility supplying the power to the college noted the fact that the lamp only used 110 volts, which was unlikely to kill someone, never mind charring the body beyond recognition. Nonetheless, the official verdict remained death by accidental electrocution. Lesches would live another 12 years in the state hospital before his body was laid to rest. His spirit apparently has not yet found peace, for students living on the third floor of Heffron Hall began telling stories in the 1940s of strange goings-on in the dorm.

According to numerous reports, the sound of footsteps and the tapping of a cane are heard in the hallway, there are inexplicable cold drafts and notices on the bulletin board will be seen wavering, as though blown by a breeze when no such waft is present. There has also been more than one report of a student being prevented from entering the floor by some unseen force.

Perhaps the most detailed account of something mysterious occurring came in 1945, when seminarian Mike O'Malley heard footsteps late one night outside his room. The footsteps stopped outside his room and he heard a knock on his door. Opening it, he observed a cloaked figure, whose face was covered by the cowl of its robe.

"What do you want, Father," O'Malley asked the figure, believing it to be one of the priests. A startled O'Malley reported hearing a guttural, otherworldly moan. Even more agog, O'Malley again asked what the figure wanted and his blood froze as the cowled figure stammered, "I – Want – You!"

Frightened, the student punched the indistinct figure, breaking his hand. The commotion awoke his roommate, who just managed to catch a glimpse of the face of the cowled figure, reporting it to have a claylike appearance.

Officially, college discipline records say a student did break his hand, but in a cafeteria fight. There are no records showing anyone at the college with any facial injury from a fight.

So many other stories of supernatural occurrences were recorded at Heffron Hall that the student newspaper decided in 1969 to verify the stories or lay them to rest permanently. Staff members descended on the third floor of the dorm with ghost hunting equipment and spent a number of nights monitoring the floor.

The student reporters detected consistent drops in temperature in the corridor in the wee hours each night. Because Lesches is known to have died at 1:45 a.m., his spirit seemed a likely candidate for the cold spots that were recorded moving east to west at a rate of 100 feet in 30 seconds. The cold was confined to spots, rather than the entire corridor feeling chilled. The cameras also recorded blurred spots that showed clearly on the photos.

Their investigation, however, was deemed inconclusive, leaving many students confused by the seeming contradiction of concrete evidence being overridden by opinion. Many continue to believe the tales of a haunting in Heffron Hall right to the present.

Based on the many legends surrounding the haunting, in 1989 *USA Today* named Heffron Hall "Minnesota's most legendary haunted place."[22]

Turning again to the *St. Paul Pioneer Press*, we find a May 14, 1996, article by columnist Don Boxmeyer that tells of the ghost of a boxer who regularly worked out in Glancey's Gym in a St. Paul suburb. Owner Jim Glancey, a retired asbestos worker who opened the gym in 1992 and found success teaching the fine points of pugilism to young boxers, soon discovered that he was not alone when he retired to his upstairs quarters after closing the gym in the evening.

He regularly heard the sound of something working on the speed bags, but found no one in the gym when he checked. Experiencing this phenomenon numerous times, Jim Glancey came to expect the rapid fire sound of a speed bag being used by an expert pugilist. He nicknamed the phantom boxer "Mutt" after the comic strip character and openly told others about the spook in his gym.

The gym was located in a former meat-packing plant and provided the gym with ample space for the various activities that boxers need in training exercise, from heavy and light bags to a pair of rings for sparring practice and lockers in which to keep the paraphernalia of the sport.

The ghost story actually begins prior to Glancey's, however, when the building housed the Anderson Meat Company. Located at Beech and Forest streets in St. Paul's East Side, the building was crowned by a 60-foot smokestack that becomes a grisly part of the story.

It seems that Anderson Meat received a mystery call on a Tuesday in April 1983 that a burglary had been attempted in their building the previous Sunday. The anonymous caller also informed the company that the would-be burglar might still be in the building, adding that company personnel might want to check the chimney.

When police responded to Anderson's, they found a rope tied to the top rung of a ladder built into the outside of the smokestack.

It ran down inside the chimney's flue and was taut. Upon further investigation, the officers determined that the rope was tied to a body dangling at the end of the rope. Later investigation would determine that the body was that of 30-year-old Clyde Mudgett, who was already known to police.

Apparently Clyde's ill-conceived plan for entering the meat plant was to lower himself via the rope and chimney and crawl out a clean-out door at the bottom of the smokestack.

Unfortunately, he underestimated the height of the chimney and his rope was about 20 feet short of the bottom. Hanging and wedged inside the confined enclosure, he died of asphyxiation from heat and fumes generated by the furnace and water heater.

As police and firefighters attempted to raise Clyde's 6-foot-1-inch body to the top of the chimney, the rope proved to be inadequate for a second time, this time breaking and sending his 190-pound body plummeting to the bottom of the flue. As an ironic postmortem to Clyde's scheme, the clean-out door located there was too small to allow removal of the body and the firefighters had to chop a hole in the chimney to effect removal of the corpse. A medical examiner would conduct an autopsy, determining the cause of death as asphyxiation and noting that the three days of heat and fumes in the chimney resulted in partial mummification of the body.

The final irony in Clyde's ill-advised stab at burglary is that Anderson Meat Company executives told police there was nothing worth stealing in the building.

But Clyde's incompetence in the breaking-and-entering effort wasn't his first gambit into crime. His record showed that he had earlier served 18 months in an Indiana State Reformatory for a burglary conviction in that state. His record also showed that he was a two-time state champion in Indiana Golden Gloves, had turned pro in the mid-1970s and was the owner of a 30 wins-22 losses record as a light heavyweight and heavyweight professional. Among other venues, he had boxed at Madison Square Garden on national television.

Flamboyant in the ring, he was known to toast the fans from the ring with a beer. Resembling Burt Reynolds, he was a friendly, talented boxer who would, it was said, fight anyone – but who hated the training sessions required for his craft.

When Jim Glancey began converting the building in which Clyde perished into a boxing gym, it was just natural that Clyde's spirit might take an interest and want to compensate for his earthly distaste for workouts. No sooner was the gym refitted with bags, weight-training equipment, boxing rings and other amenities of the pugilistic craft than the Mutt's spectral night workouts began. Living upstairs gave Jim ample opportunity to reflect that the phantom boxer was a skilled puncher, rattling the light bag with the rapid fire bapa-da-bapa-da-bapa of one who has experience on the speed bag. Indeed, so "spirited" was one of those workouts that ceiling plaster in the bathroom fell into the tub where Jim was taking a bath.

Long after Jim detected and named the specter "Mutt," he learned the details of the body extracted from the building. Given the circumstances of his life and death, Mutt's presence was hardly surprising. Jim's seemingly random choice of the name Mutt for the phantom boxer also seems more than a little coincidental, since it could quite easily be a derivative of Clyde's last name, Mudgett.

Having heard of the haunting of Glancey's, *Pioneer Press* columnist Don Boxmeyer, photographer Bill Alkofer and University of Minnesota photojournalism student Kirk Monpas made arrangements to visit the gym on a ghost watch. This was nothing new for either Boxmeyer, Alkofer or the newspaper, since they had all been on ghost vigils previously, including one in 1969 at the Summit Avenue Griggs Mansion in which the newsmen were so unnerved by ghostly goings-on that they quickly abandoned the vigil in the middle of the night. (See Griggs Mansion story in the next chapter.)

The three men and Glancey were particularly watchful of a speed bag attached to the ceiling and the floor by bungee cords, which apparatus Jim assured them was Mutt's particular favorite. Boxmeyer reported that nothing unusual seemed to occur during the several hours they sat quietly awaiting some sign of the Mutt's presence. In a later interview with *City Pages* writer Mike Mosedale, Alkofer told the reporter that they did see some of the heavy bags moving as though by themselves. "At first, I thought Boxmeyer was playing a prank on me, so I made the bag stay still for a while, then the thing started swinging again. I thought to myself, 'Maybe there is something to this – it's a little spooky.'"

In the lighthearted article he wrote, Boxmeyer reports there was nothing to see or hear and the ghost vigil began busting up at about 11:30 p.m., by which time Glancey assured them, Mutt would have finished his workout.

Boxmeyer writes, "I took a couple of pokes at the Mutt's favorite little double-ended bag, which was stretched tautly between ceiling and floor swivels. I left the room to join my colleagues. When I looked back at the bag, it was swinging in the darkened room.

"When I checked, the bottom bungee had been detached. I didn't do it. Alkofer says he didn't do it. Kirk Monpas swore he didn't do it, and Jim Glancey says he didn't.

"The Mutt didn't say a word."[23]

But Alkofer was assigned later to return to Glancey's on an unrelated photo shoot. Standing on a table shooting pictures, Alkofer told Mosedale of the *City Pages*, "All of a sudden out of nowhere all four legs collapsed and I came crashing down. I saved my camera equipment, but I got a big gash on my leg."

After completing the assignment, Alkofer says he inspected the table and found that the screws affixing the legs to the table had been loosened or removed. "I think old Clyde was playing a trick on one of the newspaper guys who had the audacity to poke fun at him. I carry the scar on my shin with me to this very day to remind me of something my mother always told me, 'Never speak ill of the dead.'"[24]

Despite, or perhaps because of, the disruption of Mutt's nighttime workout routine, Glancey's Gym was a major success, regularly sending a stable of boxers to the Upper Midwest Golden Gloves Championships and producing a generation of young boxers known for their civility and clean living. In 2000, the gym generated more boxers in the Upper Midwest tournament than any other regional training facility and the gym was named the blue ribbon winner in its category in 2001 by the *City Pages*' "Best of the Twin Cities" issue.

Despite that success, by May 2002, the 73-year-old Jim Glancey was growing weary of traveling to boxing events and the daily routine of watching over his gym and its boxers. He closed the gym and sold the building inhabited by Mutt the Spirit Boxer. Jim does continue to publish his quirky boxing newsletter, *Winners Never Quit.*

It's not yet reported if the Mutt took to the new owner's use of the building as a wood shop, but for more than a decade he provided the aspiring young boxers, coaches and Jim Glancey with enough experiences to truly become one of Minnesota's legendary hauntings.

On the western end of the Mesabi Iron Range in Coleraine, the ghost of a purported witch named Bertha Maynard haunts the old Lakeside Cemetery. Northern Minnesota Paranormal Investigators obtained videotaped evidence of something ghostly in the vicinity of the cemetery and Brian Leffler of that organization says that both their videotape and electronic voice phenomena audiotapes seem to support the posit that the ghostly presence is indeed Witch Bertha's spirit.

Because she was thought to be a witch, her grave is located away from the other internments in the cemetery. Claims that the headstone moves around or can't be found during daylight both proved false, but the video and audio tapes obtained by the investigators certainly seem to support the idea of a haunting.[25]

Perhaps no haunted public place in Minnesota is more widely reported than the Wabasha Street Caves along the Mississippi River in the downtown area of St. Paul.

The limestone caves have seen a variety of uses since they were first used to mine sand for early roads in the 1840s. A bit later, they sheltered a mushroom farm. In 1933, the world's first underground nightclub, the Castle Royal, opened in the caves and immediately became a popular watering hole for St. Paul's party crowd, as well as the most notorious gangsters of the era.

To prepare the caves for the nightclub function, elaborate interior work included a large fireplace, tiled floors and other nice appointments. The Castle Royal is said to have attracted many of the most famous big bands of the time for dancing enjoyment.

But it was the underworld clientele that kicked off stories of hauntings in the caves. In 1934, a scullery maid cleaning up after hours heard the sound of arguing in a back room and went in to investigate. There she found four men engaged in increasingly belligerent discussion. A few minutes later, three of the men were shot down in front of a fireplace in a hail of gunfire.

By the time the police arrived on the scene, however, the bodies had disappeared, the blood was cleaned up, and the only evidence that anything untoward had happened were the pockmarks of slugs in the face of the fireplace. Those pockmarks remain to the present.

But the bullet holes in the masonry, it is said, are not the only evidence of the shooting. There are reports that the ghosts of the three victims remain on the scene. A fourth apparition of a man in a panama hat who has been seen to vanish through the cave wall is also said to inhabit the caves, as are the spirits of a man and woman who make an occasional appearance in the barroom at about 3 a.m.

At present, the establishment is part of Down in History Tours Inc., which offers tours of the enchanted caverns. Deborah Fretham of that company has reported numerous ghostly occurrences since her affiliation with the caves. Quite early in her association with the caves, she and a tourist were in the rear area, which remained in somewhat original condition, and encountered a misty area that evolved into the vague image of the upper torso and head of a man. As the apparition moved toward the women, they were overwhelmed by a feeling of malevolence that permeated the space around the vague figure. Huddling together, the women feared for their safety, but experienced only a sudden chill as the apparition passed through them, leaving behind its sense of evil purpose.

On another occasion, while sitting at the bar as a patron with friends, Deborah distinctly felt the icy, unfriendly grip of a hand, which turned her around on the stool, despite no one being near her. Others in the vicinity witnessed this happen and were astonished not to see anyone nearby.

But there also seems to be a friendlier spirit in the caves, since Deborah reports at least a couple of occasions when her wine glass has been refilled when no one went near it.

Finally, Deborah also reported an encounter with a costumed ghost of a woman dressed in an 1800s-period costume that simply walked up to her, then disappeared through the wall of the party room.

The caves still offer a licensed bar, a coffee house, a variety of entertainment programming and serve as a venue for reserved parties, receptions and other events both private and public.[26]

Very recently, writer Kris Janisch reported in the October 14, 2005, issue of the *Stillwater Gazette*, that the Warden's House Museum in the downtown area is haunted by the ghost of a former warden's daughter, who died shortly after giving birth to a son. She is said to have even been spotted in recent times, searching the building for her lost child.

Built in 1853, the solidly built structure has housed the families of 11 wardens of Stillwater State Prison before being converted into its present role as a museum.

Given the fact that the house is on the grounds where hardened criminals once uneasily served their time, it's little wonder that employees at the museum often have reported eerie feelings in the master bedroom, or encountered blasts of icy air when no source was apparent, or the report by an intern of hearing mysterious humming when no one else was present, according to Chad Lewis, co-author of *Minnesota Road Guide to Haunted Locations*, as quoted in the newspaper account.

In addition to museum workers, construction employees at the nearby Terra Springs condominium development on the former prison grounds told of seeing a man in prison clothing who roamed the halls of the Warden's House.

Brent Peterson, executive director of the Washington County Historical Society that operates the museum, admitted to the reporter that he's heard several stories of visitors' shoulders and hair being pulled by something, but stated that he'd never experienced anything unusual himself.

Despite Peterson's disclaimer, when the Warden's House Museum closed for the 2005 season at the end of October, the Minnesota Ghost Hunters Society was scheduled to conduct an investigation to check out the ghostly reports. As this is being written, no report has been found about the results of that investigation.

Although he couldn't confirm the ghost at the museum he supervises, Peterson revealed to Janisch another story of a Stillwater haunting. The story goes that the house, though built circa 1960 and relatively new by standards of ghostly lore, is haunted by an apparition whose shadow has been sighted roaming inside and outside the building. Particularly active when remodeling or renovation is taking place at the house, the ghost has been known to move power tools from where the work is being done into the bathroom.

Still another ghostly sighting that has been reported in Stillwater is the spirit of a Confederate soldier at the Water Street Inn. Employees at the establishment have reported smelling body odor and hearing unexplained noises that have been attributed to the long-deceased rebel.

The inn's owner, Chuck Dougherty, is skeptical of the tales, saying the 1896 building was office space until being turned into its present use in 1995.

"Unless somebody went up to someone's office and died,..." he pondered, concluding, "I've never heard anything."[27]

If we can put any faith in a story published by the October 27, 2005, *Minnesota Daily* student newspaper of University of Minnesota, the State Capitol in St. Paul is inhabited by the ghosts of both Cass Gilbert, the architect of the building, and the spirit of Colonel William Colvill Jr., the commanding officer of the First Minnesota Volunteer Infantry Regiment when that unit was decisive in the Battle of Gettysburg on July 2, 1863, in what has come to be accepted as the most critical and decisive combat of the Civil War. With a casualty rate of 82 percent of its 262 troops, it also ranks as the most deadly action by any Union regiment in the Civil War as well as one of the deadliest in U.S. military history.[28]

Gilbert's ghostly presence in the stately building may be understandable, since it could have been one of the designs in which he took enormous pride (not forgetting that he also designed many other imposing edifices like the U.S. Supreme Court Building), but reports of Colonel Colvill's presence there are considerably more perplexing.

The sidebar notation in the *Daily* incorrectly ascribes Colvill's ghostly presence to the fact that he was the first to be buried in the Capitol rotunda, but that is simply untrue. He is in fact buried beside his wife, Jane Elizabeth, in Cannon Falls, where a statue and monument honor the memory of his service to the United States. His body was the first to lie in state in the rotunda after the Capitol was completed shortly before his death in 1905, but that hardly seems reason enough for his spirit to hang around the building. A monumental statue in the Capitol honors his memory, but that also seems an unlikely reason for his spiritual being to take up residence there.

But, even without a ready explanation for this hero's haunting of our Capitol, this ghost story inspires me to record the story of the Battle of Gettysburg and disclose here why the First Minnesota Volunteer Infantry Regiment is so acclaimed in historical circles. It also gives me the opportunity to relate a family story that may or may not have spiritual overtones.

On July 2, the second day of the Battle of Gettysburg in 1863, the First Minnesota was located atop Cemetery Ridge, overlooking the center of the heaviest fighting, while supporting an artillery battery after a lengthy forced march in midsummer heat to reach the battleground. The Third Corps of the Union Army had unwisely taken up a position far in advance of the rest of the Union defense forces and the Confederate troops under rebel General James Longstreet boldly attacked and routed the exposed troops of the Third Corps, who retreated in disorganization and confusion.

The situation became critical as the center of the Union army collapsed. Without reinforcement, that center would give way completely, Union troops would be divided and the battle would almost certainly be lost.

At that moment, Major General Winfield S. Hancock arrived and, quickly assessing the gravity of the situation, rode up to the First Minnesota and asked what unit they were. Colonel Colvill identified the regiment and himself as commanding officer. Without hesitation, Hancock ordered, "Charge!"

Tempered by action in a number of previous battles, the 262 disciplined Minnesotans fixed bayonets and moved en masse down the hillside, following Colonel Colvill's lead into the heart of ferocity, pausing to fire a musket volley into the Confederate ranks, then breaking into a run as they approached the somewhat sheltered positions that the Confederate soldiers occupied. A dry creek bed called Plum Run at the bottom of the ridge was crossed in the midst of withering fire from the rebel troops. Fallen comrades littered the area behind them, dead and wounded, including their commander and his horse, but the remains of the regiment lowered their bayonets to meet the enemy with nothing more than steel blades, pressed forward by their own bravery and momentum.

Unhesitating in the face of the bloody carnage they were incurring, every Minnesotan who could still advance continued his charge into the front line of the enemy, fighting hand-to-hand and breaking through to face yet more losses from musket fire in the hands of Longstreet's second line of troops, which they also vanquished. The center of the Confederate line was broken, but fewer than 50 men of the First Minnesota remained standing. Nonetheless, they held the vastly larger enemy in check until reinforcements could be brought up, at which point the Confederates retreated, leaving the field to the victorious Union Army.

An ironic sidebar to Colonel Colvill's story is that he had been relieved of duty and was under arrest just prior to the battle. He had disobeyed an order on June 29 to have his men wade across a shallow stream and allowed them to avoid wet feet by crossing on a log or a footbridge. He was only returned to command the morning of the attack.

Before his troops reached the dry creek bed in their charge, Colonel Colvill was felled by two severe wounds that would leave him partially crippled the rest of his life and required months of recovery. Despite that fact, he later re-enlisted in the First Minnesota Heavy Artillery Regiment and was commissioned as colonel of that unit, serving in the Chattanooga area until the end of the war. His continuing invalidism also did deter not him from later public service in his adopted state and he was successful in business, both in his law office at his hometown of Red Wing and as publisher of newspapers in that area. He was appointed state Attorney General in 1866-68 and was twice elected to the state legislature. In 1887, President Grover Cleveland appointed him registrar of the Duluth Land Office and he moved to that city and also opened a law office there. After his wife's death in 1894, he retired to a homestead he acquired seven miles northeast of Grand Marais in an area that bears his name to the present time. A plaque was dedicated to his memory by the North Shore Historical Society in 1936.[29]

All of which has still not presented any reason for his spirit to continue haunting our state Capitol, so we'll simply leave it at that, but perhaps my family's connection to all of this will add a suitably spiritual twist for which I'm sure the reader has by now grown impatient.

Since my childhood, I've heard my mother's family talk about an ancestor named John D. Logan of Pennsylvania, who came to Northfield in 1855 as a 17-year-old youth. In 1861, he enlisted in Company G of the First Minnesota and was promoted to corporal in that unit later that year. Somehow, he was wounded while on picket duty, but would return to duty and serve honorably until 1863.

The version of the story that I've always heard now deviates slightly from that posted on the Web under his name at http://FirstMN.phpwebhosting.com.

In my family, it was said that John D. suffered sunstroke during the long forced march of the regiment to join the Battle of Gettysburg. According to our story, his comrades laid him in a shaded spot and continued their march in the humid midsummer heat to their date with destiny.

Apparently, the official records do not substantiate our version exactly, stating only that he did suffer severe sunstroke in June 1863 from which he never fully recovered. Thus he missed the First Minnesota's valiant charge in the Battle of Gettysburg.

He would be discharged for disability in January 1864, never having returned to active service, but for some reason having been demoted to private.

The implication, of course, is that the fortuitous sunstroke likely saved his life or averted the severe injuries that would have been likely in that battle.

Might John D.'s guardian angel have resorted to somewhat desperate measures to save him from the coming carnage? My family always seemed to nod in that direction, but what is for certain is that without the sunstroke, he would have been in the midst of the desperate battle and might not have lived to establish a successful sawmill business on the railroad line midway between St. Cloud and Little Falls 15 years after the war. Here he also surveyed, platted and promoted the townsite of Royalton, taking a leading role in public affairs there and serving as the first president of the village after its incorporation, as well as serving as organizer and first commander of the Phil Sheridan Post of the Grand Army of the Republic.

If his guardian angel interceded to save him, that spirit appears to have done well. John D. would go on to live 44 years after missing the First Minnesota's charge into the certain destruction that saved the battlefield at Gettysburg. He would die peacefully in August 1907 in the town he created and fostered throughout his later life.[30]

While these tales of hauntings in public places certainly do not exhaust the trove of such ghostly goings-on in *Haunted Minnesota,* they do explore the most commonly reported occurrences.

CHAPTER 3

Haunts on the Home Front

As if ghostly encounters in a public place aren't scary enough, imagine the dread that a wraith could create within the "safety" of your own home, apartment or dormitory room. Of course, that would depend to some degree on how malevolent you perceived the presence to be. In some instances, those spirits have come to be perceived by people as actually being kindly, even beneficent, to them. In others, the specter is always encountered with fear or loathing.

Surprisingly, or perhaps not considering that a good deal of activity of a spiritual nature goes on there, St. John's University at Collegeville just west of St. Cloud seems to harbor several specters, including that of Murro, a bear that was an early mascot to the school.

Perhaps the most ominous ghost at St. John's is that of an angry and vengeful mother whose son, a young monk at the abbey, was killed in a fall from scaffolding during construction of the Abbey Church. The mother was said not to have accepted the explanation by the abbot, even interrupting the dedication ceremony for the new building to engage in further argument.

Finding no satisfactory explanation for her son's death, the distraught mother boarded a buggy and left the campus in a huff. The buggy overturned into the small lake adjacent to the road and she drowned. But her spirit maintained its animosity for the place where she and her son died and shortly after her death, wet footprints began to be found traveling the center aisleway of the church. No longterm remedy for her presence was ever efficacious and when the new church was built in the later 20th century on the same spot, a long crack opened in the center aisleway during the dedication rites.

The lake in which the spectral woman drowned is also part of the story of two other hauntings. Brother Anselm Bartolome is said to have drowned there sometime after the anguished mother. Brother Anselm also makes his presence known by leaving wet footprints in the building where he taught students and his ghostly presence has been infrequently sighted at night walking along the lake's shoreline.

Then there is the sad story of Murro the Bear. A student was teasing the school mascot near the lake and whacked the bear with a boat oar. Not taking kindly to that treatment, Murro attacked the student, killing him. Authorities had little choice but to have the animal shot, but its angry spirit apparently continues to seek retribution by prowling the shoreline of the lake.[1]

Finally, the Stearns County History Museum gets credit for digging up the following relatively recent story of something supernatural at St. John's. The article appeared with 11 other ghostly stories published in *Graffitos*, an alternative newspaper.

The story states that in the late 1980s, a group of young monks at St. John's gathered for a serious discussion about a topic of mutual interest to them. While the pros and cons of the matter were being weighed and each of the monks had the chance to share his view, the others listened in silence. Suddenly a pitcher of water on the table in the meeting room levitated upward. Startled, the monks' attention was riveted on that rising pitcher and, as they watched, the pitcher circled the room three times, then crashed to the floor, broke and splashed the water all around. No one could think of any possible explanation for this eerie event.[2]

But coming as it does from the site of so many older haunts, this recent incident should come as no surprise, since there is no reason to believe that we in the modern era are any more immune to paranormal events than were our forebears.

In Minneapolis, *Star Tribune* home and garden writer Connie Nelson told the story of a house that Twin Cities psychic and ghostbuster Carol Lowell said contained 12 spirits.

At that time, the 101-year-old house was the home of Virginia Van Dusen. Over the years that Virginia's family lived there, a number of them reported such ghostly goings-on as unexplainable problems with lights or appliances, the sound of footsteps when no one was there, small items gone missing and so forth.

Thus Virginia was not at all surprised by Lowell's declaration that the home was haunted, but she was a bit dazzled by the number of spirits the ghostbuster identified. The psychic was also able to identify some of the specters, telling Van Dusen that four of the spirits were a family that died of a plague in the house in 1910.

In discussing what to do about the ghosts, they decided that Lowell should eliminate 11 of them, if possible, leaving one benign presence with Virginia's blessing.

"I've never been afraid of ghosts," Virginia told Nelson. In fact, after the ghostbuster rid her home of most of the spirits, she shared a number of her stories in her neighborhood newspaper.

"I'll bet there are a lot of ghosts in these old Kenwood homes," she said.[3]

In West Duluth, a century-old home yielded a 1997 Halloween ghost story for writer Celia Tarnowski of the *Reader of Duluth/Superior*. Calling the family "the Baxters" to preserve their real identity, Tarnowski says that they had lived about 25 years in the house when she wrote the story. Apparently little of interest occurred to the family of four during their first years in the house, but after that peace and quiet, they began to notice strange things going on in their home.

Mrs. Baxter surmised that the ghostly activity might been spurred by one or both of the events that happened almost simultaneously four years after they moved in. Rummaging in the attic, she discovered two early photographs that she liked and planned to have cleaned, reframed and hung in the dining room. At that same time, renovation work began on the house. It wasn't long afterward that the unexplainable began, too.

Television and lights would go on and off on their own. A heavy plastic bucket filled with wooden puzzle pieces inexplicably fell off the shelf where it was stored and crashed noisily on the floor. The toilet flushed when no one was near it.

Tracking back to when these odd occurrences began, Mrs. Baxter decided to try putting the two pictures back in the attic. The strange happenings abated, at least for a while.

But whenever the family would consider an inside remodeling project, peculiar things would resume. Once, a large toolbox too heavy to lift was placed on a countertop flush to the wall. For no apparent reason, it suddenly crashed to the floor. Coughing noises were heard coming from an empty upstairs bedroom a number of times. Doors opened and closed, footsteps were heard going up and

down the stairs when no one was there, even the smells of pipe smoke, perfume or freshly brewed coffee would be encountered in empty rooms.

One night when she went to the bathroom, the posters in the daughter's bedroom were all taken down and stacked neatly in a pile. Early one morning, they awoke to a racket downstairs in the kitchen. Upon investigating, they found the blender, stand mixer and electric can opener all running – on their own – when no one was yet stirring from the comfort of their beds.

The daughter was the only one who actually saw the ghost. Returning from school, she noticed a gray-haired woman wearing a blue dress sitting in the dining room. The girl went into the kitchen and asked her mother who the visitor was. They went to the dining room to investigate. The woman had simply vanished.

No one in the family sensed any malevolence on the part of the spirit and at times the ghost even seemed to help out, as when Mrs. Baxter dropped the bathtub drain plug behind the clawfoot tub. After attempting to retrieve it using a towel, which also ended up behind the tub, she went into the bedroom to ask for her husband's help. When they returned to the bathroom, the towel she'd dropped was neatly folded next to the tub and the drain stopper was lying atop it.[4]

One of the most famous of Minnesota's haunted houses is the Griggs Mansion on Summit Avenue in St. Paul. Built in 1883 by

Chauncey W. Griggs after he accumulated a fortune in the wholesale grocery business, the house is said to be haunted by the specter of a young servant girl and by that of the long-deceased gardener and caretaker.

Reportedly, in 1915 the young woman committed suicide by hanging herself near the landing of the mansion's fourth floor. Upset over a failed love affair, her spirit has haunted the mansion ever since, and encounters with her have been reported numerous times by a variety of people over many years. There apparently are others, but that of Charles Wade, the gardener/caretaker, is the other common ghost wandering the mansion. His spirit is said to favor the home's library, where he was a frequent visitor and borrower of books.

In 1938, the Griggs Mansion was donated to the St. Paul Gallery and School of Arts and became studio space for emerging artists to learn their craft. As part of the remodeling for the change, a skylight was added to the top floor where painting classes were held. Students and teachers alike complained of an uncomfortable feeling of being watched by someone, or something, as they used the classroom.

In 1950, Dr. Delmar Rolb was hired by the academy and moved into an apartment in the front basement of the building. He reported several encounters with something "not normal" while living there, including the apparition of a tall thin man who appeared in his room one night. By the time Rolb left in 1959, it was understood that the mansion contained something that was ghostly, although there were no episodes suggesting any malevolence, just the discomfort of not feeling quite alone in the building.

After Rolb left the art faculty, two students moved into the apartment. One night, one of the students awoke to see a child's figure floating above his bed. Who or what that child might be is unknown, but the student was quite certain of what he saw and reported.

The mansion would serve as the home of the art school for 25 years, but by 1964 a new location was prepared for the school and the mansion was put up for sale. Fittingly, occult publisher Carl Weschke bought the haunted Summit Avenue building in 1964 and ordered extensive renovation of the aging facility.

An interesting character in his own right, Weschke is described by one biographer as a magician, a Tantric practitioner, a pagan and a former Wiccan high priest who played a leading role in the rise and spread of Wicca and Neo-paganism in America during the

1960s and '70s. By 1961, he was president of Chester-Kent Inc. of St. Paul and purchased Llewellyn Publishing Ltd. of Los Angeles, California, moving the company to St. Paul. At that time, Llewellyn published books on astrology and a few other New Age topics, but under Weschke's leadership the imprint would blossom into the premiere publisher of titles dealing with the Wicca religion, alternative health and healing, psychic development, earth-centered religions and almost any other occult or mystical topic.

But back to our story about the Griggs Mansion. Shortly after the remodeling work began there in 1964, the rumored haunting of his property seems to have made itself known to Weschke. Stopping by the house to check progress on his way home, he discovered an open window on the upper story. He closed it, but found it again open the next day. Checking with the workers, he was assured that they did not open it. Weschke again closed the window, but the persistent spirit continued to reopen that window for several days before Weschke in exasperation nailed the errant sash shut. Even that did not deter the force that wanted that window open, for the next time he visited the mansion, it was again open.

Weschke wasn't alone in perceiving something supernatural at work in his house. Workers on the crews reported strange noises and shadowy figures roaming the hallways. When he lived in the house, Weschke reported that he would often hear odd noises at night, doors slamming shut on their own and footsteps ascending or descending the stairs. On one occasion while working at his desk at the mansion, he reported seeing "a thin, long-faced man with white hair, dressed in a black suit" who faded away after less than a minute. A total of at least six ghosts have been reported by several sources to haunt the mansion.

So prevalent were the rumors of the Griggs Mansion haunting that three members of the *St. Paul Pioneer Press* staff were invited by Weschke to spend a night there to personally experience the haunting for a ghost story on which they were working. The three settled in for the night and all reported hearing strange footsteps moving around the house and seeing terrifying images of spirits. Not surprisingly, they hurriedly left before their vigil was scheduled to end the next morning and one of them later proclaimed that nothing would get him to go back inside that house.

In the early 1990s, Weschke sold the mansion to another private party who had little interest in occult or supernatural occurrences. It remains in private ownership and does not welcome visitors, but tales of the haunting continue to surface from time to time.[5]

On I-35 near the Iowa border, the Jensen House in Albert Lea sits atop a hill outside of town and has apparently been haunted since before it was completed by James Jensen in 1893. Earliest habitation of the site was a log homestead by an 1862 settler.

Jensen reported that he sensed something peculiar whenever he was working in a southwest upstairs bedroom of the unfinished home. He told family that he could feel someone following him and looking over his shoulder anytime he was in the room. None of his family ever agreed to occupy the room and it remained a spare room the entire 53 years that the Jensens lived in the house.

When the Jensen family moved out of the home in 1946, it was rapidly occupied by 14 different owners over the next 18 years. Neighbors' tongues began to wag in wonderment at the rapid succession of owners coming and quickly vacating the property.

By 1964, after the house sat unoccupied for the previous three years, Dick and Anita Borland moved their nine children into the rather ramshackle home. Its peeling paint and broken window panes would require a considerable renovation, but they believed they were equal to the task. That labor would become less important as they began the work. Before they even moved in, they met the first of the ghosts that they would encounter.

Several Borlands were in the yard cleaning up the place when one of them noticed a lady standing on the upstairs porch, outside that accursed southwest bedroom that the Jensen family refused to occupy. Rushing inside, the family members found the house empty – there was simply no one there.

A few months after they moved in, two of the kids encountered a woman in the upstairs hallway. She was tall, thin and wore a flowered dress and an apron. Seemingly searching for something, she implored Rebecca and Richard in a chilling voice, "Help me! Please help me!" Scared half to death, the kids ran downstairs and told their mother what they had seen. Thinking they were imagining things, it didn't take long before she had her own encounter with the strange womanly specter, who turned into the southwest bedroom and hovered near the closet. A number of other family members felt her presence in the same location, sometimes seeing her enter the closet and vanish.

Never seen downstairs, the womanly spirit appeared to be attached only to that one pesky bedroom. Another apparition, however, appeared downstairs near where a pantry had once been located. Much older than her companion ghost, this spirit would appear and then gradually fade away. After seeing the ghost several times over the next 1¹/₂ years, Anita believed that it was the same spirit the family had encountered upstairs, perhaps just in an incarnation of her later life.

Anita talked with a relative of the Jensen family, who recognized the description perhaps as "Grandma Jensen," a compassionate ancestor who matched that description. There seemed little likelihood that the two apparitions were of the same person, leaving the family to wonder just who the upstairs ghost could have been while it occupied the temporal world.

Meanwhile, as a private residence, this haunted house is off limits to visitors.[6]

Back in northern Minnesota, a woman related a story to the author of an unusual haunting in her rural Duluth home. The family has come to call this specter Richard, after her great-grandfather, who died in an underground mining accident. The rationale for the name becomes clearer when she explains that he seems to prefer to spend most of the time in the basement of their home.

The woman first became aware of Richard's presence when they were occupying a mobile home on the property as they started to build their permanent residence.

"Mainly, Richard makes his presence known by moving things from where they should be, but I first became aware of him one evening when I was in bed with the door to the bedroom nearly closed. I heard the door opening and when I started to turn to see who could have gotten into the house, something stopped me and I couldn't turn or move. After a few moments, I just drifted off to sleep. I didn't know what had happened, but there was definitely something ghostly going on."

She says that she had hoped that after they moved into their new house that Richard wouldn't follow them. But from the time they moved in, they were aware that he had joined them. They would often find a basement door open that they all knew had been securely closed. The problem of the repeatedly opened door was finally solved when they installed a solid lock on the outside of the door.

"I don't think the lock would stop him, if he wanted to open the door, but it seems to have convinced him to just stop," the woman says. Meanwhile, the family feels comfortable going to the basement during daylight, but none of them, including their dog, is comfortable descending at night. When necessary, two or more go down together to do whatever needs doing after dark.

Richard's presence is not particularly scary, just mainly annoying. The woman says he seems to seek acknowledgement of his presence by hiding things. When she finds some item missing, she often shouts at Richard and, within minutes, will usually find the object.

Richard is much less likely to make his presence felt if she simply acknowledges him by occasionally greeting him aloud. She admits that several times when she is upset with him and shouts her frustration at him for moving some object, she will later discover that she is the culprit. On those occasions, she always apologizes to the apparition.

Her daughter is the only family member to have actually seen the ghost of Richard briefly. She describes him rather humorously as being the vague image of a partially dressed man in Fruit of the Loom-brand underwear and work socks. From that brief sighting, however, her description of the apparition does match her grandmother's memory of the appearance of the living Richard. The daughter also tells me of an evil presence that she and a fellow employee have sensed in the file room of a medical facility where they work. That story accompanies her grandmother's account of a malevolent spirit in the workplace at the beginning of the next chapter.

That three generations of this family are gifted with sensitivity to paranormal presences also raises the probability that this characteristic is inherited in some families.[7]

While the stories of the vengeful hauntings at St. Mary's and St. John's universities are longstanding and documented in numerous sources on paranormal events, they are certainly not the only tales of ghostly activity in academic settings. There are numerous eerie stories from a variety of Minnesota colleges and universities, fitting properly into this chapter because the hauntings are most commonly sited in campus residence halls.

In central Minnesota, three buildings at St. Cloud State University are said to be haunted by women who came to untimely ends at the college. In at least one instance, students, faculty members and janitorial personnel have all reported the sound of high heels in a hallway where there was no one present.

In nearby St. Joseph at the College of St. Benedict, the ghost of a nun buried in the convent cemetery appears to troubled women students who walk by the graveyard. There is also a room where the ghost of a student who died continues to reside. Sounds of moaning and crying have been reported and are said to have become so disturbing that the room was eventually sealed off.

Concordia College's Hoyum Hall in Moorhead seems to have a ghost of a somewhat mischievous temperament, perhaps more correctly a poltergeist, a troublesome imp, than a full-blown ghost. The women residents in the hall have reported hearing their names called out as they were sleeping. A number of them also report flooded bathrooms, papers that have been moved or tampered with and radios or televisions turning on by themselves.

Mankato State University in southern Minnesota has a respectable list of ghostly reports. One specter is fond of stealing rolls of toilet paper from the main storeroom and another ghost seems to be perpetually locked inside his room, ringing the buzzer to get out. Perhaps the most interesting report is of an apparition that gets his kicks by going on panty raids in the dorms.[8]

At the South Campus of St. Thomas University, Cretin and Grace halls may also be haunted, according to a report in *The Aquin* newspaper of November 1, 2002.

Perhaps the most chilling occasion of a ghostly encounter was reported by a woman student who was lying in bed approaching sleep when she felt a presence in her room. Frightened, the woman nonetheless demanded that whatever was present show itself. In the twinkling of an eye, a face appeared in the wall, mouthing unheard words to the girl. It took her no time to obtain housing in another dormitory on the main campus.

Another odd occurrence involved a male student who was on his way to do laundry in Cretin Hall. Stopping at a soda machine, he inserted his money, but the beverage refused to fall. He banged and shook the machine to no effect. Pausing, he was about to depart, when the can simply dropped into the slot.

Since residence hall advisors had warned students during orientation that if anything unusual happened, it was only polite to thank whoever rendered the help aloud. The student said his thanks and went on to the laundry, where he found the card-swiper flashing "welcome" on the screen.[9]

In the previous chapter, we mentioned the kidnapping of Hamm's Brewery scion William Hamm Jr. by the infamous Barker-Karpis Gang. It figured in the probable haunting of St. Paul's Landmark Center by the ghost of underworld figure Jack Peifer. It develops that the home where Hamm Jr. spent part of his boyhood also appears to have ghostly presences.

The mansion, built in 1892 at 668 Greenbrier (then known as Cable Avenue) by William Hamm Sr., was a gift for his bride, Marie. It was across the street from the mansion built earlier by Hamm Sr.'s father, Theodore, the founder of the Hamm's Brewing Company. By the time of Theodore's death in 1903, William Sr. and Marie's family had outgrown the home they built. They moved across the street into the older mansion built by Hamm's father and mother. Over the years, a number of Hamm family members would build and occupy homes in the same area. William Sr.'s original home was used for many years by other members of the Hamm family. In 1934, the Hamms sold the mansion, and it served as a slowly deteriorating boardinghouse for 40 years. In 1976, it was acquired by Karin and Richard DuPaul, who have spent years restoring the historic mansion to its former glory.

The DuPauls reportedly had an attraction to the house even before they considered buying it. Despite being a deteriorated hulk that would require a great deal of time and restoration, their fascination with the place increased. They decided to take the plunge and buy it. Before they even had a chance to move in, they came to believe that there was something supernatural about the old mansion. Still living in their former residence, both Karin and Rich suddenly had the feeling one night that they should go to the mansion. The hunch was so strong that they complied. When they arrived at the house, they found water dripping everywhere from burst water pipes. Their intuitive feeling to visit the house avoided an expensive, disastrous flood in the building.

Another night, after they moved in, Rich was wakened by a shake and felt that he should go to the basement. There, he found that several cardboard boxes stacked next to the furnace were smoldering – despite the fact that the furnace had not been working and they were using the fireplace for temporary heat.

Such ghostly occurrences have convinced the DuPauls that something unnatural resides in their home, but it doesn't particularly bother them because they've deduced that they can live with whatever or whomever it may be.[10]

Returning to the Duluth area, we find eight ghostly tales that were discovered by former *Duluth News Tribune* staff writer Laurie Hertzel, who now writes for the Minneapolis *Star Tribune*, and published October 29, 1989, under the headline "Ghost Stories People Believe." A couple of them are paraphrased here. All were reported without identifying the original sources, likely at the request of those telling Hertzel the tales.

Told completely in first person by a woman identified only as being in her early 40s, the first story involves a haunting at a home on West Fifth Street. The woman reported that when she was about 6 years old, she awoke one night to see a man dressed in 1930s or 1940s attire leaning against the doorway with his hands in his pockets and his feet crossed.

"I remember being terrified," the woman told Hertzel. "It was sort of a test of will. I didn't want him in my room. I felt as though somehow my energy had to keep him out of that room. But I felt he could come in any time he wanted. It was sort of like he was laughing at me."

At that moment, a bit after midnight, her aunt let herself into the house after completing her evening job. The specter turned and looked down the stairway to where her aunt was entering and then simply walked away.

For years, the woman wondered who or what she had experienced, but kept the episode to herself. Saying she continued to remember the intensity of her feelings during the event, she finally broke her silence by mentioning it to her brother, who responded with a surprised, "You saw him, too?"

Her brother told her that he saw an apparition of the same description in the hallway near his bedroom at the other end of the hall. Neither of them, however, ever encountered the ghost in any other part of the house. The woman did not report that any others of her family ever told of seeing the ghostly apparition.

Since Laurie Hertzel is such a good storyteller, I can't resist one more from the same article.

A man says that he bought a 65-year-old house in east Duluth and hired his brother to paint the interior. It didn't take long for the place to spook the brother.

"In one bedroom that he was painting, he'd put a coat of paint on the wall that looked like it covered," the man told Hertzel, "but the next day the old, lighter layer of paint showed through his new coat." Eventually, the brother needed seven coats of paint to cover the old layer.

But it was on a night when the brother built a fire in the fireplace and slept in the living room that he first actually saw the ghost of the house.

"In the middle of the night, he woke up and this lady with a blue gown was standing by the fireplace looking at him. He said she had kind of grayish hair."

The brother would experience another sighting of the gray-haired lady in the blue dress a few years later while attending the University of Minnesota-Duluth, and staying at the house. This time, she was in the third-floor bedroom that he occupied and simply walked out of the room and down the hall.

The owner's wife had her share of strange goings-on in the home.

"I used to hear strange things," she told Hertzel. "I heard footsteps going up to the third floor, going up and down. It was a sound that sent cold chills up my spine."

Their son also had experiences with the ghost. The boy slept in the room that had been such a painting problem for the owner's brother. His father reported that numerous times the boy came into his parents' bedroom in terror, saying there were hands in his bed.

"He'd be sleeping and wake up scared to death and would come into our bedroom screaming that someone was trying to touch him," the owner said, noting that their son's experiences eventually ended. The owner's brother, however, had another ghostly lady encounter during a visit just the summer before the article appeared in 1989.

"He and his girlfriend stayed on the third floor and he woke up and saw the ghost walking around the bedroom, then going down the hall. At first he thought it was his girlfriend, but he got up and she was still asleep in her bed," the owner related.

Although the owner himself never saw or experienced any sign of the ghostly presence, he believed the stories told by his brother, wife and son. "There's a lot of stuff we don't understand very well. It's something that has definitely been experienced, and it's hard to explain those experiences," he summed up.[11]

In her 1992 *Ghostly Tales of Minnesota*, Ruth D. Hein tells of a rural Isanti County home that newlywed owners moved into in 1975, not questioning why it sat empty for more than two years, despite being a desirable home and site.

It didn't take long before the wife had her first ghostly experience. While vacuuming the floors, she thought that she could hear water running. Her husband was outside and she was alone in the house. Shutting off the vacuum, she discovered that the sound of running water was coming from the bathroom.

Cautiously, she approached that room and found that both faucets were turned on full, but no sign of who, or what, had turned them on. Thus began a 10-month barrage of strange occurrences that could only be termed as unnatural. About a month after the first instance, the newly married woman took a day off, planning to finish organizing her first kitchen. Busily rearranging things, she was startled by a roaring rumble that she could not identify.

"I went to check the basement. When I opened the door, a wave of hot air hit me. I thought the house was on fire and slammed the door. I started for the phone, wondering who to call and what our fire number was."

After calming down, she reopened the basement door and found no evidence of smoke that would indicate a fire, just the insufferable heat. The roar that had frightened her was the furnace running.

"But why was it running?" she wondered. It was a 72-degree F. June day and the thermostat was set at the lowest setting, 52 degrees. With nowhere else to turn, she called the fuel oil company and a repairman advised her. Nothing he suggested shut down the errant furnace. He finally told her to unscrew the fuse to shut it off. It was the only instance in the couple's long residency in the house that the furnace performed erratically.

But the running water and furnace weren't the end of strange happenings in the home. Shortly after the furnace episode, the wife was relaxing in the kitchen with a cup of coffee when a booming crash broke her solitude. After spilling coffee all over the kitchen, she dashed upstairs to see what was happening. She discovered that a troublesome window that she had forced open a month earlier had slammed shut. That seemed peculiar, since she had attempted to close it during a rain storm and had difficulty getting it shut.

To that point, the incidences of unnatural goings-on only involved inanimate objects. Then, a month or so after the window slamming, the couple's black Labrador puppy snuck up into a large overstuffed chair. He knew he wasn't allowed on the furniture and the woman chastened him by saying, "Hey Gus, you'd better get your little bones out of that chair! You know you can't be on furniture!"

Turning for just a moment to dry her hands on a towel, she heard a sharp yelp and a thud. Turning and hurrying into the living room, she found Gus spread-eagled on the floor in front of the chair, a look of sleepy astonishment in his eyes. Since he'd been snuggled well back in the seat of the chair for his nap, she had no idea how he suddenly fell to the floor. Unfortunately, Gus wasn't talking about the incident.

No one seemed to believe the woman when she tried to describe the strange occurrences, at least not until her husband was present during another strange happening involving another upstairs window. Trying to find relief from a hot, humid August afternoon, their peace was suddenly interrupted by a loud bang and the sound of shattering glass. Rushing upstairs, they found that the bedroom window had imploded into the room. Glass was everywhere. They tried to determine what caused this episode. There were no clues as to what force had caused the window frame to burst into the room, and her husband was suddenly willing to consider that their home was haunted.

It wouldn't take long for his suspicions to be solidified. The couple had just returned home from work and were going through their mail when a large window fan sitting on the floor turned on. Engrossed in the mail, the wife told her husband they didn't need the fan, since it was a comfortable temperature in the room.

"I know," he said. "Why did you turn it on?"

She answered that she hadn't switched on the fan, accusing him again of turning it on needlessly.

Turning from their mail, they looked at the fan whirling at top speed. It was eight feet from either of them and neither could have reached the switch.

With the onset of winter, the wife woke one night to hear tapping in the hallway. Fearing skepticism from her husband, she didn't mention it the next day, but again heard the tapping that night. Waking her husband, she shushed him, saying simply, "Listen."

"What's that tapping?" he asked. With no logical reason for a tapping sound, they concluded that there had to be something supernatural in the house.

The couple then checked with old-timers in the neighborhood and were told that the builder of the home had been a bachelor who was terrified of thunderstorms. Since the area was prone to such turbulent storms, he took the precaution of building a root cellar in the back yard near the house, where he could take shelter. During a severe 1953 storm, he retreated to the cellar. A giant pine tree was uprooted and fell directly onto the protective shelter, smashing the roof, which fell into the cellar.

After the storm, a neighbor found the bachelor in his root cellar, backed tight against a wall and quite dead. With no serious injuries evident, the neighbors concluded that he died of fright.

The bachelor was not the only suspect in the haunting. The couple later learned about a 1960s occupant who lived with his wife and children in the house. This husband and father was taking medication for high blood pressure. The blood pressure meds of the time had a serious side effect, depression. As he continued taking his medication, he sank into deeper and deeper woe.

The man's wife worried about his deteriorating personality, but daily chores had to be done and she took the kids to town to get groceries. Returning an hour or so later, they could not locate the

man. Fearing the worst, the woman ordered the kids into the house and called a neighbor for help in her search.

The neighbor found the husband's body hanging in the barn. The couple speculates that he might be the unearthly incarnation haunting their house.

But either their research into possible sources for the haunting or the wife's confronting of the spiritual presence shortly afterward seemed to have a salutary effect. In her ghostly confrontation, the woman reported saying, "Now look. We aren't going to get scared and run. We love it here and we plan to stay. Don't you worry, we'll take good care of your place for you and for us, since it's our place now. So you can just leave. Please go and be at peace!"

Her assurances to the spirit were evidently salutary, since the couple and their children lived the next 17 years in the house without anything of a wildly unexplainable nature happening there. Their family grew up in the house and would occasionally hear or see something that was a little different. Their parents would off-handedly explain these goings-on as simply their ghost checking up on them.

Growing up, their kids indulged in a game anytime they heard a tapping. They'd tap back to see if the spirit would respond. However, they quickly discovered that the tapping they heard was sometimes one of their parents playing a trick on them.[12]

As a writer, I try to maintain a certain level of healthy skepticism about information that comes to me. However, I am also a family man and have found several stories of supernatural happenings within my own family circle. I am not the sort to openly declare my family to be untruthful or unstable, so I share some of the family lore here.

My daughter has told us numerous times of a man in her bedroom. The first time was shortly after we moved into our home in Two Harbors and our preschool daughter asked at breakfast, "Who was the man in my room last night?"

We looked at one another in puzzlement. "What man?" her mother asked.

"The man with the long hair and shirt like a checkerboard," the daughter responded. "He was looking at me when I woke up."

With a bit of a chill, her mother remembered an episode that she'd had in the upstairs bathroom, across the hallway from our daughter's bedroom. With no breeze or other disturbance, she'd been spooked to see both the shower curtain and the towels moving as if being manipulated by a pair of hands.

But she assured our daughter that no one resembling her description of the man had been in the house during the night.

The child would report numerous instances of seeing the strange man through the years – always at night and always in her bedroom. As the years passed, a number of her overnighting friends would likewise report waking suddenly in the darkness to see a misty long-haired presence wearing the plaid shirt standing over our daughter's bed looking down at her.

Of the friends who saw the ghostly presence, only one was actually unnerved by the encounter. Even years later and after many visits in our home, she still refuses to go to the second floor where the bedroom is located. She'll drive to a convenience store to use the bathroom, rather than go to the one on the second floor.

Our youngest son also tells of some kind of ghostly activity when he came home to an empty house one day as a boy. Hearing an unusual whirring noise, he decided that it came from the basement and went down to investigate. As he rounded the corner from the stairway into the area where an antique sewing machine was located, he observed the machine running, despite it being unplugged and barely functional to start with. As he entered the area, the machine stopped humming, although the needle assembly continued its up-and-down motion for a few moments before complete silence descended on the scene.

While one of the girls did feel frightened by her encounter with our ghost, we have been unable to track down any information that would lead us to believe there is any danger from our supernatural being. Indeed, the origin of the spirit remains a mystery, since it doesn't match descriptions of anyone connected to the house prior to our ownership. By Two Harbor's standards, at less than a century old, the building is young and, while a number of former owners have passed on, there is nothing in local lore to suggest any reason for one of their spirits to linger in our home.[13]

On the Mesabi Iron Range, Brian Leffler of Chisholm is a founding member of the Northern Minnesota Paranormal Investigators (NMPI) and has posted photographic and videotape evidence of several paranormal or supernatural Iron Range presences on the Web.

At Christmas 2002, Brian shot a number of still photos at his son's preschool and in his home. The photo at the Hibbing Parents Nursery School and Daycare shows a misty area in the lower right corner and an orb at left center of the picture, but his brief description accompanying the photo says that a number of pictures in his house also astonished him by revealing a number of orbs and mists. After examining the photos, Brian says he carefully checked his camera for any abnormalities that might explain the paranormal images and found nothing that would explain them. He did find a speck of dust that consistently appeared in the same place on the upper corner of all the pictures, while the orbs and misty areas were found in a variety of locations on the photos.

Speaking of the photos in his home, Brian writes, "We have had several odd occurrences there. We've heard many thumps and crashes that we can find no explanation for, along with several of us hearing the voices of a woman and little girl talking to each other and calling our puppy. The puppy barks and growls at nothing on frequent occasions. We find tightly shut doors that have popped open, also without any reason. A friend who is somewhat psychic has visited the house and said that there is at least one ghost here. We call one of them Amanda, which just popped into my fiancee's head one day while she was heading to the basement."

Brian's fiancee at the time submitted two photos in May 2003 showing peculiar mists and orbs near a china hutch in their house and reinforced his story of strange happenings in the house.

Brian was one of a group of NMPI investigators checking a Mountain Iron apartment leased by one of the group's newest members. The investigation took place on December 13, 2003, after the woman revealed to the group that she had seen a little girl of about 5 years of age.

They set up a Sony Handicam in the apartment hallway with the night shots option on, and one of the investigators sat on the floor in a bedroom attempting to communicate with the spirit of the little girl. Another member, identified cryptically in the Website report as "pbodle," was directly behind the camera. Brian was to the left of the camera looking at the fold-out screen. He gripped his still camera in his right hand.

"Phil and I witnessed a flash go across the screen and I commented to him that there was a flash and did he see it. He responded that he had."

Rewinding the videotape, they were able to see something amorphous when they played back the tape and Brian made still pictures of those images, which appear with the report of the investigation posted on the Web.[14]

One final Iron Range tale came to Ruth Hein for her 1999 volume, *More Ghostly Tales from Minnesota* from Paul of Hibbing. Paul, in turn, heard the story from a couple who were living in a very old house built atop an abandoned underground mine between Chisholm and Buhl. Although less renowned than the Mesabi's famous open pit mines, several of the areas of the range did employ underground mining in earlier times to extract rich veins of iron ore buried deep beneath the surface.

As related by Paul, the couple were quietly reading before bedtime when a figure that they could only describe as an early underground miner suddenly just rose silently through the floor into the room where they sat. As reported, the apparition's clothing was gritty and dusty, he wore an old-fashioned miner's helmet with a lantern attached and his boots were so worn and supple that he made no sound during his brief moments in the house. He barely paused before disappearing through the wall of the room.

The couple nicknamed the apparition "Zeke" and deduced that what they had seen was the shade of one of the old timers, who apparently thought his underground shift was over and was headed home for the night. The couple never saw the ghostly miner again and subsequently moved out of the house into somewhat less disquieting quarters.[15]

Back in my home territory, two brothers from Two Harbors told me about an apparition their entire family experienced at one time or another in their family home. With a number of siblings and their parents, their mutual experiences seem to be ample evidence that something spiritual was going on in their home on a quiet residential street.

As experienced by various members of the family, the ghost might merely be recognized as footsteps where no one was present, or occasionally as a hazy or misty "something" of which they'd catch a glimpse from the corner of their eye, or the sound of someone going up the stairway – again, when no one was in that part of the house.

Dan, the brother who told the bulk of the story, had the spookiest encounter with the entity and told me of that episode.

"I was upstairs sleeping and remember that it must have been pretty late at night, because I felt like I'd been asleep for quite awhile. Suddenly, I felt something plop down on my bed and throw an arm and a leg across me. That got me wide awake in a helluva hurry, and I kicked out and squirmed to get away. When I started that, whatever it was just stopped without making any sound.

"None of us ever got a good enough look at the ghost to figure out if it was a man or a woman and that was the least of my worries when it had its arm and leg over me, but it seemed pretty strong. 'course, I was just a kid when it happened, and some of the women in those days were pretty strong, too."

Turning to his brother, I asked if he'd heard that tale before. "Sure, ever since we were kids," he says.

Dan hesitates a second and then says with a grin, "I guess I'd feel a little better about it if it was a lady ghost that tried to climb in bed with me, but I guess I'll never know, 'cause none of us lives in the house anymore."[16]

A woman from Alexandria posted her story of haunts in her home under the title "Knocks, Shadows and Apparitions," on the Ghost Village Website in September 2005, saying her experiences started in March 2001. The story is of particular interest because it pulls together several threads that seem to appear in many other stories. For example, they were greeted by the ghostly cohabitants shortly after moving in. The episodes of encounters appear to have tapered off as the spirits and people became accustomed to each other. Finally, as in many ghost stories, the several spirits infesting the house did not outwardly manifest either malevolent or benevolent intent, perhaps merely being curious to meet the new folks before deciding what to do about them.

Saying that she had never believed in ghosts, preferring to believe that stories of such things could be easily explained by natural events, the woman indicated that she was changing her mind after 4½ years of living in the house that she, husband and two daughters occupied. In the interim, a baby daughter joined the family and was 18 months old at the time of the story.

"Within a month of moving in, my husband and I started hearing footsteps upstairs when we were downstairs. Our bedroom is downstairs, our kids' are upstairs. Every time we hear the footsteps, either nobody is upstairs or our kids are sleeping. This first time we heard the footsteps, the kids were at their grandparents, I was sleeping and my husband was in bed watching TV. He heard someone walking down the upstairs hallway and start down the stairs. He grabbed a golf club and headed for the stairway and could still hear the footsteps on the stairs when he swung around the corner, but no one was there.

"The next time, we were talking in bed and it sounded like someone was walking all over the upstairs, as if looking for something. Our kids each had a friend overnight and I told my husband I'd go see what was going on, thinking one of the kids must have gotten up to go to the bathroom. By the time I got there, the footsteps had stopped and all four kids were sound asleep."

Saying she blamed the noises on the air conditioning, she was satisfied with that conclusion until she heard the footsteps and the AC was off.

As time passed, other weird noises that they heard sounded like heavy weights being dropped or falling, knocking in the stairwell and what sounded to be her husband coughing in the downstairs bathroom when the observer was in the upstairs bathroom directly above. All of these strange noises occurred when there was no one around to explain their origins.

Before long, the daughters told their mother they were seeing "people" in the house. Unsure whether to believe the girls or not, the woman said that the girls told of seeing images ranging from fuzzy to perfectly clear. The oldest daughter said she saw an older, heavy man sitting in a living room chair, standing in the hallway and outside by a swing set. Of the last incident, she reported that he waved to her.

The younger daughter told her mother that she had seen a little girl and talked with her. Her mother told her to tell the ghostly girl to go be "with God," which apparently worked, since the girl ghost has not returned. Another time, this daughter reported seeing an older man, a young woman and a teen-age boy, all in suits, ties and a stylish dress. It seemed that they could see her and they looked around the room with interest, as they distracted her from the television she had been watching.

Though her husband never reported seeing anything of a ghostly nature, the woman says that she believes she caught a momentary glimpse of a tall, thin man with dark hair walking across their lawn. Her mother was more positive of her sighting during a visit with the family, telling the woman a week or two later about a "figure" she saw walk through the kitchen. It had no features, but she recognized it as a tall, thin man, raising the speculation that it might have been the same one the woman thought she saw outside.

At the time of the report in September 2005, the several spirits in her house had apparently quieted down, perhaps finally having accepted their presence in the home.

"What kind of freaked me out two nights ago is that our 12-year-old was in her room with her little sister and out of the blue the 18-month-old turned and looked toward the corner. She kept waving and saying, 'Hi,' and then pointing and laughing. Her sister looked but saw nothing, so now I'm wondering if the younger girl is seeing those things," the woman concluded.[17]

A Duluth woman, who prefers not to be identified, grew up in Little Falls and says that her grandmother's home in that city was "very haunted." Nearly every member of her family reported incidents of strange goings on while at Grandma's place. While she did not report any instance of apparent malevolence or maliciousness on the part of whatever it was that occupied Grandma's house, she did say that there was always a feeling of apprehension by those who experienced encounters with the "ghost."

"Probably the most common thing that happened is that we'd hear creaking on the stairway that went upstairs, but no one was ever there when we checked on the noise," the woman reported. "Then there was the door of the bathroom that would open by itself, even though everyone made sure we latched it tightly shut when we were in the room. It would just slowly open up by itself."

Her sister was staying at Grandma's to work on a school assignment. Grandma went out for a while in the evening, and the sister was alone when she heard the sound of water running. Looking around, she found the faucet that was slowly running and turned it off. Returning to her homework, only a few minutes had elapsed when she again heard the sound of water running and again turned off the troublesome tap. Doggedly returning to her

assignment, she was startled a few minutes later to hear the faucet suddenly turned on full blast. After she turned it off, she decided she'd delay the homework and wait outside on the front porch for Grandma's return.

Several of the woman's siblings experienced being followed by an unused wheelchair stored in an upstairs bedroom. They thought perhaps the floor of the room sagged a bit, causing the wheelchair to move on its own, but that was before a couple of them had the chair follow them out of the room and turn the corner to continue chasing them in the hallway.

"My uncle and his new wife stayed at Grandma's house when they got back from their honeymoon while Grandpa and Grandma were gone on a short trip. They were asleep and his wife woke up and could hear papers rustling and saw a light coming from downstairs. She thought that Grandpa and Grandma must have gotten home and went back to sleep but was surprised the next day to find that they weren't there. She mentioned it to my uncle, and he must have told her then about the strange things that happened in the place because she would never stay in that house again."

Of her own experiences, the woman says perhaps the oddest occurrence happened after her grandfather passed away and Grandma was alone in the house. She called her grandmother just to say hello and pass the time of day. As they talked, she could clearly hear pots and pans rattling in the background in her receiver from Grandma's end of the call. Thinking one of the family must be visiting, she asked, "Who's with you?"

Grandma answered, "There's no one here. I'm here all by myself."

"Oh, that's funny. I can hear pots and pans rattling in my telephone."

"Well, it isn't me, and there's nobody else here," Grandma informed her.

She pauses a moment and says, "I clearly heard the noise, but Grandma said it wasn't her, so I don't have any idea what I heard – except maybe the ghost wanted to be sure that I knew it was still there in Grandma's house."[18]

Each year at Halloween, the *St. Paul Pioneer Press* always seems to come up with a new story or two of hauntings or other paranormal activities in Minnesota.

In the October 30, 2005, edition, writer Ellen Tomson reports on her interview with Annie Wilder (a pen name) about her haunted house, which is featured in her book entitled *House of Spirits and Whispers.* Described as a lifelong believer in angels, spirits and lost souls by Kelly Hailstone, a publicist for Llewellyn Publications which published the book, Wilder is also credited as being especially open to supernatural perspectives.

Wilder related that from her first visit to the house, she felt a spirit watching as she and her real estate agent examined the building. Located south of the Twin Cities in a Mississippi River town identified as "Sibley" in her book, Wilder said that the Victorian-era house was melancholy and gloomy at that time, but she bought it nonetheless and moved her two children, the family's belongings and the family cats into it.

In no time, she began experiencing moments of inexplicable fear, frightening dreams and out-of-body experiences for which she had no explanation. A member of her town's Heritage Preservation Commission, Wilder determined to delve into the history of her home, believing that every building with a past has some story to tell and that the actions, emotions, beliefs, hopes and fears of former occupants and their dormant memories may linger in the structure and "come alive again."

She quickly perceived that one of the strongest spirits in her home was that of Leon, the previous owner who had died six months before she purchased the house. A carpenter by trade, Leon's handiwork was found throughout the home and in her book she says that he made his presence known by knocking on walls, turning on lights, closing doors, walking noisily around, even by helping workmen renovating the house. The family also noted the frequent scent of cigar smoke or chewing tobacco. Once, Wilder even heard Leon clear his throat and another time he chuckled in her presence. She has seen him twice, looking quite regular – "a nice old guy."

She came to believe that the spirit of Leon was clearly visible and not transparent because he was only recently deceased and had occupied a physical body just a short time before her encounters. This seems to be borne out by a subsequent appearance of an apparition from a much earlier era that was holographic or transparent. The latter spirit sat motionless on the foot of Wilder's bed looking deeply despondent and hopeless – apparently grieving for a young man that Wilder perceived might have been her son. Despite considerable research, she was not able to identify any former resident or event that might account for the sad female ghost.

She was, however, able to identify three young sister-spirits whom she identified as belonging to a prominent family who occupied the house during the late 1800s-early 1900s. But that story also had a puzzling aspect to it, since the spirits she encountered were young women, whereas two of the sisters had lived to ripe old ages and died only a decade or so before she purchased her home. Why was she encountering youthful spirits instead of middle-aged or elderly apparitions?

Pondering that question, Wilder came to believe that she was seeing the sisters as young women because part of their everyday happy energy from when they lived in the home as young women remained in the structure and they thus appeared as they were at that stage of their lives.

Raised as a Roman Catholic in a family that all share strong intuitive abilities, Wilder earned a bachelor's degree in communications and film at the College of St. Catherine in St. Paul.

She told *Pioneer Press* reporter Ellen Tomson that she uses a pen name and the fictitious name for the town where she lives as a precaution because, "I don't want people to come by and antagonize the ghosts. It's a little bit of humor – but also the truth.[19]

Student reporters on the staff of the *Concordian*, the college publication of Concordia College in Moorhead, discovered several recent stories of hauntings on that campus that were reported in the October 29, 2004, edition.

Mikki Eken recorded the sad story of a ghost said to haunt Fjelstad Hall, a women's residential facility housing up to 135 freshmen and upper-class students.

The residence is also said to be occupied by the ghost of Dolorita (Dolly) Larson, a 20-year-old junior who hung herself during an episode of deep melancholy during the mid-year finals of 1953. An obvious achiever, Dolly was an honor graduate of Canby High School in 1950 and was active in church work, Luther League, the church choir and many other activities. She enrolled at Concordia and attended classes starting in the fall of 1953, continuing her active schedule by joining the Lutheran Student Organization, Lutheran Girls' Society, the college band, Nu Sigma Rho Sorority and the Ski Club. Whether such an active life contributed to her finals week depression is unknown.

Depending on the version of the tragedy you hear, Dolly either hung herself in her dorm room or in the attic chapel that was then used by residents of the dorm. The fact that the attic chapel was permanently closed to students shortly after her death would seem to validate that location and, indeed, would also seem to be borne out by the fact that special permission was required by reporter/photographer Mikki Eken to shoot a photo of the attic interior for the 2004 story.

Whichever story may be the truth, Dolly's troubled spirit is said to still inhabit the residence hall, causing strange happenings like doors opening and closing by themselves, the volume on televisions and radios to change inexplicably or objects that move mysteriously to the window sill. Eken's 2004 photo also inexplicably contained several strange bubbles or orbs of light that are often said to indicate spiritual energy in an area where spirits are suspected.

A 1984 renovation of Fjelstad Hall makes it impossible to identify the room she occupied at the time of her death, but the many instances of mysterious encounters with "something" certainly seem to make the story of Dolly's haunting credible.[20]

Other Concordia residence halls said to harbor the spirit of the same female ghost are Hoyum and Brown halls. The origin of this woman's lingering presence is uncertain, but is suspected to be a suicide in which she hung herself outside Hoyum Hall room 616. Eken ascribes several stories to the college archives, all describing the haunting in the same way.

According to one of those tales, three male students in Brown Hall had arranged their beds three high to save a bit of space in their room. The fellow in the bottom bunk was out for the evening in question and his two roommates had gone to bed and were peacefully sleeping when the one in the top bunk felt a definite, strong tug on his blankets. Yelling to his roommate to stop annoying him, he turned over and went back to sleep.

Shortly after, his roommate was wakened by the same powerful tug on his coverings. After several repetitions of these rude awakenings, the fellows decided the tugging on their bedclothes must be the result of their missing roommate playing a joke on them. But just at the edge of returning to sleep, one of the fellows rolled over to spy the pale face of woman staring at him. A black cowling or cloak covered her head and her presence lingered next to his bed. Needless to say, he definitely reported the ghostly incident the next day to campus authorities.

Not to imply that Concordia is prone to unhappy affairs of the school's female hearts, but one more story is related in Mikki Eken's story for the Halloween issue. This one relates a tale of a co-ed who fell hopelessly in love with a professor who, perfectly properly, rejected her advances. The unfortunate, unidentified woman composed a love letter to her beloved and leapt to her death from a fourth floor window of the Old Main Building, but continues to roam that floor in spectral form, whence her spirit is said to compose a love letter each year on Valentine's Day. It's said to be an exact replica of the letter the distraught woman left before her death. Strangely, in cases where the recipient decides to show the spectral letter to someone else, it simply vanishes, much akin to the spirit of the unhappy student herself.[21]

In a number of instances, destructive incidents or ghostly activity appear to be attributable to poltergeists, which are generally described as troublesome imps that create minor mayhem, rather than more serious destruction or death.

A Duluth woman tells of seeming poltergeist activity in the Eveleth home where she grew up.

The most annoying recurrent activity in which the imp indulged involved a tackle box that was faithfully returned to its proper shelf in the back porch after each use. Soon afterward, it would fly across the porch, crash against the wall and fall to the floor with a terrific racket.

Tackle would be mixed and tangled, requiring care and patience to straighten it out and return the contents to their proper slots in the box.

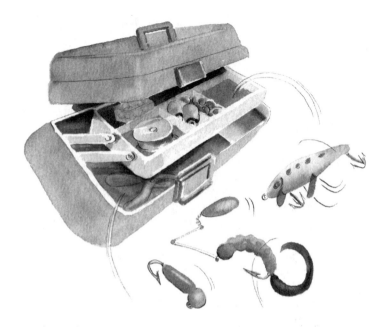

This poltergeist was most likely to wreak its havoc on the son of the family, but everyone in the house experienced the eeriness of the flying bait box at one point or another.

The woman telling the story also observed a weird episode of a spoon that was lying on the kitchen counter that suddenly began to rattle on the countertop, then abruptly zipped across to the tabletop and bounced onto the floor, narrowly missing a friend who was visiting her.

"There was never any serious damage done by our poltergeist," the woman stated. "He was just kind of annoying, the way a practical joker can be."[22]

A Two Harbors man told of several incidents of seeming poltergeist activity. Tableware or other items would inexplicably fall from seemingly secure cabinets or from perfectly level countertops, crashing to the floor. While troublesome, causing the couple to ponder what was happening in their house, there seemed nothing malevolent about them.

Their somewhat casual attitude toward this annoying spirit would all change with one frightening incident that occurred when he and his wife were upstairs and their young child was napping in the living room. They suddenly heard a bang and rushed downstairs to check on the baby's safety. In the living room they found that the entire acrylic front of their entertainment center had exploded outward, sending shards throughout the room.

The baby was unharmed, but had wakened and was staring intently at something in the now-empty space where the acrylic panel had been.

"There was nothing in the cabinet that could have caused the acrylic to explode," the man states. "The equipment inside was all okay, but the whole living room was covered with pieces of the front panel. We also wondered what the baby had been staring at in the cabinet. After talking about it, we agreed there was some kind of ghost or unnatural force causing these things to happen and we should try to get rid of it. We asked around for advice and were told we should try telling the spirit to leave while we walked around the house with burning incense. It must have worked because we didn't have any more weird things happen after we did that."[23]

While the latter story is rather indeterminate as to the source of the weird things that occurred, poltergeists have been blamed for prankish activities similar to those one might expect of a somewhat psychotic practical joker or by an impious child. One wonders if such pranks should be taken seriously, or merely be accepted as annoying. And at what point do such activities take on overtones of a more serious nature? Was the shattering of the entertainment center panel merely the result of an overly boisterous poltergeist, or a manifestation of a more sinister spirit who had been drawing attention to itself earlier with the less-destructive incidents?

To some degree, the comfort level that is felt by those experiencing such "pranks" may be one gauge we can use to determine the appropriate response. Since many people who experience hauntings record a sense of dread or apprehension, can we infer that if no threat is perceived, it's likely that none is present? In such cases, the victim of the haunting may either accept the inconvenience it causes – or, like the couple in the latter story, undertake an exorcism on their own, or even engage "ghostbusters" like the several Minnesota-based paranormal investigative groups to send the spirit to the other side.

CHAPTER 4

Haunts Where We Work

 In the previous chapter, I promised two stories about malevolent spirits lurking in workplaces. They come from a North Shore woman whose grandparents still inhabit her home (see Chapter 8) and her own Duluth-area granddaughter who reported seeing the spirit of Richard in her parents' home (see Chapter 2). I relate them early in this chapter, before I overlook my promise.

The woman told me, "Several times I've encountered a spot of nearly unbearable cold in a place I work where there are no drafts or other reasons for such a chill. They aren't in the same place every time, but seem to take place in out-of-the-way areas like the back room. I definitely have the feeling there is something evil or mean about the ghost."

Just as disconcerting, she has occasionally also heard a quiet sound of sobbing, but is not able to discern whether the crying is a man or a woman. Because she knows the spirit is evil or mean spirited, she would rather avoid any contact and has made no effort to communicate with or discover more about the presence.

"All I know for sure is that I've had several encounters, and they always give me goosebumps. The crying may have something to do with the meanness I sense. Perhaps the ghost regrets something that happened when it lived or maybe its death was violent or unpunished. All I know is that it gives me chills every time I sensed its presence. I don't want to try to find out anymore about it."

Mentioning her first encounter to fellow employees, her tale of the haunting drew laughter, and she quickly quit discussing it with them. But later, she drew a measure of satisfaction when one of the scoffers came around to her side of the story. Working alone at a desk one evening, the fellow was badly shaken by what he experienced.

"It was after dark and I was working in another area of the building," she says. "A bit later when I went into the room where he was working, he was pure white and shaking. He looked very frightened.

"It took him a few minutes to settle down, but he finally told me, 'Just before you came in, there was something sitting in that chair across from me and I could tell it was angry or wanted revenge for something. As you came in, it just disappeared.'"

His poking fun at her story ended abruptly and, in fact, he told her several times afterward that he had seen the ghost again, but would never vouchsafe the information to anyone else, remembering the scorn that she had encountered.

"He said the ghost always frightened him, even though he came almost to expect to run into it," she says.

Unfortunately, the man who could corroborate her story passed away before I could check with him on any other information he might have been able to reveal.[1]

Meanwhile, the woman's granddaughter spoke of a Duluth-area workplace spirit that was frightening to her and a fellow employee.

"I don't know anything about its history, but the fellow I work with and I both feel creeped-out when we have to go into one aisle of filing cabinets in the storage room," the granddaughter says.

"He usually finishes work at 8 o'clock in the evening, and if I have to go into that room after he leaves, I get freaked. He told me that he's heard strange noises when he's in there and that it sounded like an angry woman's voice yelling at him.

"I've never heard anything, but a while ago I was leaving the storage room and felt something like a cold finger reach into the neck of my shirt and give it a jerk backward. When I turned around to see what was going on, there was nothing there. That was especially scary because we had already figured out that the ghost was angry about something."

Unable to discover anything to which she can attribute the spiritual presence, she said the storage room may have been the scene of a long-ago murder or possibly the rape of some woman who once worked there, since the ghost seems to concentrate most of its anger against the fellow employee. Whatever the origin of the ghost, being jerked backward by the nape of the neck has made her perfectly aware that something happened to create an unhappy spirit that maintains its vigil in the workplace.[2]

In researching haunted workplaces, one is impressed with how many spirits are identified on farms. There are several likely explanations for this. Many farmsteads are in rather isolated locations and sizable numbers have been abandoned in the last 60 years as the population shifted from an agrarian emphasis to an urban existence. Abandoned, isolated locations are especially rich in potential for imaginations to run wild. Thus, some of the stories may be purely creative. But there also seem to be some stories that carry the ring of truth.

One of the most noted haunted farm sites is some 20 miles southwest of New Ulm at a farm called the "Old Twente Place." Dating from the 1880s, this tale of a haunted gravesite on the farm features a 6-year-old girl named Annie Mary Twente, her insane father and strong evidence that Annie Mary was buried alive in 1886.

Depending on the source telling the story, Annie Mary either died of "lung fever" or was a lingering survivor of an accident. Either way, the young girl was in a deep, extended coma, which led everyone involved to believe that she had died. Her initial interment was at a town cemetery, but for some reason the Twentes were uneasy about the burial and had their daughter removed from her original gravesite. Some stories state that the reason they opened the gravesite was the result of her mother's recurring dream that the girl had been buried prematurely, while others indicate the father's unstable mental state was the reason for the disinterment.

Whatever the reason might have been, upon opening the casket, the Twentes were horrified to find the inside of the coffin scratched and marred. Annie Mary's fingernails were torn, broken and bloodied as evidence of her struggle to escape, and her face was said to be a mask of terror at the realization of what had happened to her.

Needless to say, the truth of their daughter's fate did not rest easily on her father Richard's unsettled mind. Annie Mary's reburial was atop a hill overlooking the farm, a relatively common practice in those times. Richard initially built a stout wooden fence around the grave, but was dissatisfied with it and replaced it with a 4-foot-high stone wall and locked iron gate at the opening.

Soon thereafter, stories of strange goings-on near the burial site began to circulate. People reported sighting a wandering specter in a white dress. It was said the spirit wandered whenever the iron gate

was opened. Horses on the nearby road were said to refuse to pass the grave. Later, stories arose of cars stalling on the nearby bridge and headlights that inexplicably dimmed or failed in the vicinity of the burial site.

But the specter seemed incapable of preventing vandalism on the site of her burial, for the gravestone was stolen numerous times and the carefully built and locked iron gate disappeared. Trees and weather uprooted the sturdy rock wall that Richard Twente erected to protect the grave. Through the years, the site became less and less hallowed as a result of both natural forces and vandals.

Eventually, the owner of the property was petitioned by descendants of the Twente family for permission to again disinter the remains of the little girl and rebury her with her parents in a northern Minnesota gravesite where vandals would be unlikely to disturb the site and a caretaker maintained the grounds.

After her remains were removed from the farmland, the burial site was turned into crop production by the farmer who owned the property. Nothing remains of the stone wall, the trees planted on the gravesite or the headstone, which was re-erected at Annie Mary's latest burial site. In essence, the legend of Annie Mary's horrific burial and haunting of the vicinity of her grave is all that remains from this tragedy, since no recent tales of a ghost in a white dress have been reported at either the original gravesite or the cemetery that now contains her mortal remains.[3]

Outside of Duluth, a man told Laurie Hertzel of the *Duluth News Tribune* about a ghost that bothered him in a farmhouse his father had purchased after the death of "Axel," the reclusive former resident who died in the house. The man's father and uncle lived on the farm, but the narrator apparently had already moved into his own digs.

Axel had erected a concrete pillar with his name on it beside the driveway to the house. One day after purchasing the place, the man's father accidentally knocked the pillar down with his tractor and it remained on the ground. His father and his brother lived for some time at the place, but strange things began to happen after the pillar was overturned.

The brother would sense someone else in a room when no one was there. Both of the men heard footsteps on the stairs or the attic door slamming, again when no one seemed to be there. One weekend, the father asked his son, the story's narrator, to housesit the farmhouse during his absence.

"The first night I stayed there, I had just gone to bed. It was a calm night in the summer, and the attic door just slammed," the narrator told Hertzel.

Not thinking much of the episode at the time, he'd had time by the next night to ponder what had happened. He closed the door to the bedroom before retiring, figuring that way he wouldn't hear whatever was padding around.

"I was sleeping and having a dream that someone was knocking on the door – knocking and knocking and knocking. I woke up and there was still the knocking, but after a couple of times it was quiet. Then something grabbed my leg and started pulling. I took my other foot and kicked a couple of times and it was gone. I looked, but there was nothing there."

But the kicks apparently worked, for he had no other episodes with Axel afterward. He did not, however, say whether his father and uncle continued to be plagued by the cantankerous ghost of the old farmer, or if they replaced or removed the concrete pillar.[4]

In far southern Minnesota near the Iowa border, a respected Rochester businessman told of strange events while he was growing up during the mid-1930s on a farm established by his grandfather. At the time, his uncle was living with his family, helping out with farm chores and work. They shared an upstairs bedroom. At night, after shutting the door to their room, they would shortly hear the doorknob turn and the door would open about a foot. No matter how persistent he and his uncle were about shutting the door a second or third time, the knob stubbornly turned and that door swung open a foot or so. Even after they began locking it, the key would turn, fall to the floor and the door would open.

Other odd occurrences in the farm home included the night-time setting of the breakfast table by some unseen force. In the morning, they'd find everything for breakfast laid out in its rightful place, but no sign of who, or what, had done the settings.

Another time, when his father was gone for the night, the rest of the family was assembled in the kitchen after dark and one of them happened to look outside and saw what appeared to be a figure carrying a kerosene lantern from the barn toward the house. Thinking perhaps that the man of the house had changed his mind and was returning home, he and his uncle went to the back door to greet him. They plainly heard footsteps crunching in the snow, but when they opened the door and his uncle called to his father, the lights and figure had vanished.

Lighting a lantern, his uncle went out into the yard to make sure no one was there. When he reached the spot where the figure and lantern had disappeared, he saw footprints in the snow that simply stopped where the vanishing act took place.

On pleasant summer nights, a number of people reported hearing violins playing and lights moving about in a grove near the house. "It got so people would even come out from town and park along the road to listen. Some beastly hot nights we'd take blankets out into the back yard and lie there to try to stay cool. Sometimes, we'd hear the music, the same song over and over, then it would just end."

The Rochesterite could only think of one event of any moment at the farm, that being a longtime, persistent rumor that the Jesse James gang camped at a spot near the farm. He speculated that the spirit or spirits of some gang members may have returned to haunt the pleasant little grove, where they would have found momentary respite from constantly evading the long arm of the law. No records have turned up to indicate that any of the bandits displayed musical talents, but they would certainly have had lanterns to ward off the possibility that lawmen could sneak up on them under cover of darkness.[5]

Perhaps one more story of a haunted farm site will suffice to support my contention that farms seem particularly prone to hauntings.

A location outside of Willmar called Deadman's Hill has been reported to be haunted for nearly 150 years stretching back to well before the Civil War. In that long-ago era, runaway slaves were often shuttled through Minnesota on their way to freedom in Canada. Although the northern states did not condone ownership of slaves, it was legally permissible for bounty hunters to pursue runaway slaves in the north. If they succeeded in recapturing the fugitive slaves, they could return the unlucky runaways to their owners in the southern states.

From such machinations is the legend of Deadman's Hill created. The story goes that a freedom-seeking slave was successful in reaching southwestern Minnesota and was camped at the top of the hill near a pleasant farm site. Unfortunately for the runaway, he was captured by a slave hunter who had been on his trail for weeks to earn the reward offered by the slave's owner.

The bounty hunter chained the slave to a nearby fence post and lay down for a much needed night's sleep. During darkness, the slave managed to wrench the fence post from the ground and began his escape. The slave chaser awoke and the two men engaged in hand-to-hand combat until the slave managed to behead his tormenter with the bounty hunter's own sword.

Upon waking the next morning, the family in the nearby farmhouse discovered the slave's cadaver sprawled near their front porch. He had, apparently, been seriously wounded in the fight, but managed to crawl to the house, dragging the fence post and chain along with him.

The family followed the drag marks to the top of the hill, where they discovered the body of the slave chaser. They buried the body at the top of the hill while the slave was interred near the house, where they planted a tree to mark the grave.

Apparently the ghost of the runaway slave was not content to have eternally escaped his enslavement, for within a short while unfortunately two innocent lives were taken on Deadman's Hill.

The first killing resulted in the death of a man living on a nearby farm, paying rent for the property by sharing his harvest with the owner of the land. A trail in the snow led investigators away from the corpse, but inexplicably showed signs that whoever left the footprints had also been dragging something behind it – something that would be about the size of a fence post.

A second death ensued, this time claiming the life of the man hired by the dead sharecropper's widow. Again, a distinctly telltale trail led away from the dead man's body.

Only one conclusion could be reached … the ghost of the dead slave had obviously taken the lives of both these worthy farmers. It also came to be known that the family that discovered his corpse experienced many odd occurrences, like objects that disappeared for a time before turning up in unexpected places. They also reported hearing the ghostly sound of movement on many occasions. The sounds were said to start near the hill and advance upon the house, accompanied by moans and the sound of something dragging on the ground. Rattling chains were heard.

Never seen, the presence of the ghost remained frightening for many years to everyone who heard the sounds of his labored movement. Even to the present, peculiar things have persisted in taking place, but fortunately there have been no further killings attributed to the specter of Deadman's Hill. No rationale has ever been put forth for the two deaths shortly after the initial episode either, which may suggest that the runaway slave's spirit was wreaking revenge on the two dead men for complicity in the bounty hunter's success in capturing him. Like any good tale of spiritual goings-on, no earthly reason is ever required for a haunting or other ghostly activity to take place. After all, ghosts play by their own rules.[6]

With Minnesota being home to one of America's busiest ports and having already devoted several pages to rustic specters inhabiting Minnesota farmlands, perhaps a few maritime ghost stories are now in order.

As an introduction to our seagoing ghost stories it's appropriate to look generally at the idea of ghost ships sailing onward eternally over the bounding main. The term that is generally applied to all such spectral vessels is *Flying Dutchman*, originating from the loss of an actual Dutch salt-water vessel that disappeared on a voyage around Cape Horn, South America (some accounts say Cape of Good Hope, South Africa). The ship did not originally carry the name *Flying Dutchman*, which was appended to it later by sailors after it came to be common maritime knowledge that sighting a vessel that was definitely known to have foundered was an absolute harbinger of doom for ships and sailors.

Ever since, sailors have attached the foreboding name of *Flying Dutchman* to these sightings and most believe that they foretell dire conditions for those who labor over the waves.

Despite such a dire reputation for sailors, in his book *Haunted Lakes*, maritime historian Frederick Stonehouse reports that two Great Lakes ships were actually christened *Flying Dutchman*. One of the vessels wrecked within six years of launch, but the other served out a prosperous career – which would seem to prove that it is not the name that is cursed, but the ghost ship itself.[7]

The most persistent ghost ship sighting on Lake Superior is without doubt the doomed steel steamer *Bannockburn*, which simply vanished from the lake's calm surface on November 20, 1902, northwest of Keweenaw Point, Michigan. Taking all hands with her, she had been downbound from Port Arthur (now Thunder Bay), Ontario, with a cargo of grain.

The *Bannockburn*'s tie to Minnesota is not tenuous. Often a visitor, its prime cargoes were grain, and more often than not, the starting point of any voyage was the port of Duluth.

Moments before her disappearance, the ill-fated ship had been under the eye of Captain James McMaugh of the upbound *Algonquin* in swirling fog about 60 miles southeast of Passage Island, Isle Royale, Michigan. McMaugh took his eyes off the ship for a few moments to tend to navigational duties, and when he turned back again to the *Bannockburn*, he was startled to find that it had simply slipped from view. Although intermittent fog could have shrouded the doomed ship, McMaugh later said that he doubted that possibility and stated that a boiler explosion could have taken the ship to the bottom. He also said that his ship was close enough that such an explosion should have been loud enough for his crewmen to hear it.

A field of wreckage was all that remained of the Canadian-flagged vessel. A single life jacket from the ship was found on the beach by a member of the U.S. Life-Saving Service at Grand Marais, Michigan, but the sturdy ship would never again be seen in its mortal form.[8]

That doesn't mean the ship ceased to sail. Numerous stories can be found of sightings by seamen who report the ice-like apparition of the vessel driving through misty seas on its unending voyage toward Sault Ste. Marie at the eastern end of Lake Superior. So little wreckage was found and was so scattered that the location of this wreck has never been determined.

Remaining shrouded in its own mystery, the occasional sighting of the *Bannockburn* by storm-threatened seamen prompts mariners to say that its disappearance left the souls of 22 sailors seeking their own redemption.

The sightings of the ill-fated steamer have not been shown to overtly relate to any subsequent wreck, but frequently do portend impending storms and foul weather. If nothing else, the reincarnation of this ghostly vessel serves as a stark reminder to all seamen of the perilous nature of their profession and how much they depend on the particular ship on which they sail.

And one can be sure that any lonely seaman on midnight watch who espies the spirit of the *Bannockburn* on its ghostly voyage will pay heed to his rounds, wondering if this time its appearance does prophesy some disaster waiting to take his life or destroy the vessel on which he depends not only for his livelihood, but his life itself.[9]

While the Lake Superior wreck of the Canadian-flagged *Bannockburn* in Michigan waters makes any connection to Minnesota arguable, the wreck of the 730-foot SS *Edmund Fitzgerald* is inextricably tied to Minnesota. The steamer wintered many years in the Duluth-Superior Harbor, was a constant visitor in Silver Bay for taconite pellets that were mainly destined for Toledo, Ohio, and had several crewmen who were Minnesota residents.

There are stories by sailors who tell of seeing the ghost of the *Edmund Fitzgerald* battling its way toward safe anchorage in Whitefish Bay, Michigan. The ship never made that refuge on November 10, 1975, when it took all 29 crewmen to their deaths on its dive to the bottom, where it rests today in more than 500 feet of water.

But the *Fitz*'s strong ties to its winter sojourns in the Duluth-Superior Harbor may help to explain the following story of the doomed ship's hold on one of its would-be rescuers, the Duluth-based U.S. Coast Guard Cutter *Woodrush*, and its captain, retired Captain Jimmie Hobaugh.

Hobaugh commanded the *Woodrush* when it made a storm-tossed 22-hour voyage from Duluth to the eastern Lake Superior site of the wreck. Some 30 years after its foundering, the *Fitzgerald* continues to exert its hold over the former Coast Guardsman. Ironically, that hold continued long after he retired from the service and became manager of the Museum Ship *Valley Camp* in Sault Ste. Marie, Michigan, where some recovered items and the two wrecked lifeboats of the doomed steamer are displayed on the grounds.

In the large seas following the monumental storm that sank the *Fitz*, Captain Hobaugh and his crew remained over the sunken freighter for three days and four nights, utterly frustrated at being unable to do anything but watch for wreckage or bodies. Within minutes of their arrival, a life ring and a light popped to the surface and were the last items to come off the *Fitzgerald*.

For a *Lake Superior Magazine* profile written by Dixie Franklin, Hobaugh remembered, "All I could feel was futility and anger, wondering why those 29 guys had to die."[10]

A little more than six months later, the captain and his ship were back at the scene to serve as the base for the underwater survey and photographic record of the wreck using a remote-controlled, unmanned submersible. Again he encountered huge seas as a terrible storm blew in the first night that they were anchored over the wreck.

"That first night, the winds blew so hard that the buoys marking our anchor lines were pulled under and crushed by the pressure," he said, indicating that they were probably submerged 200 feet or more to cause such an implosive force.

In the days that followed, as the crew went about the task of guiding the submersible over and around the wreck, the *Woodrush* was an amazingly quiet ship.

"You just didn't know what those cameras were going to show," explains this plain-spoken man who rose through the enlisted ranks to win his commission as an officer. "It was very eerie and quiet in the monitoring area when those images were coming in, because you never knew if you'd spot bodies or what."

The expedition proved conclusively that the wreck was that of the *Fitzgerald*, but found no evidence of any bodies. As they departed the site, Hobaugh assumed that his association with the wreck was over and resumed his routine duties as captain of his ship.

The *Fitzgerald*, however, had other plans for this Minnesota-based vessel. Somewhat later, Hobaugh found himself escorting three Canadian ships through ice in Whitefish Bay. Late in the day, they got stuck in ice 10 miles from the sunken freighter. Unable to do anything else, Hobaugh and his crew tried to relax for a night of being pushed hither and yon by the shifting ice, awaiting the arrival of the U.S. Coast Guard ice-breaker *Mackinaw* to release them.

The ship's mascot, Sougee, was a fun-loving black Labrador retriever who enjoyed the run of the ship and was a friend to every member of the crew. That night, however, the Lab was uncomfortable, staying in one place and cowering away from some parts of the ship "like he was in a funeral home," the captain remembered. Being a somewhat superstitious sailor, Hobaugh could only wonder what the dog sensed that he would like to know.

The next dawn revealed the answer to that question, for the shifting ice pack had moved his ship directly over the *Fitzgerald* wreck site.

It might be noted that many old-time sailors believed that sighting a black dog on the deck of a ship was an omen of something dreadful. So, might big, black Sougee have had some spiritual foreboding of what weather and fate were accomplishing? Given his love of sailors, was he uncomfortable at the impending encounter with the spirits of the *Fitz*? Being unable to speak for himself, he could only show his feelings by his actions, which were distinctly unlike his usually happy antics aboard the ship.

Of his own association with the doomed freighter, Hobaugh said, "Sailors have a special feeling for each other and a reverence for any ship, but for me the *Fitzgerald* just seemed to be a ship that would not leave me alone. Hardly a day goes by that I don't think about those 29 poor sailors who went down in that wreck."[11]

Other stories about the mystical power of the *Edmund Fitzgerald* and other *Flying Dutchmen* vessels are found in Frederick Stonehouse's *Haunted Lakes* and *Haunted Lakes II*, but most occurred well away from Minnesota's north shore of Lake Superior.

Stonehouse does, however, document two reports from witnesses who told him they saw an old-time steamship working its way past Lester River toward Duluth's ship canal. In each instance, the witness said that they pulled off the highway for a better look and discovered that the steamer and its trail of black smoke had just vanished, despite bright sunny weather and calm seas. Neither narrator had any ready explanation, since both believed that the ship should have been easily visible from their pull-off vantage points.[12]

Since their sightings were momentary, neither witness could provide enough details to identify the phantom ship(s), but it is interesting to note that the *Benjamin Noble* foundered in this general vicinity, and was only found 90 years later in 2005 by a team of Duluth-based divers and shipwreck enthusiasts.

Spirits from sunken vessels may be somewhat easily understood, but what should we make of recent reports by two winter workmen of a haunting aboard the Great Lakes Fleet's 858-foot ore carrier *Roger Blough?* I uncovered these tales in research for my 2003 book *Haunted Lake Superior.*

One of the storytellers was serving as night watchman and heard distinct footsteps on the main deck. Since he thought he was alone on the ship, he went up to see who had come aboard, but was surprised to find no one. A light dusting of snow had fallen since the last workers left the ship for the day and he scanned the deck for footprints, but found none. With good lines of visibility in all directions from the lay-up berth, he looked for any sign of someone in the area who may have come aboard. Again, he saw nothing that was unusual, and no sign of anyone anywhere.

Back down below only a short time, he was again startled by footsteps overhead. "Who's there?" he shouted, feeling sure that no one could have come aboard in the few minutes he'd been below deck.

At his bellowed question, the footfalls halted and silence again reigned on deck. The watchman hastened topside, only to find it empty, with no sign of anyone having been anywhere nearby.

A little unsettled by these events, the remainder of his night watch was uneventful, but he was more than a little happy to see daylight the next morning as other workers came aboard.

Later, another winter worker was doing a job in the vicinity of the engine room when he heard a single weird electronic oink of a klaxon. A few moments later, the klaxon sounded again.

Investigating, the workman determined that the weird sound could only have come from the chief engineer's office. At lunch, he asked another worker who was familiar with the ship what caused the sound. He was told that it only occurred when the engine room telephone receiver was either lifted or replaced. He found that a little hard to believe, since he had been alone when he heard the sound.

When he returned to his worksite, he checked it out and, sure enough, when he lifted the receiver, the klaxon sounded and honked again when he hung up.

Continuing with his job, he heard the oink several more times before he finished. Knowing that no one else was in the area, he could but wonder who – or what – was playing with that telephone.

A few days later, the two men were chatting at lunch and the second worker told of his experience with the mysterious beeping. The man who'd heard footsteps on the main deck hesitated before he blurted out his story. The men agreed that they didn't know what it was, but that something spooky was going on aboard the *Blough*.

For the casual shipwatcher or uninformed skeptic, it may be useful to know that in June 1972, barely a month before its scheduled launch, the nearly completed *Blough* was ravaged by an engine room fire while initial fueling was taking place. Four workers in the engine room lost their lives in the disastrous conflagration.

With that extra bit of information, the question arises: Is some poor soul still on board, tramping the deck at night in an effort to escape his fiery fate? Might the klaxon beeps have been caused by the spirit of a doomed workman deep in the belly of the *Blough* – still futilely trying more than 30 years later to make a phone call for help in escaping that flaming engine room?

For now, at least, the questions beg an answer, but for persistent skeptics looking for a loophole in the tale of a haunted *Roger Blough*, I will simply offer the following anecdote as another scrap of evidence that there is, indeed, a haunting aboard the ship.

Shortly after the publication of *Haunted Lake Superior* in the spring of 2003 in which I revealed the above stories, I ran into an acquaintance who sailed on the *Blough* and was getting some R&R in Two Harbors while the ship was being loaded. After a few minutes of conversation, I casually asked if he'd ever heard of any weird happenings while living aboard the big ore boat.

"You mean the guy in the tunnel who always disappears when a crewman sees him," he immediately answered.

My ears must have perked up an inch or more when he said that, but when I began to pursue the subject, he immediately clammed up. Knowing that I was a writer and might expose him to ridicule as the source of information for some future story or article, he probably felt he'd said too much already.[13]

I've had no good opportunity to pursue the subject with either him or other crewmen from the *Blough*, but the immediacy with which he answered my casual question seems to indicate that at least some crewmen have had encounters with something not quite natural on the *Roger Blough*.

The Cuyuna Iron Range in mid-Minnesota is now inactive, its rich ore mined out and its once bustling mining towns now primarily devoted to tourism and services for those who chose to remain there after the mines shut down.

But in the first half of the 20th century, the Cuyuna was an important source of specialty manganese ore that was used to produce high-quality steel for armaments, tanks and industrial products to keep the nation growing.

Because of the special nature of its iron ore, even mines whose tonnages would have made them marginal on Minnesota's Mesabi and Vermilion ranges could be profitable on the Cuyuna Range.

Thus it was that the 200-foot-deep underground Milford Mine north of the city of Crosby had 49 miners at work in the mine shafts at 3:25 p.m. on February 5, 1924. Barely into their shift, the miners set off a blast in one of shafts and were startled a few moments later by a sudden, almost overwhelming rush of wind that extinguished the flames of the carbide lamps on their hats. In the blink of an eye, the electric lights also went out and rapidly rising water and mud chased the miners down the shafts as they ran for their lives to find the ladder to the surface. Only seven would reach the ladder and get to the surface.

The 42 fatalities in the accident made the Milford Mine disaster the worst in U.S. mining history.

Later investigation indicated that the blast had created a rift between the mine and nearby Foley Lake, allowing millions of gallons of lake water to rush into the mine and quickly inundate the dewatering pumps that normally kept seepage under control. In the ensuing darkness and flooding, disoriented miners were overtaken by the onrushing water, slammed into the mine walls or simply knocked down so savagely that they were either killed instantly or were immobilized and drowned. The water would all but completely flood the entire complex, reaching to within 15 feet of the surface.

At the bottom of the mine ladderway, skiptender Clinton Harris had been called in from days off to substitute for another skiptender who was, luckily for him, sick that day. By the time of the accident, Clinton had already sent a load or two of ore to the surface in the mine's skip, a hoisting device that transferred the ore from the mine's lowest level to the surface.

As the person nearest the shaft's ladderway, he might have effected a quick, relatively easy escape from the looming disaster, but chose instead to remain at his work location and sound the alarm whistle to alert others of the danger. That alarm whistle continued to wail for four hours and eventually had to be disconnected to silence its mournful call.

Although there are at least two versions of the Milford Mine haunting, it's the spirit of the courageous Clinton Harris that is most commonly identified as the mine's ghost. I'll get to those stories in a minute, but first a bit more history.

The aftermath of the disaster is well documented. A special investigative panel was appointed by the governor and came to the conclusion that the flooding was "an act of God" and that no one could be blamed. Labor and safety advocates begged to differ with that opinion, pointing out that the mine had probably been too close to, even possibly under, Foley Lake.

Meanwhile, the record tells of a monumental seven-month effort that encompassed 12 days of pumping to drain the lake before work to dewater the mine could get under way and allow teams to get to the grisly business of recovering the bodies of the dead men.

Once the water was removed from the mine, workers would shovel thousands of tons of mud by hand in order to reach the corpses of their comrades. This ghastly effort consumed months, but eventually all the bodies were recovered.

It would only seem logical that one of the first of those recovered corpses would have been that of Clinton Harris, since he was just at the bottom of the entry ladder into the mine and had taken on heroic proportions for ignoring his own safety while remaining on duty in an effort to save others.

The story goes that a sharply increased demand for manganese iron ore spurred the reopening of the Milford Mine after it was cleaned up and the dead miners removed from the shafts. Having been without a paycheck for months, many miners were more than happy to get back to work, even though the odor of putrefied flesh was rampant in the mine.

But as the first of the miners reached the bottom of the shaft to begin their first shift, they caught a glimpse of a figure just at the edge of their lantern light. Turning their lights on that figure, they recognized the form to be that of a badly decomposed Clinton Harris, with the cord of the alarm whistle still knotted around his waist, hanging by one arm on the ladder and gazing upward with blank eyes toward the surface. Knowing that the skiptender was dead and his earthly remains long since removed and buried, the miners scrambled for the surface in haste and panic. Midway up, they heard the mournful wail of the warning whistle sounding in the shafts of the mine, even though that whistle no longer existed. It's said that none of the men from that first shift ignored this doleful warning of eternal perdition.

Not a one ever returned to the mine.

A report published within a few years of the disaster tells of miners in the lower levels of the mine hearing the warning whistle at midnight and rushing for the exit. Still another tells of miners hearing a woman's screams echoing through the underground shafts. That story indicates that the woman was the widow of one of the dead miners and had attempted to throw herself headlong into the black water that swirled within a few feet of the shaft's surface outlet just after the disaster. She died a few months after that episode, and her ghost is believed by some to have regularly visited the mine's nooks and crannies in search of her fallen husband, shrieking out her grief each time she visited the location where he drowned.[14]

Given the sometimes perilous nature of their work, it seems perfectly rational to believe stories of ghosts of military personnel and Minnesota is said to be inhabited by spirits of long dead soldiers involved in the Civil War and in the 1862 Sioux Uprising in the southwestern area of the state during that conflict.

Located in the central part of the state near the modern cities of Little Falls and Brainerd, Camp Ripley has served as a training facility for military men since it was first erected in the mid-1800s. Its first function was to serve as a residence for soldiers charged with keeping peace on the nearby Ho Chunk/Winnebago tribal reservation when that originally Wisconsin-based tribe was moved briefly into Minnesota from Iowa. The reservation only remained six or seven years before the Winnebagos were displaced to a reservation in South Dakota and then were subsequently relocated one more time to northeastern Nebraska, where the descendants of those people remain today.

As the Civil War heated up, Fort Ripley became a training ground for troops needed to sustain the U.S. Army's troop levels. In the killing fields that were the battlegrounds of the Civil War, many of those brave men would meet their death from ferocious cannon and rifle fire, as well as intense hand-to-hand combat.

It should also be remembered that, at the beginning of the conflict, volunteers filled the ranks of the Army, but a year or so later the United States adopted conscription legislation that enacted an unpopular draft of men for the war. Certainly, one might think, the spirit of unwilling draftees might be more likely to continue haunting the place of their induction than would the ghost of a willing enlistee. Among other inequities, that first draft law allowed those who could afford it to hire replacements, if their name came up for unwanted military duty.

It is not surprising, then, that the ghosts of men clad in Civil War uniforms are occasionally sighted and reported in the vicinity of the original Fort Ripley, which was located on the huge Camp Ripley refuge that today serves as a National Guard training facility for units from much of the Upper Midwest.

According to various reports, the indistinct, ghostly soldiers are often spotted along roadways near dusk, plodding onward in their spiritual journey to a less than happy destiny.[15]

John Savage of the Minnesota Paranormal Investigative Group has also received strong indications of paranormal activity in the area of Fort Ridgely State Park in southwestern Minnesota, which is the site of the Army post that was twice attacked in the Sioux

Uprising of 1862. The fort was staunchly defended by the troops there and the incursions were repulsed until reinforcements arrived and quelled the uprising. The uprising ultimately resulted in the removal of Lakota/Dakota people from Minnesota to the Dakotas.

John indicates that he believes the spectral encounters that he's had in that area include both Army troopers and Native American spirits, but says that his organization needs more study to definitively identify what he's sensed in the battlefield areas of the uprising.[16]

A workplace haunting that I have never heard until this book was being completed involves the building in which I've worked for more than 12 years and comes to me from Bill Meierhoff, the owner of the Waterfront Plaza building in Duluth's Canal Park. Bill says that he believes the building has two ghosts, one of whom he's almost certain is the spirit of a longtime maintenance man named Herb Crawford.

For the first 37 years after being built in 1920, the building housed a warehouse and the headquarters for Marshall Wells Hardware Company, the largest hardware wholesaler in the world before it went out of business in 1957. It was during this time that Herb came to work in the building.

"Herb came with the building when we bought it in 1966 and was a good employee for us for a number of years," Bill remembers. "One of his jobs was maintaining the elevators and when there was trouble with one of them he'd lay on the floor and listen to it run. He almost always figured out what was wrong with it.

"He ended up having some health problems and then died in an elevator. It took us a while to realize that he wasn't just laying on the floor troubleshooting a problem, but had passed on," Bill says.

He says Herb is likely the ghost that his son, Thomas, encountered in the basement of the building.

"It was dark when Tom went in there and bumped into someone. He said, 'Excuse me,' and flipped on the light, but there was nobody there. There was water on the floor just in front of him, but there weren't any wet footprints anywhere in the basement. Whatever he bumped into had just vanished without any evidence."

The other ghost apparently likes the sixth floor offices that we occupied in the building and several night cleaning people have told Bill of encounters they've had with something spiritual.

In addition, several Lake Superior Port Cities Inc. employees tell of strange goings-on in the women's room. One hot-water tap would turn on while a woman was in a stall. One of the stall doors was almost always closed, even though no one was in the stall and the door would normally stay in the open position once it was opened. After becoming aware of these strange doings, the women checked that the faucet was shut off when they entered, but would often find it trickling when they exited the stalls.

Then, too, Huckleberry Finn, our late lamented office dog and greeter, would occasionally and uncharacteristically break out barking at – something. We couldn't discern any reason for his outbreak, but he obviously knew something that we didn't.[17]

As this volume is being finished, the top three floors of the building were undergoing renovation into upscale housing units. The bottom four floors were earlier remodeled into the Hawthorn Suites Hotel and three restaurant establishments. Despite all of that remodeling disruption, which is often said to animate greater spiritual activity, Bill did not report any incidents from workers involved in the job. Save one.

Prior to the demolition of one of the emptied office spaces, Bill's son Dan was inside, inspecting the space. Progressing toward evening, one of the other workers happened to walk past the office in the hallway. when he looked in, he saw Dan and another person looking around. When asked later who the second person was with him, Dan answered that he was not with anyone else. He was alone.[18]

We wished Bill good luck in trying to sell condos in a haunted building, but he wasn't worried, saying "Almost all buildings with any history have some ghosts."

CHAPTER 5

Haunts by the Unexplained

While ghosts and uneasy spirits rarely assume earthly forms that can be readily identified or documented in any coherent manner, there is a good deal of evidence that creatures of a more solid nature have called Minnesota home since the earliest days.

To begin at the beginning, the earliest ancestors of many tribes of Native Americans were the *Lenni Lenape*, who migrated east from the far western region of the continent over a long period of time – perhaps beginning in the last Ice Age. Some dropped out along the way and established tribal groups in the territories they adopted, but the Ojibway, Delaware, most eastern tribal groups and some Midwestern tribes are all said to have descended directly from the Lenni Lenape, who reached the eastern shores of the continent centuries before the French settled there.

Ojibway lore then tells of their ancestors returning westward to take up residence in the Upper Midwest, following a sacred sea shell they called *miigis* that led them on the journey via four stages from the East Coast to Wisconsin, much as the pillar of fire led the Jews out of Egypt to their Holy Land.[1]

But it is the Lenni Lenape's eastward movement that we're interested in here, for the lore from that era states that at some point in their migration, they reached a river that marked the boundary of territory controlled and inhabited by people of gigantic stature who lived in fortified townsites in the region and appear to have developed quite an advanced civilization. At first, the Lenni Lenape asked to reside amongst these giant people, but were refused permission. They were, however, given leave to cross

98

the river and traverse the land controlled by these formidable folk, who were named the *Alliigwi* and gave their name to the Allegheny Mountains, the river of that name and a Pennsylvania county.

As the Lenni Lenape began crossing the river, however, the Alliigwi became alarmed at their numbers and obvious strength and fell upon the unwary earliest arrivals, killing many. Needless to say, this did not sit well with the Lenni Lenape. After making an alliance with the Iroquois people from the north, they entered into a protracted war with the giant people. Savage fighting occurred over many years, but eventually the Lenni Lenape and Iroquois bested the Alliigwi and took possession of the land that the giants had previously controlled in the Allegheny Valley and upper Ohio. The hapless Alliigwi made their escape down the Ohio River to the Mississippi. The Lenni Lenape moved on to the eastern seaboard, directly begetting the Delaware tribe, among others.[2]

Unfortunately for the tribe of giants, when they reached the Mississippi in the general vicinity of Minnesota they encountered the Dakota people, who wanted nothing to do with the idea of sharing their territory with these tall interlopers. Initially impressed by the Alliigwis' stature, the Dakota are said to have quickly discovered that the giants were basically cowardly. The Dakota rather easily vanquished the remnants of the Alliigwi tribe. There were said to be many dead on both sides in this final Alliigwi confrontation.

Thus we come to the crux of this tale, for a number of early archaeological digs at Native American burial mounds in Minnesota and other Midwestern sites reported skeletal remains of giant humans. In some, these giant bones are intermixed with remains of more normal proportions, leading to speculation that the victorious Dakota people may simply have hurriedly stacked all of the decaying bodies together and covered them with earth to dispose of them.

That could explain the discovery of giant skeletons in south central Minnesota digs, for which there are newspaper articles confirming the discoveries. A June 29, 1888, report in the *St. Paul Pioneer Press* stated that seven large skeletons were unearthed in a burial mound near Clearwater, just south of St. Cloud. According to the report, the skulls were enormous and mysteriously revealed double rows of teeth in the upper and lower jaws. The skulls were large enough to fit over the heads of more normal-sized humans and also revealed unusually low, sloping foreheads. The remains were buried in a sitting position facing the lake.

A few years later, the *St. Paul Globe* of August 12, 1896, reported that the skeleton of "a huge man" was uncovered on a farm near Lake Koronis south of Paynesville. In notes of the Paynesville Historical Society, Dolores Hislop states that area resident Charles Zapf had a keen interest in Indian culture and confirmed in a 1925 paper that he wrote that burial mounds were opened in the area by relic hunters between 1879 and the 1896 discovery of the huge skeleton alluded to above. Zapf also said in his paper that a second skeleton of an 8-foot-tall man was discovered during roadwork in the Paynesville area in somewhat the same time period.[3]

While the previous reports of giant skeletal remains were all located in south central Minnesota, an earlier story in the *St. Paul Globe* of May 23, 1883, states that 10 skeletons of "both sexes and gigantic size" were discovered in a burial mound at Warren in the northwestern part of the state.[4]

No solid evidence points to these giant skeletons as being those of the vanquished Alliigwi people and none of the skeletal remains appears to have survived to the present in museums or other public viewing areas, but the oral tradition of the Dakota and Delaware people of warring with giants is certainly one possibility for the existence of giant skeletons uncovered in Minnesota. Such large skeletons have also been reported in burial mounds ranging from Pennsylvania and Ohio through the Upper Midwest.

It should also be noted that some Web chatter accuses none other than the prestigious Smithsonian Institute of skullduggery in the disappearance of such an abundance of giant human remains. The veracity of those sites is a challenge to ascertain.

But other explanations of giant skeletons are also possible.

For generations, native people and pioneers reported seeing humanlike creatures that became known variously as Bigfoot, Sasquatch, Yeti, the Abominable Snowman or a number of other various and/or regional designations.

Originally identified in the United States by tribal people in the Pacific Northwest, the legend of large, hairy, extremely reclusive creatures is also recorded among Midwestern tribes like the Ojibway and Dakota – although some scholars interpret Ojibway lore about Bigfoot as also being intermixed with their belief in the *windigo* (in some references spelled *wendigo*).

As described, the windigo actually assumed several identities in Ojibway belief. One tells of a giant spiritual creature variously described as pure white and 15 feet or more in height, but there are other stories of a large sinister creature that feasted on human flesh, but could never be sated because as it devoured the flesh, it grew larger physically and its appetite increased proportionately.

A third form of windigo described in Ojibway lore is identified as any human being who ever resorted to cannibalism as a means of surviving some exigency. Cannibalism seems to have been common in legends as late as the mid-1800s. In his landmark book, *Kitchi-Gami: Life Among the Lake Superior Ojibway*, Johann Georg Kohl devotes considerable space to discussion of this human form of windigo, recording instances in which native people clearly identified people who indulged in cannibalism as late as 1854.[5]

Whether Bigfoot and the windigo are interrelated in Ojibway lore or not, at least one Website claims that as late as the 1920s a windigo that had hung around Roseau since the 1800s was spotted and reported. The site also states that every time such a sighting occurred, an unexpected death followed in the community. After the 1920s, there were no more reports of encounters with the ghastly creature.[6]

But the Ojibway legend of windigo is only another possibility for stories about large, humanlike creatures inhabiting Minnesota's out-of-the-way places. The Dakota (eastern) and Lakota (western) tribes of Siouan people both have legends of supernatural or spiritual beings that they refer to as Big Man or Great Elder Brother

(*Chiye-tanka* in the Lakota dialect and *Chiha-tanka* in Dakota). In some views, sighting a Bigfoot is cause for concern, since failure to respect this being can lead to misfortune. Conversely, others believe that they are brothers whose touch brings good luck to those blessed with the contact. In most expressions from the Dakota/Lakota, there is both a spiritual and a physical side of Bigfoot and a sighting is always regarded as important.[7]

Native people are not the only believers in Sasquatch, however, and the Internet is rife with first-person accounts of supposed sightings, ranging from hearing simple vocalizations of unknown origins to outright encounters in which facial/physical features are described in some detail. In some of these stories, the reporters also tell of an overpowering, sickening odor accompanying the beast like that somewhere between rotting flesh and the spray of a skunk. In fact, in some other areas of the United States, the Bigfoot/Sasquatch is named Skunk Ape for this unpleasant characteristic.

Depending on the eyewitness's tale, the animal that is encountered ranges from nearly white to quite dark brown or black, with fur also variously described as being quite long to relatively short. When they can be discerned, facial features are said to resemble those of higher primates like chimps or great apes. The height of the creatures also varies from report to report, with some descriptions being no more than 6 feet to extremely tall specimens estimated at 9 feet or more.

An August 2002 report on the Bigfoot Field Research Organization (BFRO) Website (from which the following stories are taken, largely because each is supported by follow-up reports by investigators who made contact with those who claimed sightings) comes from from a woman with a bachelor of science degree in Roman Archaeology who at the time of her story worked as manager/director in an investment firm. The BFRO investigator stated that the woman prided herself on her observational acuity, despite the fact that her story took place 24 years earlier when she was 13 years old and her corroborating sister was 8. The woman also mentioned an unpleasant odor, perhaps sulphurous or rancid, associated with the sighting.

According to the woman, she and her sister were playing tag with some cousins in a cornfield on her aunt's farm in Isanti County near Dalbo in central Minnesota. They burst out of the corn near the edge of a swamp, about 20 feet away from a large animal standing manlike and staring at them. Staring back, the woman stated that the encounter lasted perhaps a minute. She at

first thought the animal was a bear, but the longer she looked at it the more it was apparent that that was not the case.

"It stood like a man, was shaped like a very large man (estimated at about 7 feet in height) and had mannerisms that were like a man," she stated. Covered in coarse-looking, dirty, matted hair, it stood in swamp water up to its ankles and stared at them, at one point making a throaty sound that startled them. At their movement, the Bigfoot took a step toward them and the girls simultaneously and hurriedly retreated into the cornfield, hightailing it back to the farmstead, where they talked adults into accompanying them to check the site where they had encountered the Bigfoot. By the time they arrived back there, the big critter had disappeared, apparently without a trace. She admitted in her report that the adults believed that the girls had made up the episode, but she maintained that her encounter was real and took place when there was light enough for the critter to be quite plainly visible.

The investigator whose analysis accompanied the report found nothing to cast doubt on the girls' stories of staring down a Bigfoot, while noting that the woman also indicated in later conversations that the being was definitely male, since she had the opportunity to observe the genitals of the creature, describing them as "not large, but present and visible."

Also in August 2002, a man reported on an October 1985 sighting that he and a friend and hunting partner had as teenagers in a forested area near Silver Bay on Minnesota's Lake Superior north shore. As they moved through the woods, they heard something moving in the brush and then sighted a large unidentified creature.

They were some distance from their car. Their initial sighting spooked them, but not as much as a few seconds later when the creature howled, raising the hairs on the back of their necks and causing them to duck to the ground and load slugs into their 12-gauge shotguns to defend themselves if attacked. Intermittent howling continued. They could hear the animal moving a couple of hundred yards away, but directly in line with the path they needed to follow to get back to their car.

Despite their youth, both were experienced hunters and woodsmen, knowing that this was no bear, moose, timber wolf or other native animal of the northern forest. Taking no chances, they dropped the three ruffed grouse they'd shot and cautiously moved to the trail, continuing to hear movement to their right as they sidled for the car.

"I remember being terrified, and it was clear that it was a large creature, but it moved very fast – faster than any bull moose I had ever encountered. It followed on our right for a few hundred yards. It was approaching dark and we had lights with us. I turned to my friend and pointed. At that moment, we could see a complete outline of this creature because we were in the growth and it was following, but emerged with a clearing of bright light behind it," this hunter stated.

At their sighting of the beast, they both again ducked to the ground, the thought of shooting the animal not even entering their minds.

"We were scared. I had worked as a wilderness guide and this was nothing that I had ever seen before. It walked on two feet and stood at least 9 feet tall. We continued on our way, all the while hearing this thing in the brush following us. It was amazingly stealthy.... It finally stopped following us as we crossed a ridge toward a more traveled trail. We both remember the day like it was yesterday and recently spoke of it. I was not much into this sort of thing until I saw it. I am still not a 'Bigfoot kook' or anything, but I am a college-educated outdoorsman and from all I know, there could be hundreds of them and we humans would never know."

Noting that both the young hunters were experienced beyond their years in the outdoors, the BFRO investigator of this episode said that he was told during an interview that the young men stopped to listen to the sounds in the bush and discovered that the creature stopped too in an effort not to be heard. When they reached a point from which they knew they'd catch a glimpse of the animal, they were shocked to see the large, upright walking creature. They also perceived by that time that it seemed to be more inquisitive than threatening, as it had first been, a real relief to the teens.

"I don't care what you think, and I don't care what you say. I have witnessed it with my own eyes. Bigfoot is real," he stated, going on to say that, despite being a skilled outdoorsman, he felt like a kindergartner in comparison to the skills the creature displayed that day.

The investigator concluded, "What you have is apparent intimidation, followed by a conscious effort to conceal the fact that it was shadowing them. The man reporting the incident summed up his perception by saying, 'The way I look at it, the creature warned us and then discreetly escorted us out. That's how I felt.'"

A Bigfoot sighting south of Hibbing occurred during early summer and was reported to BFRO on July 17, 2004, by a couple living in a rural area off Highway 73. The husband arose about 5 a.m. and was waiting for his morning coffee when he heard strange noises outside the home. Saying they sounded like a low cry or calling sound, he knew he'd never heard anything similar before and stepped out the door, figuring he'd check to see what the noise might be as he casually strolled to the mailbox to fetch the mail from the previous day.

As he walked down the driveway, he glanced to his left into a grassy area near a grove of pines about 50 feet away and saw a figure he estimated to be 6 to 7 feet tall. The creature wore no clothing and the husband reported that it was covered in grayish-brown fur from head to foot. He was also startled to observe that the animal stood on two legs, but was definitely not a bear. He could not make out any facial features.

Too surprised to move, he watched the critter for a short period of time before it became aware of him and ran into the surrounding woods. Later, the husband went to the grassy area where the animal had been and found large footprints pressed into the grass. His father-in-law went to the area later and followed the faint tracks for a distance, coming upon feces he knew was not from deer, bear, moose or other game in the area.

Emphasizing that the sound the man heard seemed to be more of a calling than a scream or a howl, the report indicated that when the couple mentioned the encounter to others, they were told that a similar creature had been seen by another party on a nearby logging road east of their home.

"Steve" from Babbitt claims to have had three different encounters with large bipedal animals over a number of years, according to his report on the BFRO Website.

On a trip home to Babbitt from Virginia after dark, Steve, his wife and kids were traveling on County Road 21 when his headlights illuminated an extremely tall, furry critter walking across the road on two legs. He was so startled by the sight that at first he couldn't speak. When he did manage to try to call his wife's attention to the creature, it had already reached the forest along the road. His wife did not see the animal and asked what he thought he'd seen.

"I told her I saw a Bigfoot, and she later told me that she believed me. I can still see this in my mind as clear as a bell and have had recurring dreams about it, sometimes even nightmares," Steve's report states.

His second encounter with something weird in the north woods happened during deer season. He and his oldest son were tracking a wounded deer at dusk and decided to delay their search until the following morning. A hunting partner convinced them to continue the darkening search. The three first stuck together, then split up to widen the search. Steve doubled back the way that they had come and was about 200 yards from their cars when he heard a grunt.

Stopping, he heard the sound of a tree being broken nearby, followed by a loud grunt and the sound of the tree hitting the brush and ground. Loading his rifle quickly, he walked with flashlight in hand, ready to confront with gunfire whatever might threaten him. Walking in tight circles to stay alert to anything around him, he made his way the 200 yards to the cars and told his partner and son when they arrived, "He's here!"

Thinking Steve was talking about the wounded deer, his partner replied, "I know he's here somewhere, but did you find him?"

"Not the deer! *HE*'s Here!"

"Where?" his partner asked.

"Up the hill on the road, and I think he threw a tree at me."

They talked for a bit longer in the deepening darkness, called off the search and went home. Steve avoided that hunting ground the remainder of that season, only returning a year later because curiosity got the better of him. Going back to the hill, he found that the trunk of a relatively sizable sapling had been torn from its roots and was lying against a tree some 25 feet away from the stump. Although Steve never saw this second Bigfoot, the strength of the beast can be inferred by the distance it hurled the tree in its effort to scare him off. Obviously, that effort accomplished its end.

Finally, Steve's May 2002 report indicates that he and his son found a Bigfoot footprint a week before his report near a mine dump at Aurora. They gathered what was needed at home, returned to the site and took a casting of the footprint in the forested area. At the time of the report, he retained the casting and displayed it for the Bigfoot Field Research Organization investigator of his sightings. The investigator reported that the casting was somewhat indistinct, not showing individual toes, but demonstrating a very large and wide human-like foot perhaps 13 inches long.

Finally, the BFRO also received a report on February 17, 2002, of a sighting in Pine County in August 1972 about five miles east of Willow River and a couple of miles east of Interstate 35. The encounter occurred as a man drove along an unmarked gravel road to a remote lake to go fishing.

"From the car, I spotted two white Bigfeet in an open field between dense patches of pine trees. These creatures were approximately 7 and 9 feet tall. The shorter one was shaped like a gorilla and was female. The taller was a more human-shaped, muscular brute and the head was more rounded than the female's. They froze in mid-stride like deer do when caught in a similar spot," the report states.

As an outdoorsman and rural resident, the man stated that he was not particularly shocked at the sighting because there had been other recent reports of species like wolverines and cougars that had been spotted in that area that were long deemed to be extinct in Minnesota.

"I would compare the height of the animals to that of Clydesdale horses." the reporter stated. "I think they were in an annual migration from Wisconsin west into Minnesota like the bears that move westward from mid-August to October to den for the winter. I found out much later that others had seen a white Bigfoot in an area from near Duluth all the way to Webster, Wisconsin. The different bone structure of the male and female was surprising, to say the least."

Asked by the BFRO follow-up investigator why he had waited 30 years to report his sighting, the witness said that he felt a sense of ownership of the sighting and also planned to try to photograph the creatures to prove that they were real. That plan was abandoned later when he moved out of the area and became busy with other pursuits. Much later, when he purchased a computer, he discovered the interest in Bigfoot on the Internet and wrote his report for the BFRO.

The investigator spent an hour in a telephone interview with the witness and said he seemed quite honest and convincing. An avid hunter and fisherman, the man stated categorically that what he saw could not have been either humans or bears, since he got an incredibly good look at them from about 30 yards distance in bright, sunny morning light.[8]

The fact that far and away the largest percentage of BFRO-investigated sightings are concentrated in the northern half of the state and that the few in southern Minnesota occurred in forested areas indicates that the Bigfoot is a forest-dwelling, reclusive and wary creature that eschews contact with humans and prefers the shelter and anonymity of secretive habitation. The vast areas of wild land protected as national forests, state and national parks, tax-forfeitured lands and uninhabited places give ample shelter and space for these elusive creatures as they go about their primitive existence surrounded by sophisticated society.

It's also worth noting that most of the sightings occurred either after dark or at dusk, implying that Bigfoot is likely nocturnal. Several of the reports also noted that the creatures' eyes glowed in the light, much as a deer's or dog's eyes reflect the artificial lights of cars or outdoor lighting fixtures, also reinforcing that it is a nocturnal animal.

No physical remains of a Bigfoot have ever been recovered, but there are a number of photographic images, including a short film by Roger Patterson, as well as numerous castings of footprints (some, admittedly, proven to be fakes). Other forensic evidence has been presented by advocates for the existence of the Bigfoot.

Dr. Jeff Meldrum of the Idaho State University Department of Biology has collected in excess of 150 castings of large footprints and made his collection available for analysis by Jimmy Chilcutt, a fingerprint and footprint specialist from the Conroe, Texas, Police Department who initiated studies of primate fingerprints to determine if fingerprints might be used to identify a person's race.

While his initial research into determining race was inconclusive, his study of primate finger- and footprints piqued his interest in studying the castings in Meldrum's laboratory. Going in as a skeptic, after his investigation Chilcutt was convinced that a 1987 footprint from Walla Walla, Washington, was not only real, but very different from those of primates and humans.

"The ridge flow pattern and the texture was completely different from anything I've ever seen," Chilcutt said. "It certainly wasn't human, and of no primate that I've examined. The print ridges flowed lengthwise along the foot, unlike human prints, which flow across. The texture of the ridges was about twice the thickness of a human, which indicated that this animal has a real thick skin."

Chilcutt came away from his Bigfoot studies as a believer. "I can assure you there's an animal up in the Pacific Northwest that we have never seen," he told a reporter from *Field and Stream Magazine*.[9]

Meanwhile, Meldrum points to a very detailed body casting obtained in the Gifford Pinchot National Forest in Washington state as more solid forensic evidence of Bigfoot's existence.

That 400-pound bit of evidence, known as the Skookum Cast, was made in September 2000 by a team sponsored by the Bigfoot Field Research Organization. Putting a cache of apples in a muddy area, the researchers played taped recordings of noises from previous Bigfoot encounters and spread around a special mixture of human and primate pheromones that was concocted for the bait site by Dr. Gregory Bambenek of Duluth, whose deer and fish baiting products are known to fishermen and deer hunters by his trade name of Dr. Juice. Dr. Bambenek was a member of the expedition that obtained the body casting and carefully collected hair samples from the site for later analysis. He is quite convinced that the cast reveals details like a number of heel marks and achilles tendon impressions that show that the creature was not human and is likely that of a Sasquatch.

Returning a day later to the muddy site, they were excited to find quite a detailed imprint of a huge animal that had apparently laid on its side to reach the desired fruit. Examining the cast of the imprint obtained by the BFRO team, Meldrum identified impressions of a forearm, a thigh, buttocks, Achilles tendon and heel, saying of the animal, "It's 40 to 50 percent bigger than a normal human. The anatomy doesn't jibe with any known animal."

Such fragments of evidence are convincing to at least some genuine international experts. None other than Dr. Jane Goodall, renowned worldwide for her lifelong study of chimpanzees, surprised an interviewer from National Public Radio in November 2003 by saying that she is convinced that Bigfoot/Sasquatch does exist.

Despite the absence of any bodily remains, Goodall said that such archeological evidence may not be necessary, if there is good enough photographic or video evidence.[10]

But native lore and somewhat contemporary stories of Bigfoot encounters are not the only evidence of secretive primates inhabiting the north woods. Even the lumberjacks of the late 1800s/early 1900s left tales of the Agropelter, their version of what could be Bigfoot critters. Unlike most other stories of Bigfoot, this elusive critter was relatively small. About the size of chimpanzees, they are said to live in rotting trees and are wont to either clonk unwary visitors on the head with clubs or assault the unwanted tourist with a flurry of sticks, rocks and other handy missiles. In some lore, they were carnivores, preferring human flesh above all else, but other accounts indicate that they were omnivores, existing on a variety of plants and flesh, in much the same fashion as the black bears of the area do. They are also likely the result of creative evenings of storytelling in the bunkhouses.[11]

As an extension of the Agropelter lore, as a mere stripling lad in his Maine birthplace, Paul Bunyan is said to have cleared a town deacon's woodlot of Agropelters by first thinning the woods of all hollow trees, thereby depriving the critters of their preferred homesites. After they moved on, he embarked on his legendary logging career by harvesting the remaining trees and driving them down a nearby river to market, making a packet of money that set him up for his later life's work.

While many stories of Bigfoot encounters indicate no evidence or perception of physical aggressiveness or danger to the witnesses, one 1976 tale from the Lake of the Woods area of northern Minnesota that was investigated by the Bigfoot Field Research Organization and is recorded in their Minnesota Website listings seems to indicate some desire by a Bigfoot to at least intimidate, if not outright harm, three witnesses.

The reports states that the three men were camping near the Canadian border in thick forest and saw a tall hairy figure by a nearby tree staring at them. Trying for a better look, the men were surprised to see the creature run off in an upright posture on two legs. Investigating further, the men noted a fetid stench ("like rotting feet") as they approached the area where the figure had been. Other than the stink, however, the men had not perceived any sense of foreboding or intimidation. That was destined to change shortly.

Closing camp, the men followed a railroad grade going through a swampy area lying about 100 feet on each side of the tracks. As they walked, they heard the sound of something moving to their right, when suddenly a football-sized rock shot by them. Thinking perhaps that some unknown person was in the same area, they checked around, but no one else was anywhere to be found.

Remembering the size of the boulder, they also reflected on the strength required to hurl such a missile past them from the woods. It seemed unlikely that anything human could manage such a feat.

They were also aware that the rock was definitely aimed for them and was not meant as a friendly gesture. They resumed their trek out of the woods along the tracks.

Suddenly, perhaps a 100 yards ahead of them, the figure appeared from the right side of the tracks, crossed quickly, located a dry spot to re-enter the swampy wooded area on their left and disappeared. They hurried to the spot to try for a better look, but there was nothing to see and they continued on their way to where their vehicle was parked.

Later, in town, they mentioned their sighting to townspeople and learned that there were a number of similar sightings reported by locals in the area.

Disappointingly, the investigator from the Bigfoot Field Research Organization was only able to contact one of the three witnesses, but reported that the single witness was credible and further reported that the creature had a flattened face, was covered with fur, some of which was found clinging to the tree where they first observed it. He also said that there were footprints at the base of that tree, but that they neither collected the hair samples nor attempted to make castings of the footprints.[12]

While many of the stories revealed here come from past decades, a recent posting concerning Bigfoot evidence in Cook and Lake counties in northeastern Minnesota was posted in March 2005 at www.virtuallystrange.net.

According to Jim Richardson of Duluth, who is described, with his brother, Allen, on the Website as a "Fortean researcher," three people he was working with were snowshoeing several miles into the woods to spend February 12-13 in a cabin near Grand Marais. For whatever reason, they were following a wispy trail in waist-deep snow at 1 to 2 a.m., sinking more than a foot into the powdery snow.

During their traverse, they came upon large footprints that showed a 4- to 5-foot stride that crossed their trail and were visible in both directions as far as their lamps allowed them to see. The huge tracks and extraordinary length of stride spooked them, since they sank to the bottom of the snow pack and indicated not only great height but great weight for whatever left the trail.

"One person assured me that the tracks were bipedal and not moose tracks or anything like that," Richardson reported. "He was also the one who inspected them the closest of the three and said he could discern that it was a large footprint. He is really pretty certain that nothing identifiable made those tracks and leans toward a Bigfoot explanation. The other two guys are hedging their bets, saying the tracks are unidentified. What can be said with some certainty is that the experience spooked them all."

The second northeastern Minnesota report at the Website tells of another witness who went out to check on the condition of a yurt he had erected near Isabella (between Lake Superior and Ely on Highway 1), fearing the weight of the snow had collapsed it. This incident occurred on March 4, 2005, and he found the yurt in good shape, but was a bit perturbed by something else that he discovered.

Without snowshoes, the man and his dog walked through hip-deep snow about a half-mile, telling Richardson that, even as a tall person, his footprints were only about a foot apart and that the trek was exhausting for him – although his dog had a grand old time.

At some point during this tiring trip, the man came upon a single set of very large, wide and elongated human-like tracks, again displaying a stride estimated at 4 to 6 feet apart.

"Not even the tallest person in the world wearing snowshoes could stride like that through such deep snow," the witness stated.

Curious to see what more he could discover about the strange tracks, he returned on March 9, but found that the footprints, which he estimated to be 16 to 20 inches deep on his first encounter, had filled with newly fallen snow, but were definitely not those of a snowshoer. Nonetheless, photos he took were shown to the Grand Marais area witnesses, who said the tracks were the same as what they encountered on their nighttime foray into the woods.

The photos were sent to world-renowned cryptozoologist Loren Coleman, who reportedly told Richardson that little could be learned about the footprints without casts of them. While he did not outright reject the prints as fraudulent, Coleman said, "Too much melting to say much, it appears. These could be anything."

Nevertheless, the two reports did spark memories in the area of a 1985 encounter with a Bigfoot estimated to be 9 feet tall in a wooded area just north of Silver Bay, with the implication that these episodes may indicate a wide-ranging primate in the north woods of Minnesota's Lake Superior north shore.[13]

Before introducing perhaps the most famous or infamous Bigfoot story ever reported in this country, I do want to squeak in my son's account of spotting a mysterious furry creature while on a camping expedition with three friends north of Two Harbors.

I'll let Hugh Jr. tell his tale in his own words.

"All of us had summer jobs between our junior and senior years of high school, and we came to the conclusion that we had to do something fun and different before summer vacation ending.

"After talking it over, we decided that a camping trip was just what we were looking for. Sticky finagled his parents' car, I brought a few tools and a little two-man tent, Tom bought gas and Joey anteed up one of those huge military tents like they used in 'M.A.S.H.' By this time, it was already close to sunset.

"We headed north about 20 miles to Indian Lake Campground in Brimson, where the closest thing to civilization is Hugo's Bar, which is like saying that a raw crayfish is close to a cooked Maine lobster.

"It was dark by the time we got to the campground. Even scarier was that it was country dark and partially overcast, so we had turned on the headlights. As we entered the campground, Sticky slowed down to read a large sign with things posted like rules for camping, nightly fees, what-have-you. His eyes were trained on that. The rest of us were looking ahead and saw this thing run across the road just on the edge of the headlights. It ran on its hind legs like a human would, but it was about 7 feet tall, covered in brown fur, with long apelike arms.

"It took a second or two, but we all asked at once, 'What the heck was that?'

"Sticky didn't believe us when we told him what the rest of us had seen, but every one of us agreed on exactly what the thing looked like – and that it had to be a Bigfoot.

"The rest of that night was *really* fun! Initially, I tried to rationalize that maybe I had been seeing things, but all of us saw it and pointed at it at the same time, so that was out. Then I thought maybe it was a bear, but the fur was brown like a grizzly, which isn't native to that area, plus grizzlies can hardly walk on their hind legs and this thing was running quickly and gracefully into the woods, where it disappeared.

"We were all spooked, but determined to go camping. We decided to stay close to a concentration of other campers, just in case the thing came back. We drove around and there was nobody else there. This would be the one night ever, in the summer, that there was zero occupancy – and we ended up there knowing some strange creature was out in the woods. We found what we figured to be the safest spot, but it was site 13 – hardly a good sign.

"Since our planning had been hasty, we didn't even have firewood or a flashlight. We went into the woods a little way and felt around for dry wood. After stumbling around in the dark for about an hour, we had enough wood and decided to pitch camp. I was glad I had my little tent, which I could set up blind in the rain. The rest of them put up a makeshift lean-to with the big tent, but there was not much sleep in store that night. When dawn came the next day, we packed up, cleaned up the site, left the campground, and have never been back to Indian Lake since.

"After we got more comfortable talking about what we had seen, we began to hear other stories from people in the area of similar sightings of Sasquatch, going all the way back to Ojibway legends.

"From what I've since learned, the native legends say that the Sasquatch is one manifestation of the spirit of the land, that it can pass between our world and the spirit world and that when one sees Sasquatch it's a very good luck sign.

"All I know is that we didn't feel very lucky that night that we were camping in the Bigfoot's back yard!"

In talking with the boys, the author has been impressed by the similarity of each boy's version of what they saw. Adding eeriness to their story is the fact that in the mid-1980s, a late-night traveler simply disappeared in the same general area. His nearly new pickup was parked on the shoulder of the road and there was no sign of a robbery, struggle or violence, but nothing has ever been found to indicate what happened to him. It's an unsolved mystery to the very moment this book is being written.[14]

No chronicle of Minnesota Bigfeet would be complete without the saga of the so-called Minnesota Iceman, a large cadaver frozen inside a three-ton block of ice. Although two tales of the Iceman do invoke a Minnesota origin for the beast, the most widely accepted story of its origin is that it was discovered floating in the Sea of Okhotsk northwest of Japan by either Japanese whalers or Russian seal hunters. The discoverers are said to have smuggled the block of ice with its strange contents into Hong Kong, where it was purchased by a millionaire from the western United States. After storing it in a deep-freeze plant for some period, the millionaire then inexplicably rented the curiosity to a Frank D. Hansen of Winona, who displayed it as an exhibit at expositions and fairs. From that scant Minnesota tie came the designation "Minnesota Iceman."

Many "facts" about the Iceman are open to dispute, but there is no doubt that Hansen did, indeed, tote the icebound exhibit from

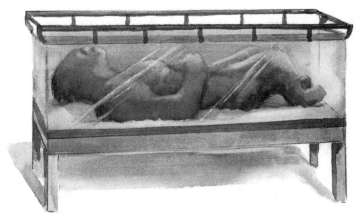

fair to fair in a refrigerated truck, charging people 25 or 35 cents to view the creature for a few minutes.

At a December 1968 appearance at the Chicago International Livestock Exposition, the curiosity was spotted and briefly studied by Milwaukee zoologist Terry Cullen, who found the story and the remains of the Iceman credible enough to send a report to the Society for the Investigation of the Unexplained, a civilian research group based in New Jersey.

There, the society's director and head investigator, Ivan Sanderson, became interested and began looking into the case, finding that there were enough details in Cullen's report of the corpse's appearance to justify further study. Sanderson was a serious student of scientific phenomena and had been a collector of rare and previously unknown animal specimens for zoos and museums. He also happened to be the science editor for *Argosy Magazine*.

During the winter of 1968-69, Sanderson enlisted the cooperation of Dr. Bernard Heuvelmans of the Belgian Royal Academy of Sciences to investigate the Minnesota Iceman. Heuvelmans was a 20-year scholar of manlike creatures who had written a book entitled *On the Track of Unknown Animals*, a scholarly examination of "abominable snowmen" and other unusual species of fauna.

Together, the scientists traveled to distant, frigid Winona to examine the apelike creature frozen in its block of ice at Hansen's rural home. By that point, the block of ice had been trimmed to a bit less than 7 feet in length by 3 feet in width and 3 1/2 feet in height and was preserved by the winter cold inside its glass coffin.

Their first day of examinations revealed that the cause of the Iceman's death had been a gunshot through the right eye that also dislodged the other eye from its socket. What they saw convinced Sanderson and Heuvelmans that they were viewing and documenting a genuine "abominable snowman" of recent rather than ancient origins.

They spent the next two days making many drawings, shooting color and black-and-white photos and intensively studying the corpse using powerful lighting to penetrate the layers of glass and ice that surrounded the body. Spotty areas of opacity in the ice made their examinations more difficult, but they did ascertain that the massive hands resembled modern human hands more than those of apes and that the big toes on the feet lay beside the other toes, rather than being opposed as they are in apes and other primates.

In his later paper for the Institute of Natural Science in Belgium, Heuvelmans said he clearly detected the faint stench of putrefying flesh emanating from the glass viewing coffin. Both he and Sanderson agreed that they were viewing a primate of an as-yet undiscovered, unidentified species and that the remains were recent, rather than fossilized or mummified.

Sanderson would break the news to the public of their findings in a May 1969 article published in *Argosy*. Heuvelmans' scientific paper appeared to reinforce Sanderson's story and, together, their findings generated a great deal of interest in both the public and scientific communities. Indeed, so much publicity was generated that none other than the Smithsonian Institute showed temporary interest in investigating this large "primate" encased in ice. The Smithsonian scientists quickly lost their interest after hearing that there was evidence that the corpse had been killed by a gunshot and that the original Iceman had been reproduced for display and that the original was no longer available for investigation.

Based on the latter reports, the Smithsonian dropped plans for any study, pointing out that if a fake could be made after the fact, perhaps the original had also been phony.

Sanderson and Heuvelmans were at first disappointed at the Smithsonian's reaction, but were later said to be embarrassed by the fact that they had been so completely suckered by a huckster who was only out to make a few bucks.

Following the Smithsonian's refusal to have any further part in the Iceman saga, the whole episode came to be generally viewed as a sham. Despite that fact, Bigfoot/Sasquatch researchers remain intensely interested and one need only search the Internet to find a multitude of sites that examine the story in minute detail. The Internet also provides the full texts of both Sanderson's *Argosy* article and a more detailed follow-up paper he wrote.

After the reproduction of the Iceman was exposed, all further traces of the "original" Minnesota Iceman simply dropped off the radar screen, although Hansen did apparently continue to show the "Iceman" reproduction around the Midwest at fairs and carnivals before retiring it and moving on to other carnival exhibits.

Despite the fact that the Minnesota Iceman was eventually declared an outright fraud, some abominable snowman researchers continue to speculate about exactly what it was that Sanderson and Heuvelmans examined in the cold winter storage truck on the farm outside of Winona, since the two men were veteran scientists dedicated to studying little known or unidentified species. They obviously believed they were seeing a genuine "missing link" that had previously been unknown among the primates.

Then, too, one has to wonder what it was that created the odor of putrefying flesh that both researchers noted in their reports. If the Iceman were a complete fake, it seems unlikely that the stench would have been present during their frigid investigations and such an odor would hardly have been an added attraction for the crowds of curious fair-goers, so it seems to lend some credibility to this entire tale.

The truth of the entire Minnesota Iceman story remains cloudy and grows more so with each passing year. We may never know if Hansen actually had a once-living creature, as Sanderson and Heuvelmans believed, or if he was simply one of the more skilled hoaxsters calling our fair state home.[15]

Strangely enough, in light of the Iceman story and given the next chapter in this book, some scholars of the paranormal have begun to link sightings of Bigfoot-type creatures with concurrent appearances in the same area by Unidentified Flying Objects and/or alien beings. Prior to the 1970s, most discussions of UFO and Bigfoot were totally unrelated, but that began to change. In their 1982 *The Bigfoot Casebook*, Janet and Colin Bord appear to be the first to link sightings of UFOs and Bigfoot in proximity to each other.

Students of the paranormal point out that such linkage could offer a plausible reason why hard physical evidence of Bigfoot's existence has always been scanty. That theory goes something akin to an "alien culture" that would easily be able to retrieve their "Bigfoot" companions busily exploring earthly environs under almost any circumstance and would presumably have a variety of superior resources available from their culture to assist in those retrieval efforts. Thus, no skeletal remains, no captured specimens, no positive proof that there is an actual "wild child" closely related to the other primates.

While that debate goes on apace, the idea of a Bigfoot/UFO connection has attracted a following estimated by one Bigfoot convention promoter at 25 percent of the people who believe in the phenomena of Bigfoot. While the UFO connection seems to introduce elements that detract from the idea of an elusive, reclusive Bigfoot creature (or several species of primate relatives) inhabiting this world, it is another aspect of the paranormal that gains credibility among followers.[16]

Haunts From the Firmament

In the early 1950s, Wayne Gatlin, who would ultimately attain the rank of major general in the Minnesota Air National Guard, was flying a routine training mission with another Air Guard pilot when they spotted an unusual sight over Lake Superior.

"A light – a bright light," Gatlin, who would go on to serve as commander of the Duluth Air National Guard and also as a senior member of the Minnesota Air Guard, told *Duluth News Tribune* staff writer Chuck Frederick. "We were on (the west) side (of the lake) and it was on the other side. We took off after it."

An experienced aviator by that point in his career, Gatlin knew that many such sightings are caused by meteors, planetary phenomena, high altitude weather balloons or other easily explained causes. He quickly deduced that what he and his fellow pilot were seeing was none of those possibilities.

"It wasn't a star or a meteor or anything like that. It was just a big bright light. It started to move away from us when we gave chase. It was definitely something – I just don't know what."

Despite flying one of the fastest aircraft of that period, an F-51D Mustang, Gatlin said, "We never could catch it. We didn't tell anyone what happened for the longest time, either. We figured they'd think we were crazy. I probably shouldn't even be talking about it now."

But this eyewitness testimony from an experienced senior officer of the military does seem to lend credibility to others' stories of seeing UFOs (unidentified flying objects) over the fair state of Minnesota.[1]

Perhaps the same flying object was responsible for a November 24, 1951, report by Air Force pilots W.H. Fairbrother and D.E. Stewart of a "milky-white" object shaped like a flying wing with no visible fuselage or tail. Spotted in the Mankato area, the pilots were also flying P-51 Mustangs and reported that the UFO had about an 8-foot span, flew straight and level and was visible for about five seconds. Reported to and investigated by the U.S. Air Force Project Blue Book, this sighting was classified as "unknown," meaning the Air Force could find no reasonable explanation for the object.[2]

As noted at some length at the end of the last chapter, paranormal researchers have recently begun to find linkages between sightings of Bigfoot and Unidentified Flying Objects, but such was not always the case. There is also a tendency by many people to believe that the UFO phenomenon is a figment that began in the last half of the 20th century, but this is far from correct. There have been reports of "something weird in the sky" almost from the day the first settler landed in Minnesota.

Indeed, so numerous are early reports of UFOs that in his 1998 book, *The M-Files – True Reports of Minnesota's Unexplained Phenomena*, Jay Rath uses 17 pages to note alphabetical listings of sightings dating back to a very early sighting of a bright nocturnal light at Stillwater in 1871, an 1878 encounter with a mystery airship at Hastings and another Stillwater report of a nocturnal light in 1890.

But by far the most reported UFO in Minnesota history was an 1897 "mystery airship" that was sighted in virtually every part of the state between what is thought to have been its first appearance on February 6 at Taylors Falls and a rash of some 40 sightings all over the rest of the state during early to mid-April.

As described by eyewitnesses after viewing the craft on the night of April 11, their first alert of the ship was a bright light that changed from red to green to white, then repeated the sequence. Businessman R.G. Adams told the *St. Paul Pioneer Press* that he viewed the craft through field glasses near the corner of Lake Street and Nicollet Avenue and observed that the lights were attached to a cigar-shaped fuselage. He saw it flying low at about 8 p.m. heading toward Lake Minnetonka and said that his mother and father had also observed the oddity. A number of other seemingly reliable witnesses agreed with Adams' description of the ship.

"I saw an object that appeared to be 18 or 20 feet long. It was shaped like a cigar and in the middle and on top was a square light....

He was going at a high rate of speed when I saw him. He would dip and shoot down for, say, a half-mile with a green light and then mount with the speed of a rocket showing a white light. As he floated, he changed his light to red or green," Adams told the newspaper.

Another reliable eyewitness, a pharmacist identified only as Mr. Newell of Excelsior, talked with the newspaper as the craft headed for his location at approximately 8:50-9 p.m.

"It seems to be coming toward Excelsior from the direction of Hotel St. Louis," Newell said, referring to a location that I'm unable to identify. "We can see a green and a white light. Sometimes it takes a shoot down and we see the green light plainly. Then it rises slowly up. It dodges around and sometimes seems to go almost in a circle."

Also in Excelsior, a woman identified as Mrs. Dr. Small viewed the craft through a field glass and was able to see a "dark body which moved with the light. It would move very erratically, shooting downward and to one side, and then rising with a succession of jerky movements."

Surprisingly, by 10:30 p.m. that same night, a similar sighting occurred about 100 air miles away at Albert Lea near the Iowa border. If the time sequence is approximately correct, the craft would have had to travel in excess of 65 miles-per-hour to accomplish that trip – not highly impressive by today's standard, but quite fast in 1897 when steam locomotives might occasionally reach that speed. Either that, or there was more than one airship involved in this brouhaha of sightings.

And the airship's schedule would accelerate after its appearances in the Twin Cities. As noted earlier, about 40 assorted sightings were reported from a wide area ranging from Virginia and Duluth in the northeastern part of the state to Bigelow on the very southwestern border and from Fergus Fall in north central to Waseca in the southwest, with the greatest concentration radiating outward about 150 miles from the Twin Cities. Those sightings were nearly all reported within a two-week period, meaning that it was moving fast and frequently if there were but one craft.

Because the descriptions were quite straightforward and reported by a number of sober and serious people, it is tempting to believe that there was "something" in the air in April 1897. On the other hand, the "mystery airship" had elicited a great deal of attention all across the western United States and it's tempting to attribute the many Minnesota sightings to a kind of mass hypnosis or hysteria that may have taken control of the populace.

Given the crude state of aeronautics in that period, it's unlikely that balloons could have been the source of the sightings, and dirigibles were only being developed and perfected at that time, making them also an unlikely source for the reports.

In his book, Jay Rath also explores the possibility that Ringling Brothers Circus of Baraboo, Wisconsin, created the airship as an attraction to draw in the public, but there is little evidence supporting that possibility and no record of bigger crowds being generated for the brothers' circus. Thus, the origin of the many reports remains shrouded in more than a 100-year fog of history.[3]

One of Minnesota's most widely publicized UFO encounters came on August 27, 1979, when Marshall County Deputy Val Johnson had a "close encounter of the second kind," which is defined in UFOlogy as an event in which an unidentified object interacts in some way with the viewer or the environment – perhaps evading intercepting aircraft, interfering with a car's operation or leaving evidence on the ground like charred markings or debris.

Deputy Johnson was on patrol in a rural area not far from the North Dakota border at around 1:40 a.m. Seeing a glaring light to the south through his side window when he stopped to intersect

with Minnesota Highway 220 from County 5, he determined that the light was too bright to be that of an automobile. He thought perhaps that it might be the landing light of a small plane either on or flying near the ground. Trying for a better look, he took a left on Highway 220 and was startled to see the light moving toward him at a rate of speed that nearly instantaneously brought it directly upon his location. Blinded by the light, he heard glass breaking before losing consciousness.

By 2:19 a.m. he had regained sufficient consciousness to recognize that his car was stalled and had skidded across the road. He radioed for help and another officer soon arrived, calling an ambulance for Johnson, who remained shaky and sluggish. At the emergency room, a doctor diagnosed him as being in a mild state of shock. His eyes were irritated in a way that resembled a mild case of welder's burn that made him extremely sensitive to bright light.

Back at the scene of the encounter, investigators began to sift through the evidence to determine what had caused Johnson's episode. They noted that almost all of the damage to the patrol car from the incident was located in a linear pattern on the left side, recording a smashed inside left headlight. The outside left light remained intact. A crack in the windshield ahead of the steering wheel ran top to bottom and evidenced four impact points, some from the inside and some from the outside. Examination of the car's hood revealed a small circular, flat-bottomed dent close to the cracked windshield. The squad car's electric clock was 14 minutes late, and they would later discover that Johnson's mechanical wristwatch was also off by the same 14 minutes, causing one to wonder what it was that would interfere with both the electronic and mechanical actions of the timepieces.

Further examination showed that the roof antenna was bent at a 60-degree angle about six inches above its base and an antenna on the trunk was bent at 90 degrees near the top. The antenna for the car's AM-FM radio was located on the right front fender and was undamaged, again showing that the bulk of the damage had occurred to the left side.

Immediate investigation by the sheriff's office also showed that Johnson's patrol car ended up 950 feet from where the broken headlight glass indicated it was damaged. The last 40-50 feet of that line of travel was marked by skid marks from sudden, hard braking. Johnson had no memory of any portion of that time.

After the initial investigations, authorities could assign no cause for the event – including collision with another vehicle or a low-flying plane. It was also concluded that the incident was not a hoax on Johnson's part.

Experts from Ford Motor Company and Honeywell examined some damage where their experience might help solve the puzzle. One of the Ford personnel, Meridan French, was a recognized windshield expert who puzzled over the damaged windshield for several days, finally admitting, "I still have no explanation for what seems to be inward and outward forces acting almost simultaneously. I can only (conclude) that the cracks were from mechanical forces of unknown origin."

In addition, the experts could not find any cause for the clock and Johnson's watch losing 14 minutes, nor the peculiar antenna damage.

Because the incident occurred only about 40 miles south of the Manitoba/Minnesota border, Chris Rutkowski of the UFOlogy Research of Manitoba (UFOROM) group in Winnipeg became interested in the case when he heard radio reports several days after the incident. Remembering that his UFOROM associate Guy Westcott was vacationing in Minnesota, Chris induced his friend to set aside some time to visit the site of the encounter to see what he could discover. Both believed that Allen Hendry of the Center for UFO Study in the United States would have already been called in to consult in the case, but Westcott told Rutkowski that by the time he completed his investigation Hendry still had not been there.

Later, Westcott would return to the scene and obtain a taped interview that was printed in its entirety in the UFOROM's *Swamp Gas Journal* newsletter of January 1980. An extended examination of the case written by Rutkowski was contained in both that and the April 1980 newsletter. In his taped statement, Johnson verified all the salient points already outlined.

From his investigations, Westcott came to the conclusion that the light Johnson had observed was "ball lightning," a phenomenon that is said to consist of a powerful electrical charge formed near electrical lines during hot humid weather. Those conditions were all present near the site of the encounter.

Val Johnson reported his own impressions of the incident by saying, "It was as if someone had hit me in the face with a 400-pound pillow." Yet, he repeatedly said that the only pain he felt was from his sore eyes.

Unknown during the immediate investigation, but reported later, Johnson had had an extensive dental examination a week before the incident, including a full series of dental x-rays. Those x-rays revealed that his bridgework and the caps on his front teeth were all intact and in good shape. A week later, his dentist found that the bridgework was broken at the gum level, but without causing either swelling or pain.

Later investigation also revealed that the car's battery would not hold a charge, but Gauss Meter readings showed that there was no change in the magnetic pattern of the car, as might be expected from a sudden electrical burst. It was agreed that ball lightning might have been the cause of some of the damage, but could not explain the circular, flat-bottomed dent in the hood, the internal and external impact marks on the windshield nor the bent antennas.

Called the "perfect witness" due to his background as a police officer and trained observer, Johnson himself said he believed he had seen something he was not supposed to see, and that his powers of observation had been "neutralized" by someone or something that did not want to be seen or observed in action. He also admitted to repeatedly finding himself thinking the same three word phrase: "I am committed," something he had never experienced before the incident and for which he could offer no rational explanation. It was seemingly meaningless to him, yet it persisted in intruding upon his thoughts.

No final conclusions were reached as to what had happened to Deputy Sheriff Val Johnson, except that he was apparently unconscious, or as he chose to describe it several times, "neutralized" for a period of 39 minutes and suffered eye damage similar to burns caused by an arc welding machine. The damage to his vehicle also gave no conclusive hint as to what had happened. The incident remains as "unknown."[4]

While Deputy Johnson's encounter with some kind of ball of light was relatively recent, in her 1992 book, *Ghostly Tales of Minnesota*, Ruth D. Hein tells of a much older story of a ghostly light that paralleled Fred Schuster in the early 1900s as he made his way home by horse and buggy from a date with his girlfriend.

As was common with horse transportation, Molly the horse knew her way home, so Fred had the opportunity to relax and gaze around. Something in a field off to his left caught his attention, and he focused on the bright light that seemed to be moving with him some distance away. He whoaed Molly, and the light similarly stopped. When he giddyupped the horse, the object resumed its tracking, looking like a round ball of orange fire rolling along the ground, although the field did not catch fire and he saw no evidence of smoke.

It also appeared to reflect its light from something beneath it, although there was no water or anything else that would give that effect. Not knowing what it was that he was seeing made him nervous and he clucked at the horse to hurry it a bit. Molly quickened her pace, but the ball also speeded up, maintaining its position beside him at some distance out in the field.

As he neared the lane to his home, he grew apprehensive that the thing might follow him right to the farmstead. Knowing no was going to believe him, he was relieved when Molly turned into the lane and the ball of fire maintained a straight line, rolling along the ground until it vanished.

"It looked like a tumbleweed on fire, but it wasn't," Fred summarized. "I never saw it again and I never could figure out what it was, but I was mighty glad that thing didn't follow me into the yard."[5]

In my 2003 book, *Haunted Lake Superior*, I synthesized a story I'd heard several times from different workers of strange encounters with colored lights and "space ships" by crewmen aboard Erie Mining Company trains running from the mines at Hoyt Lakes to the company's dock at Taconite Harbor on Lake Superior's shore. The 73-mile mainline railroad passes through a large unpopulated and forested area and trains are quite isolated as they wend their way lakeward and back.

As an employee of the company at that time, I know that a colored drawing by a talented artist working for the company was made of what one of those train crews told him they saw, but the drawing disappeared shortly after it began to make the rounds of management.[6]

Haunted Lake Superior had barely hit the bookstores when I got a call from a fellow in the Cotton area north of Duluth telling me that the story perfectly described what he saw while deer hunting near the Duluth Missabe and Iron Range Railroad tracks in the Cotton vicinity.

"I got to my deer stand well before daylight, climbed up to the stand and was just settling in when an ore train came down the tracks with its headlight shining toward me. As I watched it, I suddenly saw colored lights above it and could make out some sort of object that seemed to be trailing the train down the track. I've never figured out exactly what it was that I saw, but your story described it to a tee," the caller reported.

Thinking this would make an interesting sequel to the story that I had synthesized from more than one source, I asked a couple of questions and then asked his name and telephone number.

"Oh no," he protested. "You don't need that. Just call me a believer in UFOs since I saw that thing."

His refusal to identify himself puts him among the majority of witnesses, who nearly always demand anonymity to tell their stories of weird encounters.[7]

But these two tales of Minnesota northland UFO sightings take a decided backseat to the more than one dozen reports of UFO sightings along Lake Superior's shoreline beginning on April 1, 1975, and catalogued by Bob Pratt at www.bobpratt.org. Pratt was a former UFO reporter for the *National Enquirer* (1975-1981) who spent more than 30 years poking into UFO sightings and reports and wrote literally hundreds of accounts of witnesses. I found his Website listings to be especially credible because in many instances he listed the names of witnesses and other details that other reporters either cannot name or have agreed to omit to preserve the anonymity of the storytellers.

The north shore sightings appear to have begun with a lady identified only as Susie and her sons observing what she described as a number of strange lights, some behaving in a manner she said was like popcorn popping all over the place.

Susie and the boys were watching television and she went into the kitchen for a drink of water. Just out from the back of her house was a large field, and she was startled to see a string of lights rushing down and across the field directly at her house.

In a panic, she shouted for the boys to run, telling them a jet was about to crash into the house. As the boys stirred into action, she saw the lights swerve to her right and suddenly decelerate, appearing to float over the house next door. She and the two boys went to the window of the living room just in time to see the lights come into view, barely moving. Creeping out onto the front porch, they were able to identify five red balls of light hovering in a V formation, with a number of white lights trailing behind, but moving in a frantic fashion that had no apparent pattern "like popcorn popping" all around. The white lights moved so quickly, they were not able to determine how many there were, although they agreed there were at least four.

Leisurely, the entire formation of lights moved easterly toward Lake Superior, making what Susie described as a low, muffled whooshing sound that she had never heard before. At some point in this episode, she had phoned a friend in a panic and they called the Lake County Sheriff's Department.

As the lights moved toward the big lake, Deputy Fred DuFresne arrived in time to catch a quick glimpse of the weird formation. An Army veteran familiar with aircraft and helicopters, he knew what he had seen did not match either category of flying machine, but had no explanation for what Susie and her boys had seen. He was, however, strangely sympathetic to their strange story, likely because he told Pratt that 15 months earlier he and another deputy watched five bright lights in the sky about a half mile from Susie's house, moving close to the ground. One by one, the lights blinked off from left to right. He said that the two of them agreed that the lights were probably a UFO.

Once she calmed down, Susie would report that what they had seen appeared to be more than a single object, since she was able to distinguish stars between the multiple lights. She also related that she might not have been quite as panicky at this sighting, had she not already experienced seeing a single, large white light zoom across the field at about 6:30 that morning.

"It was pulsing like a heartthrob and was real low, close to the ground," she said.

Nicknaming the multiple reports of April 1 sightings as the "April Fool's Lights," Todd Lindahl of Two Harbors was one of the witnesses to tell his story. Today, Todd is a respected historian and railroad chronicler in the region, and an acquaintance of mine whose story I am inclined to take at face value. At the time, he was a 23-year-old employee at Reserve Mining Company in Silver Bay and was en route to the taconite plant with two other employees on Highway 61 a few miles east of Two Harbors to work the midnight shift. The time was approximately 9:55 p.m.

"I thought when we first saw the lights that it was some kind of April Fool's joke, but all of us saw these four lights out over the lake. They were sort of ahead of us and to the right. They were bright orange and disc shaped."

Described as spread out one behind the other, with each a little higher than the one behind it, the lights were suddenly obscured by trees along the road. Speeding up a bit to reach the elevated lakeside view provided at that time on Highway 61 from Silver Creek Cliff, they were surprised to see no sign of the lights from that unobstructed viewpoint.

They continued their journey a mile or so when the lights suddenly reappeared.

"This time there were eight or 10 of them," Todd said. "They were straight out over the lake from us and were in more of a vertical pattern. They were the same color. Suddenly, we lost sight of them again and that's the last we saw of them."

But their sighting would be affirmed by two fellow employees who were a few minutes behind them. Allen Michaelson of Two Harbors, who was driving, told the story thusly: "It was about 10:15 and Mike (only) said, 'Look out over the lake!' I could see some kind of yellowish-orange lights way off in the distance, kind of faded and not real bright. I couldn't tell how many there were and when we got up on the (Silver Creek) Cliff, they just faded out."

Just minutes before that sighting, another couple returning to Two Harbors from visiting friends in the country spotted a set of "reddish-orange lights in the sky ahead of us and to our left," the husband, a wildlife biologist, reported.

"There were a half-dozen or so in a sort of oval pattern and they were moving along but all of sudden just went out. There were no trees that might have obstructed our vision of them and I assumed they were out over Lake Superior. When we got to the top of a hill, the lights came on again and we watched for just a short while when they went out."

Of all the north shore sighting reports, 18-year-old Jerry LaVigne of Silver Bay would have one of the clearest, most detailed sightings.

"It was about five minutes to 10 and I had just come into the house and happened to look out the window," Jerry told Pratt. "I saw four lights quite a-ways out over the lake. When I first saw them, they were all on, and then they went out, one, two, three, four! Just like that, from left to right."

Calling for his sister to come take a look, Jerry continued with his story. "A few minutes later, the lights came on again, much farther to the south and in the same sequence, one, two, three, four from left to right. They didn't seem to be moving at all, but were more or less stationary. After about 35 or 40 seconds, they went out again in the same order.

"We kept watching and they came on again, only this time there were eight of them and they were even farther to the south. They were the same color, sort of a light bulb color, and they came on one at a time, left to right. After about a half minute, they went out in the same order and that's the last we saw them."

And the April Fool's UFO reports didn't end with the changing of the date, for a lady and her daughter who lived about a mile from Susie's home had a dawn sighting of an object about a quarter mile from their house.

"It was round and sort of disc-shaped," the Two Harbors resident said. "It had about three lights that were going around it. It was heading behind a big evergreen tree and just before it got there, the object tipped up on its side a bit and I could see it was shiny, metallic looking and had a rim about a third of the way from the edge. Then it was gone and we didn't see it any more."

Her husband had been in the shower and missed the encounter, but the woman told him of their experience when he emerged from the shower.

"He said, 'Well, they've been seeing them all over the Knife River Valley for the last two weeks....'" referring to a large rural area northwest of the town of Two Harbors and the locale of the sightings by Susie, the wildlife biologist and his wife and this woman and her daughter.

These multiple reports were unearthed on one of his earliest UFO assignments for the *Enquirer* and turned Pratt's admitted skepticism about such sightings into a lifelong obsession with UFOs.[8]

But UFO sightings on the north shore in the latter half of the 20th century may have had a much earlier predecessor, if we speculate about what it was that H.P. Wieland reported seeing with his Uncle Albert in October 1868. The son of the oldest of the five Wieland brothers who were leaders in the 1856 settlement of Beaver Bay, H.P. recorded his memoirs of north shore life in 1933. His Uncle Albert was at various times a merchant, captain of the family's lumber schooner, *Charley*, postmaster at Beaver Bay and a mail carrier between Superior, Wisconsin, and Grand Portage, Minnesota, the latter being the reason the two men were on Lake Superior that night.

H.P. would have been in his teens when this story occurred. His brief report of some type of sighting is printed verbatim in its entirety here.

"One dark night in the month of October 1868, Uncle Albert and I were rowing along the shore on one of our trips from Grand Portage to Superior. We had just passed the mouth of the Temperance River (about midway between the towns of Schroeder and Tofte) when there appeared a bright star northeast of us.

"The star got brighter and larger very fast and seemed to be coming straight for us. It passed about a mile inland from us and crashed to the ground about a mile ahead of us with a terrific roar. The illumination was grand, and after the crash, we were both blinded for several minutes. We resumed our rowing and neither of us spoke a word for a long time."

H.P. called his short report, "The Meteor or What It Was?" and a meteor is certainly a possible explanation, but in my book, *Haunted Lake Superior*, I speculate that it might just as easily be identified as an early UFO encounter. What he describes in some ways mirrors our other northern Minnesota UFO reports, with the exception that none of those reports include an actual landing. Certainly, the bright light and terrific roar might be consistent with the landing of a spacecraft, if we consider the decibel levels created during modern rocket launchings.

Given the fact that they had a pretty good fix on the location, coupled with the undeniably insatiable curiosity of Christian Wieland, another of H.P.'s uncles, it seems rather peculiar and regrettable that the Wieland family didn't poke a little further into the incident – especially in light of the fact that very little happened on Lake Superior's north shore that was ignored by this wide-ranging, inquisitive family. Still, they apparently simply accepted at face value the description by H.P. and Albert of seeing a meteor crash to earth.

In doing research on the story, I checked with a well-respected local geologist and was told that he knew of no records of meteorite finds in the Temperance River area, even after more than 130 years of people probing and poking around on the north shore.[9]

While most of the foregoing reports are based on brief encounters by untrained observers in unmonitored situations, author Jay Rath devotes two full chapters of his book, *The M-Files*, to sightings by witnesses whose credentials are seemingly unimpeachable. All were investigated by the U.S. Air Force's Project Blue Book while that operation remained active. It was subsequently shut down in 1969, but not before collecting 30 file drawers of material relating to unexplained encounters by reliable witnesses that were reported to the group.

In his chapter titled "The Astronaut's UFO," Rath tells the saga of a 1952 UFO encounter by a veteran Air Force officer who had flown 56 combat bombing missions over Europe and seven sorties over Japan. A post-war graduate in aeronautical engineering from the University of Minnesota, he had gotten a job with Boeing Aircraft in Seattle, Washington, before being recalled to active duty in 1951, serving as a flight test officer, technical inspector, fighter pilot and test pilot until 1959, when he was selected as one of the seven original U.S. astronauts.

After his 1951 reactivation, Donald "Deke" Slayton was assigned to duty as maintenance officer and test pilot with a P-51 fighter group in Minneapolis where, on June 9, 1959, he was test flying one of the P-51s during daylight.

Cruising at 10,000 feet, he suddenly sighted a disc-shaped object and gave chase.

"My first reaction was that it was a kite. A few seconds later it occurred to me that this could not be the case (because of the altitude)," Slayton later wrote to UFO researcher Dr. J. Allen Hynek, a professor of astronomy at University of Ohio who would later be selected as chairman of astronomy at Northwestern University. Hynek had served as an advisor for Project Blue Book and after the Air Force shut that program down, he was the founder of the civilian Center on UFO Studies.

After closer examination, Slayton continued, he determined that the object was flying at his altitude and seemed to be coming toward him. He accordingly kept an eye on it until is was directly off his left wing and about 500 feet below his aircraft. Saying that the object appeared at that angle to be a round weather balloon, Slayton did a 180-degree turn to get on the trail of the object.

"Upon getting on trail, it appeared to be a disc-shaped object, rather than round, sitting at about a 45-degree angle with the horizon," Slayton continued. "It seemed to be somewhat slower than I at that point, but started to accelerate and went into a climbing left turn as I closed on it. I lost sight of it ... and returned to home base. I made a report the following day to our intelligence section.... My only conclusion was that it was an unidentified object, at least to me, and I would not speculate as to what it might have been. Since it was a bright, clear day, I have discounted its being a weather or an optical illusion."

Later, after Slayton was promoted as the first chief of the National Aeronautics and Space Administration's Astronaut Office, his Project Blue Book report of a UFO encounter would become an embarrassment. Subsequently, when he became director of Flight Crew Operations and served as the docking pilot for the 1975 Apollo/Soyuz rendezvous, his name was recognized virtually worldwide, but the contents of his 1952 Blue Book report disappeared from the government's archives. Nothing remained but the dated folder in the files that held the reports classified by Air Force investigators as "unknown."[10]

Rath's second citation of apparently unimpeachable witnesses reporting UFOs to the Air Force investigators involves the mother of Cheerios, Wheaties, Betty Crocker and a host of other everyday brand names. In the 1950s, the Aeronautical Division of General Mills was the single supplier and tester of weather balloons for the government and military. Weather balloons were frequently said to be the cause of UFO sightings. A crack team of meteorologists, astronomers and assorted other specialized scientists worked in the division and knew many episodes of strange encounters, but prior to 1951 had elected not to report sightings to the Air Force because they did not approve of that service's earlier dismissive attitude toward the reports.

Upon his appointment to head the reorganized Project Blue Book in 1952, Captain Edward Ruppelt determined that the General Mills scientists might be a big help to his renewed UFO operation. He came to Minneapolis to personally make a pitch for their aid.

"I talked to these people for the better part of a full day and every time I tried to infer that there might be some natural explanation for the UFOs, I just about found myself in a fresh snowbank ... they had seen so many of them. One man told me that one tracking crew had seen so many that the sight of a UFO no longer even especially interested them. And the things that they saw couldn't be explained," Ruppelt said in his later book, *The Report on Unidentified Flying Objects*.

Following Ruppelt's visit to their headquarters, the General Mills scientists became much more forthcoming in reporting UFO sightings to Project Blue Book and, while he led that group, Ruppelt made sure that his troops gave credence to their reports.

"They knew what their balloons looked like under all lighting conditions, they knew science and they also knew UFOs," Ruppelt said of the talented team.

Perhaps their most reliable report was of an October 15, 1953, sighting by three research engineers while they were tracking a 79-foot balloon at 80,000 feet. Their first observation was of a vapor trail that quickly dispersed. It passed beneath the sun heading south in horizontal flight, moving at an estimated 15 miles a second (900 miles a minute).

After about 10 seconds, the UFO went into a vertical dive at the same speed which lasted an estimated 10-15 seconds, during which the object could be seen as a glow or reflection several times. The vapor trail ended during the dive and the UFO was suddenly visible as a gray mass that had just leveled off. The three witnesses agreed that it could have been a jet aircraft, but the speed was much greater than normal, the vertical dive at that speed was extremely hazardous to the point of suicidal, and the dive should have created a powerful shock wave that would have been heard for miles in every direction.

Even the most diehard skeptics at Project Blue Book agreed that this report by a team of unusually competent and qualified professionals at General Mills outlined an encounter with a truly Unidentified Flying Object.[11]

Before exiting Rath's cataloguing of UFO reports, I do want to reveal one more whose Project Blue Book explanation struck me as particularly funny.

In Moorhead on April 26, 1952, five glowing, circular objects were reported by a police officer and five other adults. The objects were said to be in a V formation flying northwest.

After its investigation of the report, the Air Force reported that what the witnesses had seen was ground light reflecting from the shiny breasts of ducks flying over the area.[12]

Lest you think sightings of UFOs are an uncommon event, perhaps occurring over a longish period, consider the autumn of 1965 when five reports were filed in little more than a month from a wide area of our state. They illustrate the varying nature of unidentified flying objects and each seems to indicate that some sort of electrical interference is involved in areas of UFO sightings.

On October 23 near Long Prairie in the west central area, Jerry Townsend's car completely failed after he spotted a 30-40 foot metallic rocket-shaped object on the road ahead. Jerry said that he got out of the car and saw three small objects about six inches high and shaped like beer cans with fins come out of the larger object and approach him. After some time, the three got back into the large object, which lifted off into the air. An oily substance was found on the road where the objects had been.

Only a couple of weeks later, on November 16, a lone motorist reported that his radio died and the car's engine coughed and sputtered as he was looking at an object flying over Highway 17 outside of Luverne in southeastern Minnesota. The observer estimated that the object was several hundred feet above the ground and said that it emitted a beam of light onto the ground. After it was gone, the car and radio worked normally again.

That same night, a driver near Cyrus in west central Minnesota was surprised when the speed of his car inexplicably dropped from 40 mph to 20 mph. Then the driver reported seeing an object on the road ahead. It was 10 feet high and looked a bit like a stovepipe with a cone at the top. There was a white glow around the whole thing. As the car came closer, the object rose into the air to the northeast, leaving a vapor trail.

Just 10 days later, on November 26, many residents of the Totem Town area of St. Paul reported seeing strange objects flying overhead, emitting blue and orange flashes. Some reported that their house lights went out as the objects passed above them. One person in a car said that his headlights and radio had failed as the objects passed nearby.

Again in west central Minnesota near Herman on December 20, a 15-year-old boy was driving a pickup truck when he saw a UFO hovering about six feet over the road. The engine of the truck died and the object began to glow red. As the boy watched, it rose straight up into the air, giving off sparks. The boy then lost consciousness, and when he awoke, he found that the truck was turned around and was resting in a roadside ditch.[13]

Does the fact that descriptions of the flying objects vary so widely mean that there are many models of UFOs? Might different models be used for differing purposes? And what are they looking for or doing here in the first place?

It all remains a mystery at this time, but perhaps we'll understand them better by and by, to paraphrase an old hymn.

Up to this point, our stories of "alien encounters" have all been of a rather benign nature – no deaths, few injuries of any consequence, little blood and guts. This Land of Sky Blue Waters has been a fertile area for so-called crop circles, alien abductions of our citizens and assorted other weird mayhem. But Minnesota was an early breeding ground of a peculiar phenomena that has become known universally as "cattle mutilations." (Skip ahead about 10 paragraphs if this isn't your cup of tea.)

In the early 1970s, an increasing number of farmers began finding dead livestock in their pastures, strangely mutilated, but with no physical evidence of who or what was doing the damage. In virtually every case, there were no footprints or other indications of anyone being in proximity to the carcasses, even though a fair number were found in wet or soft earth that should have yielded good evidence of someone being on the scene.

The vast proportion of the mutilations had some or all of the following characteristics: eyes removed, genitalia removed, as well as the udders of cows, rectum removed with other related organs, skin

over the mouth and chin removed, in some cases encompassing the entire head, and most or all of the blood removed. In every case the process of the mutilation was characterized as surgically precise, evidencing signs of cauterization or perhaps laser surgery, which was not yet available at the time of the earliest episodes. Estimates since the 1970s place the number of these mutilations at perhaps 20,000 in the continental United States and many more in foreign countries. Perhaps because of its isolation, Hawaii seems to have escaped the scourge, but most other states with populations of livestock have experienced a rash of reports.

One of the earliest Minnesota mutilation cases involved a heifer found fallen in fresh snow in Meeker County in 1974. The carcass was missing its eyes, left cheek, ears and tongue. Despite the new snow, no footprints were found at the scene, although a number of random circles of melted snow were recorded in the area, including one around the heifer. No blood was found on either the carcass or the surrounding ground. As with nearly every subsequent report, the lack of evidence for human presence at the scene confounded investigators looking into the case.

Law enforcement officials at first tried to pin the blame on satanic cults for the increasing number of livestock mutilation reports, but the absence of footprints or other evidence did not seem to support that supposition. A few such cases where evidence could be found did support a cult connection, but they were the decided minority.

Adding to the mystery of the mutilations was the fact that in nearly every case predators like ravens, bears, wolves and coyotes that might be expected to prey on the dead animals are said to have strangely avoided these easy pickings, perhaps reflecting some chemical or physical force that repelled the predators.

Speculation about the mutilations runs the gamut from highly secret government or military research to alien tampering for some reason. The former seems to be supported by a number of reports of black, unmarked helicopters with powerful searchlights being observed in areas at somewhat the same time that the mutilations took place. These theories rely to some extent on a conspiratorial belief that government and/or military research is far more advanced than either political or military events seem to show. And if humans are involved, why is there no solid evidence that proves that is the case? Also, why would the government/military surreptitiously steal animal parts from unwary farmers, instead of simply buying a herd of cattle and conducting their research under the cloak of outright ownership that guaranteed secrecy?

By the same token, proponents of alien theories are supported by numerous reports of UFO sightings at about the same time the cattle were mutilated, but skeptics point out that this explanation demands an ironclad belief that there are beings among us that are so much more advanced than our culture that they easily traverse light years to mingle on this planet. If they are that sophisticated, why are they putzing around with cows? And why don't they simply make themselves known to us, since they should easily be able to neutralize any threat we might inadvisably bring to bear upon them?

Whatever the case may be, reports of cattle mutilations continue to the present, but have declined dramatically from the heyday of the early 1980s. Most current reports seem to be focused more and more in South American countries that have sizable livestock populations. Surprisingly, given our early entry into this mysterious area, good, credible individual stories of animal mutilations in Minnesota are scarce, given the more than 30-year period that these incidents have been reported.[14]

Crop circles are another phenomena that are often linked by some people to alien occupation of Earth's environment. Like cattle mutilations, there is ample and solid evidence of the occurrence of patterns in field crops, but their origin remains clouded by both proponents of alien/UFO connections and about an equally vocal group who pooh-pooh the circles as hoaxes by pranksters.

The earliest reports of the mysterious crop downages come from England, where there seems to have been a several hundred-year history of such crop damage. Whatever their origin, crop circles have been investigated by a thoroughly trained team of Minnesota Mutual UFO Network sleuths and several have been noted as apparently authentic vestiges of UFO or other unearthly activity. Some UFO adherents attribute the formations to intelligent beings that are perhaps attempting to communicate with our species – perhaps in pictographic forms. Others among the UFO tribe shrug them off as merely the residue from spaceship landings, while a few even more occult proponents suggest a "magic" or even a devilishly designed origin.

Whatever the case may be, researchers and investigators have observed quite a range of anomalies within the circles that seem to point to something other than human pranksters.

Perhaps the foremost international research organization is named BLT Research Team Inc., a non-profit organization headquartered in Cambridge, Massachusetts, for the express purpose of scientifically studying the phenomena of crop circles. Founders of the team were businessman John A. Burke; Dr. W.C. Levengood, a biophysicist from University of Michigan; and music producer Nancy Talbott. The team's mutual interest in the scientific approach to the question of crop circles uses a group of associates as field investigators to collect physical, biological and chemical evidence at the site of crop circles.

Using his considerable laboratory experience during his more than eight years with the team, Dr. Levengood produced hundreds of detailed reports showing anomalies considered by most researchers to be unlikely from earthly causes, but also unlikely to be caused by little gray critters from space.

Beginning with the plants themselves, the researchers early discovered that some force resembling microwaves create expulsion cavities in the nodes of the stems/stalks of the downed plants. These openings vary in size depending on the diameter of the stem and can range up to several inches in length. They are said to be caused by sudden heating of the moisture inside the stalk that then escapes in a burst through the wall of the nodes.

But the team has also found other strange evidence within the circles, including much higher levels of unusually pure iron in clusters of very small perfectly round spheres of magnetic iron. In some, a black "sooty" material has been found on stems and other vegetation. They have also observed changes in crystallinity from the circles to areas outside the circles, as well as changes in clay soil characteristics compared to unaffected areas in the same vicinity.

Dr. Levengood has formed the postulate that the most likely nonhuman cause of crop circle formations is sudden brief bursts of very energetic, highly charged, ionized plasma vortices that emit bursts of either microwave energy or something quite similar. The BLT team also indicates that unusual electrical pulses and strong magnetic fields may also be involved in the vortex formation. The origin of these energy vortices is thought to be the ionosphere, high above earth, thus making them unearthly, even if not related to UFO activity.

Ironically, depending on the stage of plant maturity, after exposure to the energy in early growth stages, the plants produce few fertile seeds, but when exposed at or near maturity they are found to produce extremely hardy, productive seeds.

In Minnesota, two October 1994 crop circles were sampled by Minnesota Mutual UFO Network (MNMUFON) investigator Robert Schultz, with direction from Dr. Levengood, for analysis.

In Schultz's initial field reports on the circles, he describes the Milaca and Blaine scenes at some length, noting the Milaca formation as being three circles on an east-west line in a cornfield owned by Harold and Shirley Anderson. They were first spotted on October 1 from the air by their son, Perry, a private pilot, and demonstrated uniform patterns of corn being flattened to the ground – but inside the larger center circle (65 feet in diameter), the stalks lay in a counterclockwise pattern, whereas in the smaller circles (29 feet), the stalks lay in a clockwise direction.

When they first examined the circles, Harold and Perry told Schultz that they found no footprints or other impressions within the circles. Furthermore, they indicated that at the center of each circle there were clumps of dirt that were totally undisturbed.

On his first visit, Harold and Shirley were not at home and Schultz had to be content to simply walk into the formation and snap some pictures. The following day, he and a pilot flew over the field and took further photographs of the formations. After using the MUFON amateur radio network to inform other members of that organization of his initial findings, one of those members urged him to get in touch with Dr. Levengood to assist in the investigation. Levengood then instructed him on what he needed to know and do to collect good samples at the scene.

The following day, a Sunday, Schultz again returned to the field and he and Harold and Shirley talked at length about the strange formations. Harold said that neighbors three miles north of the Anderson farm had told him by phone that they saw a strange light in the sky several days before the crop circles were discovered.

During this visit, Schultz collected corn samples from each of the circles, together with control samples from 100 feet outside the circles, to be analyzed in Dr. Levengood's laboratory.

The next day, Shirley told Schultz during an interview for his investigation that she and Harold had observed a large bluish-white globe descend toward their farm several nights before the crop circles were found. Schultz noted in his original report that some time later British investigator George Wingfield told him that many English farmers had seen something similar in their fields the night before crop circles were discovered.

In his early examination of the corn samples, Levengood told Schultz that the circles were definitely not a hoax, as proven by the typical "microwave" damage to the corn cobs. It would be many months before there would be a final report, but from his full analysis, the biophysicist stated, "The data provide very clear evidence that a rapid, thermal energy delivered within the formations was sufficient to alter cell wall pit structures within the ears of corn. These changes were consistent within two independently obtained sample sets within matching sampling locations (R group by Sally Rayl and S group by Schultz). The distribution of the energies throughout these circle formations appears to be very complex, a situation which is consistent with what has been documented in many other crop formations."

The Milaca circles drew the interest of major Midwest media, with WCCO-TV and KARE-TV giving the story substantial coverage from the ground and by videotape from their helicopters. Bob Schultz was apparently satisfied to let Dr. Levengood's research speak for itself, for his report renders no verdict on what might have caused the circles.

He is not so reticent about his findings at the second cornfield crop circle he examined at Blaine less than a month later. Here, both his preliminary opinion and his final word on the incident after full analysis had been completed was that he believed there was strong reason to believe the circle was created by a flying saucer/space ship.

And the site was notable for providing a trove of evidence other than just the damaged corn. Indeed, the wealth of material collected so impressed Dr. Levengood that he seemed almost rhapsodic about some the samples.

One of the first things that caught Schultz's eye at the Blaine scene was that the cornstalks were flattened in a much more random fashion than the neatly clockwise and counterclockwise patterns at the Milaca site. The perfectly round circle measured 47 feet in diameter, with the cornstalks smashed to the ground near the center, but many of them at the outer edge were merely bent at about a 20-degree angle to the ground.

Closer examination of the scene revealed three 6-inch diameter holes about six feet apart near the center of the formation. Also near the center was a peculiar layer of white granular material on the ground. Smelling of pine sap, Schultz noted in his report that no pine trees were anywhere in the vicinity. Under the white granules, yellow crystals of an unrecognized material were discovered.

Within the circle, about 10 cocklebur weeds were found with scrappings observed on the stalks. These weedstalks, along with samples of the white material, dirt and corn from inside and outside the circle, were collected and prepared for analysis. At Dr. Levengood's suggestion, a magnet was also dragged through the soil to collect magnetic materials for analysis.

Because the Blaine farm couple requested anonymity to avoid undue publicity of their crop circle, there was no attention given to it by the media. That does not mean, however, that it did not yield spectacular findings when Dr. Levengood had the chance to study it.

Addressing the corn first, he noted that it showed the same cell wall pit distortions observed in the month-earlier sample from Milaca. The scrapping on the cocklebur stalks was also confirmed by the lab. Using Energy Dispersive Spectroscopy, Levengood identified the yellow crystals as being composed of a natural organic resin, perhaps aromatic terpenes which is commonly found in resins and essential oils. Being a natural material and relatively common, they were remarkable only for having been discovered beneath that white granular material, which was analyzed as being an inorganic, unusual composition of calcium, silicon, oxygen, sulphur and sodium. It was found to dissolve easily in water, but formed corkscrew shaped crystals when it dried. Looking similar to DNA helical chains, Dr. Levengood vouchsafed he had never seen inorganic material produce such helical crystals.

It would, however, be the magnetic metal that Schultz sent to him that turned the scientist euphoric.

"I've been having people drag magnets all over England this year in crop formations," Levengood fairly crooned. "No one has found any appreciable magnetic material yet, and you found a ton of it!"

Analysis of the magnetic material showed it to be magnetite (Fe_3O_4), which is deposited on earth from meteoritic iron floating down through the atmosphere. Spectroscopy indicated that the samples were a very pure form of this meteoric iron and had a high degree of small spherical globules measuring 2 to 100 microns under the microscope. That would be highly unusual in earthly samples.

Despite the weight of all the scientific analysis, Bob Schultz stuck to his original claim that what he had seen in Blaine was a genuine flying saucer landing zone.[15]

On July 29, 2004, five crop circles measuring about 27 feet each were discovered at rural Cottage Grove and again caught the attention of the BLT Research Team, which visited the farm of Gene and Louise Smallidge in early August to shoot photos and collect what evidence was available, following Gene's hurried harvesting of his oat crop to reap whatever he could from the smashed oats, which lay in the same direction in all five circles.

Because the oats were mature at the time the circles were formed, Smallidge was told by the BLT researchers that the oats from the circles might have proven to be more hardy and productive, but by that time those seeds were all mixed with those from outside the mysterious circles.

Nancy Talbot, president of BLT, stated at the time that the circles appeared to be the "real McCoy" from a photo printed in the local paper, but noted that further research was necessary to come to any definitive conclusion.

"If I'd known those seeds might be more hardy, I'd have saved them for next year," the sagacious farmer opined to Greg Moynaugh, a reporter for the *South Washington County Bulletin*.[16]

At the time this is being written, no report on the Cottage Grove circles has been released by the BLT Research team.

Laying aside the interesting topic of crop circles and the research being done on them, we turn our attention to reports of Minnesota people claiming to have been abducted by aliens.

I must admit that this is an area in which I feel distinctly conflicted. I understand and accept that the experiencers truly believe that they have encountered something unearthly and extraordinary, but I keep running into too many of my own suspicions about the stories and the storytellers.

I will admit that my own interest in the phenomenon is tainted by having spent a few years of duty at the Marine Corps Base in Twenty Nine Palms, California. By the early 1960s, the desert around that small town was liberally salted with true believers in UFOs of all stripes. As I understood it, they apparently congregated in the Marongo Valley and high desert north of Palm Springs in the belief that the higher altitude, clear desert air and open desert terrain made contacts with UFOs more likely. At any one of the town's several watering holes, one had difficulty having a conversation that didn't soon turn up one of these UFO junkies. We listened to talk by those seeking contact with UFOs. We had those claiming to have been abducted and "modified" by aliens. We had folks who could report with a straight face almost nightly contact with alien critters – even though an anti-aircraft unit at the base never spotted any questionable or unidentified bogey on their relatively sophisticated (at that time) radar and tracking equipment.

Besides that personal bias, another of the things that bothers me about these supposed encounters is that the same experiencers often tell a number of other stories about close encounters of various types – from merely seeing saucer-shaped flying objects to actually being taken aboard and having weird things done to them. Also, quite a few relate that they've "always" experienced encounters of one type or another.

I know there are theories by UFOlogists that aliens have selected some unknowing earthlings for research which could explain multiple experiences with UFOs by a particular subject, but I am also aware that university psychoanalysts have published a number of scholarly papers indicating that tests on subjects who tell such stories often turn up various other personality abnormalities.

Having fully confessed that I am a jaundiced recorder of the following tales, I will strive hereafter to keep my personal views out of the verbiage. I relied on the Minnesota Mutual UFO Network (MNMUFON) investigative reports of such encounters to compile this section, since they are the single source I could find that has conducted actual investigations into such incidents within Minnesota.

In November 1993, a 65-year-old mother of four and grandmother of nine told of her close encounter of the fourth kind (defined as involving an abduction or personal contact with an alien entity).

In her report, she said she woke about 2 a.m. to see a light in the center of the bedroom ceiling. Unsure what was causing the strange light, she sat up in bed and immediately spotted three odd critters that she estimated to be about 3½ feet in height and seemed to be floating above the floor. One of them was at the foot and the other two on the right side of her bed. Upset at the intrusion into her privacy, she remembered kicking out at the nearest one and was somewhat startled when her foot actually contacted something, proving this was not just some weird dream.

"The kick felt like it hit a light weight, not a lot of substance," she told MNMUFON investigator Craig Lang, also indicating that her kick struck the entity in the right shoulder, sending it flying backward about three feet and "landing on its rear."

Upon kicking the critter, she could remember nothing more about the whole episode, apparently either losing consciousness or being, as Deputy Val Johnson earlier described it, "neutralized."

She said she closely examined the ceiling of the room several times looking for something that might explain the strange light, but found nothing. Lang's investigation resulted in his ranking of the episode as "unexplained, of high significance or value."

This same woman, a retired real estate agent, also related to Lang seven other instances of encounters with flying objects or aliens.

Craig Lang also investigated a Minneapolis woman's story of a close encounter of the fourth kind in July 1994 at her parents' home in Eau Claire, Wisconsin, a bit more than an hour east of the Twin Cities on I-94.

According to the witness, in the wee hours of the morning she suddenly found herself in the front yard of her mother's home, in her nightgown with bare feet. She remembered that she was looking toward the house from about 100 feet away and spotted a pack of what she depicted as four of five sizable coyotes or wolves looking down at her from the roof of the house. While unable to clearly describe the beings, she recalled that they appeared to be furry.

Both scared and curious, she walked slowly toward the house, keeping the beings in sight, but suddenly felt that she was being escorted toward the house by a couple of entities close behind her. She reported she could feel them touching and gently guiding her, but had no glimpse of what they might be. At that contact, she felt a momentary feeling of illness and experienced what she described as being lifted, weightless and a rising sensation, at the end of which she found herself in a brightly lighted white hallway.

Instructed to walk down the hall to a door about 10 feet to her right, she passed through the doorway into a small room with some sort of contraption to her right. She there encountered an entity whose form she could not make out standing at the far end of the room and to the left of the strange machine she had first seen. She observed a number of mostly red and green lights on the machine and was allowed to examine it before she suddenly found herself to the left of her former position and in front of the middle portion of the machine which had no lights or buttons.

Suddenly, she saw what she said was a one- to three-inch wide trough of "green goo" flowing from the right portion of the machine through the middle portion and disappearing to her left.

The unformed entity ordered her to put her hand into the green material. Initially resisting that order because she found the goo icky, she was compelled mentally to do so and did not find the contact with the green material repulsive, saying that it felt as if her hand met no resistance, like moving it through the air.

She reported that she was unsure if the machine was part of an experiment or might simply have been a game for her amusement. She did discern that the machine had no function in operating the aliens' craft, but it appeared that it was simply there to interact with her. She remembers a real feeling of relief when her hand contacted the goo, which seemed to just merge with her hand.

Immediately thereafter, she found herself in the presence of five entities in a larger room. The tallest of the five appeared to be the leader and the woman reported that she got an excellent view of the beings' features, but was unable to draw or describe them during the investigative interview. They did seem totally emotionless and she said she likewise felt emotionless in their presence. After answering questions about her health, she suddenly found herself waking up in her bed and wondering, "What was that?"

The only other person in the house was her mother, who did not believe that anything unusual had happened and refused to discuss the entire episode.

The report was classified by Lang as "probable unexplained of intermediate significance, assuming the events described were a real experience." He did note that no known natural or man made phenomena could produce the effects described, but that if added witnesses or evidence could be located, the significance would be upgraded to high.

The woman did not report any beneficial or adverse health or physical problems following her close encounter, however other stories on the Minnesota UFO Network do indicate one or the other.

I must admit that two such stories will probably not satisfy real UFO enthusiasts, but they bring me to the end of my rope and thus bring this chapter to an end. Readers seeking gorier or more detailed stories on this topic are encouraged to type "alien abductions" or anything else they find compelling into a search engine to peruse hundreds of Web pages that their search produces. Happy reading to them and welcome respite from this subject for me![16]

CHAPTER 7

Haunts of Kindness or Benignness

A resident of Minnesota's Lake Superior north shore tells two stories illustrating both the benevolent and the malevolent species of ghost. Apparently an exceptionally sensitive clairvoyant, the woman would only anonymously relate her experiences for my earlier *Haunted Lake Superior* book, saying she met with ridicule after telling others of her spiritual experiences.

According to her, when she moved into her current home, her grandparents accompanied her and stayed in her home until both passed away. But their deaths did not affect their affection and protection of her and she says that she particularly senses their presence during periods of stress in her life.

"I've only seen them as misty kind of shadowy figures, but was able to identify them," she said. "I've had lights go on and off when no one was near the switch and sometimes they will prevent me from going into or out of a room for some reason only they seem to understand. When that happens, it's not so much a physical force as it is not being able to move. I've learned when that happens to just sit down wherever I am and talk to them as though they were there with me – because I have the feeling that they are and that they just want a few minutes of my attention."

But it is times of stress in her life when the healing presence of her grandparents' spirits makes them or itself known most significantly to her.

"Often, I don't even realize I'm uptight, when suddenly out of nowhere I'll feel what seems like a warm breath blow across my cheek or neck. I didn't know what it was the first time or two, but have figured out that they were telling me to just take a deep breath and relax – that everything will turn out as it's meant to and that I don't have to go crazy over it."

In some stressful situations the spirits also apparently try to distract her by moving things. Her cherished Raggedy Ann and Raggedy Andy dolls are especially favored objects for movement and she recounts many instances when one or both have been moved from their accustomed place to some other location in the house or have been switched in position from the way she usually displays them.

She says that objects will go missing as well. Despite intense searching on her part, she will only discover the item she's looking for by asking her grandparents what they've done with it or where it is. In nearly every instance, she'll discover the object shortly thereafter.

As for their presence in her home, she says that despite the distraction caused by items disappearing, her grandparents are always a comfort to her and that she's learned that when they disrupt her routine they are easily mollified if she simply settles down for a few minutes to think about or converse with them.[1]

This same lady had quite a different experience with a spirit that she perceived in her workplace. When she told fellow workers about her encounter with the mean spirit, they laughed at her. She quickly stopped talking about it after the ridicule, but later one of those scoffers confided to her that he, too, had encountered someone, or something, he could only explain as ghostly and vengeful. The woman's full account of her encounters with this evil spirit can be found in the "Haunts Where We Work" chapter in this volume. Her granddaughter also has had an encounter with an unfriendly spirit in her workplace and that story accompanies grandma's encounter.[2]

A story from within my family involves a youngster and came to me from his grandma, who had previously lived in the same house that her daughter and son-in-law were occupying when the following events occurred.

As Grandma tells the story, a neighbor couple agreed to babysit the 2-year-old boy in his home while the child's parents took a short vacation. A day or two into their babysitting, the neighbor lady awoke in middle of the night to hear the child talking in his bedroom. She went into the room and found the child sitting up in his bed, chatting.

"What are you doing?" the woman asked.

"Talking to Ruth," the child answered.

Looking around, the lady asked, "Where is she?"

"There," the boy said, pointing toward an apparently empty corner of the room.

"You better tell her good night and go back to sleep," the neighbor told the boy, tucking him beneath the covers. She returned to bed, but neglected to mention the incident to her husband the next day.

That night, the woman's husband awoke to the same chatter from the nearby bedroom. He went in quietly to see what the boy was doing. Again, the child was merely sitting up in his bed talking.

"Who are you talking to?" the man asked.

"Ruth," the boy again said, pointing at the end of his crib.

"Well, sprout, you better lay down and go back to sleep," the man said, patting the covers around the child.

The next morning, the husband mentioned hearing the boy talking and finding him sitting up in bed. Surprised, the wife told him that she had discovered the same thing the night before.

"Where would he have ever picked up the name Ruth?" the wife wondered. "It's sort of an odd, old-fashioned name for a little kid to pick up."

When the boy's parents returned from their trip, the woman asked the mother, "Who is Ruth?"

Pondering a moment, the mother said, "I don't think we know anybody named Ruth."

The woman explained what she and her husband had seen and heard and, surprised by her friend's story, the mother reasoned that she and her husband may simply not have been wakened by their son, if he talked to Ruth while they were sleeping.

The mother related the babysitter's experience to her mother, who had come to believe that when she lived in the house there was some kind of spirit on the premises. She had felt the presence, but had never seen it. Another of her daughters, however, did report seeing a shadowy figure on a few nights.

A few days later, Grandma told a friend who was a longtime resident of the neighborhood the story of the grandson's nighttime conversations with Ruth. Her friend's brow wrinkled in thought a moment and she said, "I remember a family named So-and-So that lived there years ago and went to our church, but I can't remember their first names. I'm going to check the early church membership books to see what her name was."

An hour or two later, the friend called and said, "I found them in the book and Mrs. So-and-So's name was Ruth."

Although this bit of information did send a chill up her spine and energized the hair at the back of her neck, Grandma says she came to the conclusion that this bit of news was more comforting than frightening.

"I think that Ruth must have come back to keep him company when she saw that he was lonely for his mom and dad. I don't know if she's the same spirit that I felt in the house, but none of us was frightened or intimidated by her presence. I think Ruth was just being friendly to a little boy who needed some company."[3]

Siiri Branstrom, a fellow writer and Lake Superior Port Cities Inc. employee, contributes the following personal story of a haunting where she lived briefly.

"In the mid-1960s, my parents, brother and I moved back to Minnesota from Reno, Nevada, and needed to find housing fairly quickly. A beautiful house in Cottage Grove was available for rent and my mom wanted to move in as soon as she saw it. There were so many special things about it, she asked the owner why he wasn't living there.

"He thanked her for her compliments, for he had built it all himself. A cabinetmaker by trade, he had wanted to build this house for his entire adult life – the house of his wife's dreams. To her exact specifications he'd crafted a fold-down ironing board from seemingly nowhere, hidden holes for appliances, a wall that was a bookcase and the loveliest woodwork imaginable. Everything she wanted, he built for her.

"But just months before they were able to move in, his beloved wife was diagnosed with terminal cancer. She did move into her dream house, but just long enough to die there. It made him too sad to live there, but he was too attached to the place to sell it, so he rented it out instead.

"Shortly after we moved in, Mom and Dad were questioned by neighbors whether they liked the house, was there anything strange about it? They learned that there had been a long string of renters before them, no one staying longer than six months

"I was 3 years old at the time and I do remember the huge book case wall and the sliding door cabinets – perfect for hiding a girl of my size. And I vaguely remember the guardian angel who lived in my closet. She was tall and looked like a young grandma, always in a nightgown. I was worried about falling asleep a lot of the time (bogey men and monsters under the bed), so every night she would come out of my closet, stand by my bed and promise to watch over me until morning came. I told my mom and dad about her and they thought it was a wonderful coping mechanism, that I'd created this angel. It was adorable, they said.

"One night after we'd lived in the house for several months, my mother had the sense that someone was watching her while she slept. She opened her eyes slowly and was faced with a guardian angel of her own. A middle-aged woman in a nightgown stood watching her. Mom sat up, but the specter didn't move. Only when she screamed did the vision disappear.

"As it turned out, Dad had seen her several times as well, usually in the kitchen, just standing there. He had chalked it up to his imagination, but clearly, it wasn't just him. They sensed no malice from the figure, and agreed that it was, perhaps, the owner's wife, just wanting to make sure that her perfect house was being well cared for.

"My parents started building their own house right away and gave the owner notice, but they never did tell him that the lady of the house had never left."[4]

In her 1999 book, *More Ghostly Tales from Minnesota*, Ruth D. Hein tells of a benign spirit that seemed protective toward his Grand Rapids area granddaughter. Hein's treatment is almost entirely in first person narrative, but is paraphrased here to gain a bit more succinctness.

The narrator's grandfather lived in his home near Grand Rapids until his death in 1971, at which time the dwelling was sold. A few years after his death, the house inexplicably burned to the ground. Between those two events in her life, the woman had her first encounter with what she perceived as the spirit of her grandfather, "Jacob."

At the time, she was living in a basement bedroom in her parents' home and woke one night to see someone standing by her bed. She sat up and asked him what he was doing and the specter simply vanished. She did, however, have the distinct impression that the apparition was her grandfather. She continued to be visited on a somewhat regular basis at night by the ghost, which on one occasion she found was touching her arm. She recalled that she had no feeling in the arm from the point of contact to her fingertips. Each time she asked what he was doing, he would simply disappear.

On another occasion when he disappeared through the closet door, she became aware that her cat was watching that door, making it appear that the pet had also seen the ghostly Jacob.

"There were many nights when I felt something moving on the foot of my bed. I'd turn on the light and there was no one there. None of my family could have been playing tricks on me, because none of them would go down to the basement in the dark."

Other members of the family also reported strange goings-on during this period, like her mother hearing unusual sounds from the basement and finding nothing that would have caused them when she investigated. The family's collection of slide photographs were kept in carousels and more often than not when they wanted to view them would be out of sequence, upside down or inserted backward.

Then there was the night that she and her mother were watching television later in the evening and simultaneously caught sight of something that appeared to be rather wispy white drift across a window outside the house. After quickly looking out the window, they put off investigating the sighting further until the next day, when there was no sign that would indicate what it was they had glimpsed. Friends staying at the house would also frequently mention hearing footsteps or movements when no one was present.

After Jacob's house burned, arson was suspected, but never proven. Her visits from Jacob also stopped for a while, but resumed after she moved into her own place in town. Even multiple moves didn't phase the old boy, as he continued to appear to her.

"He seems to be around more when there is disruption in my life. Now I've come to think of him as my protector. His presence has become quite comforting, so much so that I miss him when I don't see him for a while. He hasn't been around for a while because I'm happy and content in my current situation," the young woman vouchsafed.[5]

A woman named Mary in Texas wrote her first-person story of a kindly haunting by a spirit she says traveled with her from Ireland to her apartment in Hopkins. Saying that the Gaelic ghost was quite a flirt, she could actually detect the fragrance of a wonderful cologne she was unable to identify. Among other deeds this silver-haired, blue-eyed wraith rendered for her, she said he did the dishes for her a number of times.

But her apartment was also inhabited by other spirits that she perceived to be of a more malignant nature. The most annoying ghost was a red-haired boy who delighted in hiding her car keys when she was hurrying to get to work. She'd find the keys in unlikely places like the freezer or in a sofa, but not before an intensive search throughout the home. We might infer from her description that this could be a poltergeist, though she does not say so in her account.

Her first encounter with a spirit occurred a month after she and her husband moved into the apartment building, which was built on property she found out had previously been a swamp. In her first encounter with an unidentified spirit, she was vacuuming the carpet and prepared to move to another electrical outlet. Shutting the machine off, she unplugged it. The telephone was ringing and she answered and talked a few minutes, hung up and turned to continue the vacuuming.

Suddenly the brand new cleaner started on its own, despite the fact that the plug remained on the floor where she had dropped it.

While she had no intimation of a sighting of the spirit, the experience unnerved her to the point of hiding in the bedroom. Other instances of apparent ghostly episodes in the apartment involved the appearance on a couple of occasions of a dark stain that might have been blood on the bedroom floor.

Later, a friend with psychic power confirmed her suspicion that the building was somehow a "way station" for spirits on their way to the light.[6]

M.J. Downs of Minneapolis tells a tale of experiencing the benevolent spirit of her recently deceased mother.

Her mother passed away May 6, 2003, just four days before the wedding of Downs' daughter on May 10. She had been in poor health for a year previously, but had struggled mightily to survive until her granddaughter's wedding. Indeed, so firm was her resolve to be present for the wedding that the family included a single gardenia (her favorite flower) for her when they ordered the floral arrangements for the wedding.

At the wedding, the single gardenia was placed beside the unity candle on the altar. In honor of the grandmother, the bride wore a single gardenia in place of a veil.

After the wedding on Mother's Day and with the kids on their honeymoon, M.J. retired in total exhaustion and fell into a deep sleep.

Suddenly, as she describes it, "My mother showed up and she said, 'I was talking to your dad and he said that you had a really nice wedding. The reception was wonderful and the buns were especially good.'"

So real was the encounter that M.J. awoke and was nearly overcome by the powerful smell of gardenias in her bedroom. "There were no wedding flowers in the house, so I know it was not a carryover from that, and I could still feel the spot on my leg where she had patted it. I know it was mom, telling me that she was okay with things."

Almost as a postscript to the story, she also says that her grandmother had somewhat a similar experience over three nights after her husband died unexpectedly while anesthetized. In her episode, he was seeking help getting into heaven and she told him that he had to do it himself. Sighing, he left the room, closing the door behind him.

"I don't know if that sort of thing 'runs in the family' or what, but it does give me pause. It was a gentle experience, but definitely stayed with me," M.J. concludes.[7]

In the northern portion of Central Minnesota, Minnesota Public Radio writers Tom Robertson and Dan Gunderson found a story of kindly spirituality of a somewhat different nature.

Just outside of the Leech Lake Indian Reservation in a stand of jackpines near Bemidji, Bob Shimek has devoted himself to re-establishing a rebirth of his Anishinabe (more commonly, Ojibway) spirituality. Having grown up on the White Earth Reservation in west central Minnesota during the 1950s, Shimek can say with conviction that his had been a life far removed from mainstream America.

"When I was a kid, it was a bad thing to be an Indian. It was a difficult time, a time of extreme poverty, a lot of confusion, a lot of chaos, a lot of violence," Bob told the MPR reporters, also indicating to them that Indian spiritual ceremonies has been illegal and done under cover of secrecy with few people invited to participate.

As a prelude to his discussion of his spirituality with Robertson and Gunderson, Bob lit a small heap of sage leaves and tobacco, something he told the reporters that he always does.

"I'm burning some of that and hope the spirit helpers that watch over this medicine will kind of forgive us and help us through this conversation," he is quoted by the reporters, telling them that the smoke carries prayers to the Great Spirit while purifying his body and soul. Called smudging, this ceremony involved fanning the burning leaves with an eagle feather, cupping the smoke in his hands to bring it toward his face.

Before continuing, he prayed in Ojibway, translating his plea as: "Our highest Father, hear me, because I'm a weak and pitiful person…. Then I said, the spirits know me as Thundercloud (translated from the Ojibway *Aniimikiiwanakwad*) and I was thanking all the spirit helpers and the Great Spirit."

With these preliminaries at an end, the interview began.

As a kid, Bob was baptized into the Catholic faith, but by his eighth year he began communing with spirits that first spoke to him in an ancient Ojibway burial ground on the banks of the Otter Tail River.

"As clear as a bell as I was sitting there, this voice from somewhere said, 'It doesn't have to be this way,' in a comforting and reassuring voice," Bob told Robertson and Gunderson, repeating itself, "'It doesn't have to be this way.'"

Years later, as a troubled, angry 17-year-old, he would hear the voice again, but chose to put it in the back of his mind, while remembering it. Again after years, he was confronted by the spirits. This time, they drew him to a sweat lodge near his home.

Representing physical and spiritual cleansing, the sweat lodge is one of the most common ceremonial practices among Native American people, being central to a large number of Indian religions.

Skeptical of claims that the lodge experience would change him, Bob nonetheless attended the ceremony, where an older man began talking and singing in Ojibway.

"The whole lodge started shaking like this great big hand was over it. And the whole thing was just moving. Pretty soon, there were the sounds of these birds and these animals right there in the lodge. It was like birds and you could feel them flying, you could feel the wind from their wings as they were going around in there. And there were all these animal sounds. At some point in there, I just broke down and cried like a newborn."

It was his introduction to the spirituality of his people, a process that he described as being torn down and being reborn.

"Now, it's the foundation on which I run my life – to be Anishinabe in today's world and to be the best Anishinabe that I can be in today's world. It's important to keep these things going," he concluded.[8]

Manford Theel of Paynesville in Stearns County told Ruth D. Hein a great story of a benevolent spirit involving his grandfather. She recounts the story as "Finding the Missing Paper" in her 1992 book, *Ghostly Tales of Minnesota*.

Manford said that his maternal grandfather, William Arndt, was known by everyone with whom he had contact as an upright, stalwart, honest man. A Sunday School superintendent, he would preach to congregations in the absence of a minister, and also served as a bank director, insurance agent and assessor. Trusted by everyone, he was often asked to serve as executor of estates and willingly took on such additional duties.

Thus it was that William came to be associated as executor of the estate of a neighboring farmer, identified only as Mr. Giesel, who died in 1939. Before he could complete the estate, however, William himself died in 1941.

After laying him to rest, William's family thought no more about any of his affairs. Manford's parents lived on the family farm until 1944, at which time Manford and his new wife moved into that homestead and his parents moved to town.

In the fall of that year, a letter from the Giesel family arrived, explaining that they had never received the final paperwork for the estate that signed William off as executor. Responding, Manford's mother informed the heirs that William had died and the family knew nothing of the estate settlement.

The Giesels wrote back, explaining that oil had been discovered on property the family owned in Canada, but that they needed the final paperwork to give them clear title to the land and oil rights, urging the Theels to search diligently for the papers among their grandfather's effects, which they did. Nothing was discovered.

Meanwhile, the Giesels had contacted the Stearns County Courthouse and were told that the final paper had been mailed to William. Again, the family pled with the Theels to search once more for it, which they did. Again, nothing turned up.

Remarking that the matter considerably perturbed his mother, especially, Manford said that she even resorted to pacing the floor as she worried and thought about what might have happened to this suddenly valuable document.

The day after their latest search, Manford said that his father came out to the farm to help with the chores and told him that they had found the papers.

Asked how that happened, his father said that about 2 a.m. the previous night his wife started talking in her sleep – or something.

"She said, 'What do you want?' and sat up in bed," his father told him. Waking, she sat up on the side of the bed and said, "My dad was here."

Thinking she was joking, his father asked, "What did he want?"

Manford picks up the tale. "My mother answered, 'He came right through the wall. First he spoke my name in a low tone. Then, he called it out more loudly. The third time, he spoke sharply, calling out my name. Then, when he knew he had my attention, he told me the papers were way back in his folder briefcase, and then he was gone.'"

Getting out of bed, she walked to the closet, pulled out the briefcase, gave it a tug and a compartment opened in the very back that they had not seen before, revealing the necessary final paperwork fully completed and properly executed.

Thus, were the Giesels' rights to their oil property preserved – by the benevolence of a spirit that obviously remained as upright and honest after his death as he had been in life.[9]

I beg indulgence to tell one final tale from family lore of a supernatural happening of a benevolent, but a slightly different nature.

The family lost the youngest sister, father and mother within two years of each other. A Hibbing in-law tells this story surrounding the sad events.

"I've heard stories in the neighborhood and read about pennies from heaven in Ann Landers or Dear Abby for years, but I never really believed in them," she told me. According to those stories, the pennies are a sign to the living that the soul of their deceased loved one is at peace. Although they usually appear to be new coins, the year on the penny will correspond to the year that the person died and they usually show up in places where they would be least expected. The recipients are usually in grief or are uneasy about their loved one's death. The origin of this belief may be indigenous to Italy or Southern Europe, since her family immigrated from that area.

"I came home from work and turned on the lights and there on the carpet inside my guest bedroom was a penny shining in the light," she explains. "No one else had been in the house and the vacuum cleaner marks were still in the carpet from when I cleaned the room during the weekend, so I was surprised that I'd missed seeing it. I picked it up and the date said 1999 – the year my sister died. I suddenly remembered the stories I'd heard and knew what that penny was.

158

"I sort of went into shock for a second. Then I felt a sense of peace or relief and said out loud, 'I don't want just one penny, I need two more for Dad and Mother.'"

After carefully putting the single penny away for safekeeping, no other pennies were found over the next week or two. She had nearly forgotten her demand when she was rummaging for something she needed on the admittedly messy side desk in her office. Amidst a stack of long outdated paperwork, she found two pennies shining up at her, one stamped 2000 and the other 2001, the years her father and mother died.

"There was no reason those pennies would be on that table," she insists. "In fact, the papers where I found them were all older than the pennies, so there was no way they could have been lost there. They were the other pennies I had asked for and I made sure to save them in the same place where I kept the penny for my sister. Now, when I feel sad or upset, all I do is look at them and they make me feel better."[10]

While the previous story is evidence of supernatural or divine comforting for one in mourning, it's perhaps fitting that we discuss an aspect of kindly spiritual intercession of a Biblical origin.

It's a safe bet that many, perhaps most, Minnesotans at some point in their lives have heard of and believed in angels with the sole assignment of shielding the individual from the vicissitudes that the world presents them. Known generally as "guardian angels," these spirits are invariably viewed as good and benevolent to their human hosts. But the origin of these individually assigned spirits is a bit murky.

Indeed, as Reverend Linda C. Loving noted in a December 12, 2004, sermon at House of Hope Presbyterian Church in St. Paul, "Angels often appear at times of great danger or joy, times of real change, when life's meaning is tested or threatened. The word 'angel' originates from the Greek word 'angelos,' which means, quite simply, 'messenger.' In the New Testament, an angel was a divine messenger, straight from God. In the Old Testament usage an angel could be considered either a divine or a human messenger.

"Throughout the *Bible*, angels appear frequently, often in critical roles – visiting Abraham and Lot and Jacob in Old Testament stories; announcing the incarnation as well as the empty tomb in the New (Testament). The angels in scripture are sent by God to announce, to protect, to challenge."

Reverend Loving went on to say that the Biblical appearances of angels were almost always immediately followed by the words,

"Do not be afraid," indicating that such appearances were, at best, unsettling to the perceiver. Indeed, she stated that there are 365 such angelic utterances throughout the *Bible*, indicating an apparently massive need for this divine delivery system.

Beyond a casual interest in exactly what the rationale might have been in enumerating the angelic admonitions of not to be afraid, we are still grasping for an explanation of the concept of individual guardian angels.

For that, Reverend Loving may also offer a possible source, noting that a Hasidic Hebrew legend says that when a baby is conceived, an angel accompanies the soul into the womb.

"And in the blood-thumping shelter of the mother, angel and soul speak of the life to come and decide together on the purpose of this incarnation," the reverend explained. "What is this soul coming to contribute? What challenges will be faced? Where comes love?"

The catch to all this thoughtful, diligent angel and soul planning session is that, just as the birth pangs begin, "when the soul must fully enter the baby-self and the angel return to Heaven, the angel reaches out and presses its finger against the baby's lip. We still have this mark, an indentation that runs sweetly from upper lip to nose called the philtrum. It is the angel's last gift. 'Hush' it whispers to the stirring child, 'now you must forget.'"

It is tempting to accept this ancient legend from the most conservative Hebrew group as implying that, at least in the formative months of a person's life, there is angelic intervention, even though the living human being thus touched does not remember all the planning and must spend the rest of its life trying to remember the guidance of its angel, which so often is just beyond its understanding.[11]

While our speculation on the origin of the idea of guardian angels is simply that, speculation, renowned Minneapolis psychic Echo Bodine unequivocally states that such spirits are real and that she is guided by her spiritual guides at every step of her several psychic activities.

In the introduction to her 1999 book, *Echoes of the Soul*, Echo states that during her apprenticeship in the psychic arts, her teacher advised her to get to know her spirit guides.

"I was afraid and getting to know my guides was a slow process.... I was worried that they might start talking to me. I wondered what they would sound like. The first time I heard my guides, I was washing dishes. A very soft voice, rather like a thought, said, 'My name is Theodore, but you can call me Teddy.'

"Then a female thought came: 'My name is Anna.' These 'voices' didn't sound very different from my thoughts. I asked them to talk to me more, but that's all they said...."

Saying that she had been told by her teacher that guides are not always chatty, saying only what is important for her to know, Echo says that she so wanted to communicate again with them that she kept radios off around her, in case her guides wanted to talk with her. Slowly, as her fear of them dissipated, they began to communicate with her regularly.

These two original guides shepherded her through her earliest psychic training, but she reports that her guides changed over the years, with older ones moving on to help others and new ones taking their place – even obtaining necessary guidance from Jesus or from Native American healers, as noted in her interview in Chapter 9 of this volume.

Echo also credits her spiritual guides with influencing her to write her first and subsequent books, telling her that they would help at every step of the process. She has issued a total of six volumes dealing with the psychic arts since that 1983 spiritual imperative.

While she chooses to call her personal spirits "guides," Echo's nearly four decades of delving into the other world indicates that there are spirits whose task it is to help us on our journey through life.[12]

One final note regarding guardian angels comes from my North Shore friend whose grandparents' spirits remain with her in her home. In our interview, she told me that she is often surprised to encounter pleasant aromas like a perfume or perhaps apple pie in unlikely circumstances. She has reached the conclusion that such unexpected and nice scents are her guardian angel's way of making its presence known to her.[13]

On January 6, 1855, the night of the feast of Epiphany, Father Francis Xavier Pierz, another of the saintly pioneer missionaries, was ministering to his Ojibway Catholic flock at Red Lake in north central Minnesota when a powerful omen was given to him that not only moved his heart, but served as a catalyst in the growth of faith among his parishioners who also witnessed the spiritual phenomenon.

By the time of this omen, Father Pierz had already been long active in the mission fields of first Michigan, then Wisconsin and Minnesota, being one of the Slovenian missionaries recruited by Bishop Frederic Baraga to toil among the native people. In 1852, he established a sizable mission at the Mississippi River location named Crow Wing southwest of present Brainerd, but also singlehandedly ministered to a mission field said to require more than 1,200 miles of travel to tend to the far-flung congregations he founded at Mille Lacs, Leech Lake, Long Prairie and Belle Prairie. The perimeter of his mission field obviously also took in the Red Lake region. Father Pierz's ever-energetic, widely traveled missionary zeal is a legend within the northern Minnesota Catholic community and his name was adopted by both the town and the township of Pierz, both located south of Brainerd, as testament to the high regard in which he was held by both native and European people. His missionary zeal remains a legend within the faith.

On that cold winter night at Red Lake in the forested northland, Father Pierz told of seeing the sign of the holy cross as the moon rose over the north woods.

Of his sighting, Pierz wrote, "(It appeared as) a wonderful, heavenly, glittering light so that the cross-beam seemed to rest on the earth. For about an hour, as the moon arose higher in the sky, the cross grew bigger and bigger, both in length and width, the base always standing on the earth. The three upper extremities of the cross seemed to be bathed in the yellow rays of the sun, giving it a very striking appearance. On each side of the cross a glittering line of light could be seen; and the whole apparition was encircled by a magnificent rainbow, as with a beautifully colored halo."

Testifying that "more than a hundred people" also witnessed the appearance of the cross over the rustic landscape, the venerable priest read it as an omen of the bountiful blessing and grace poured out for that land and its people – a veritable revelation of God's love for all creation.

Father Pierz's positive interpretation about sighting the brilliantly lighted cross in the northern hinterlands would be born out in the following three years as he continued to visit the growing congregation on the southern shore of Red Lake. In 1858, he was joined in his work by Father Lawrence Lautischar, who opened a mission church at Red Lake on August 15, 1858. Father Lautischar's enthusiasm for the remote assignment was obvious in letters he wrote, but his tenure as leader of the flock proved to be short-lived, as he froze to death in a storm on December 3 while walking across Lower Red Lake from visiting a group of Ojibway people located at the present site of Ponemah on the northeast shore of that lake.

After that unfortunate incident, Father Pierz again took the helm of this far-flung mission to tend to the many Ojibway who accepted the Catholic faith, with assistance from other priests who began arriving in the area a bit later.

One can only come to the conclusion that, in light of his own narrative of the event, the saintly Father Pierz's faith in the message of the bright cross was correct, for the St. Mary's Mission that he founded in the town of Red Lake continues to serve the faithful to the present day, a fact that the blessed cross prophesied to the pioneer missionary more than 150 years ago.[14]

While the stories above indicate that at least some ghostly encounters can benefit those who have the experience, we are not likely to feel the benevolence of such spirits on our first encounter. Most people who report such hauntings tell of an initial feeling of fear or trepidation and only come to accept the kindly spirit with gratitude later. But the fact that many such kind or benign meetings are recorded should be comforting to anyone who has a fear of ghostly presences. The chances seem almost 50-50 for the spirit to be good rather than evil.

CHAPTER 8

Ghost Hunters

While most of us on this side of the light are perfectly happy to go out of our way to avoid encounters with deceased beings, psychic and medium Echo Bodine of Minneapolis makes a living by embracing, or by banishing, spiritual presences. She does psychic readings, performs hands-on healing and publishes books on these topics. She also offers classes in the metaphysical arts at her Minneapolis studio (called The Center) that are popular with a goodly number of Twin Citians.

Echo says that in her lifetime of experience in dealing with psychic and spiritual matters, she has seldom encountered a spirit that was unaware that it has died and belongs on the other side. This seems to contradict some stories concerning ghosts who unknowingly continue on this side of the light as a haunting presence after their bodies die.

"Most spirits see the light when they die, but some don't want to go for a variety of reasons. They may fear they'll go to Hell, or they may resist going because someone they don't want to meet is already there," she explains, adding almost jokingly, "They almost always know they are dead, so our job as a psychic is quite often to convince them to pass over. It's more like ghost counseling than ghostbusting."

A case in point, she recalls, is the ghost of Roy, a cranky specter of a man of perhaps 35 or 40 years occupying a family's home. He so abused the kids of the family that they continually repeated stories of his crabby misdeeds.

When she was called in and first encountered Roy's spirit, Echo asked, "Why are you still here?"

"I like this house and want to get rid of these kids so I can stay in peace," she read his response.

Chillingly, she also perceived images of him pushing the kids toward the stairway as though threatening them with injury. She notes that her brother, also a psychic, often accompanies her on such missions and on this occasion received a strong message involving the name Copper. Calling to the beyond for Copper, the ghost of a golden Lab appeared, at whose entry the crotchety Roy seemed to melt and bent down to play with this beloved ghostly pet as though he were a 5-year-old boy.

"I convinced Roy that Copper had to return to the beyond and that he would have to also cross over to remain with Copper. That was the last trouble the family had from cranky Roy," Echo says.

Less active in actual ghostbusting than she was a few years ago, Echo now works with several associates who perform those duties. She is increasingly involved in spiritual and hands-on healing, doing psychic readings for those seeking spiritual advice or guidance, teaching classes for would-be psychics and writing books on these subjects. Little wonder that she has cut back on ghostbusting as one aspect of her life work.

Despite a number of psychic experiences in her early years, Echo says she did not believe the first Twin Cities psychic who informed her that she had "the gift." As though to prove her point, the mentor informed the girl that at that moment her father was suffering from a migraine headache at home and that Echo should use her powers of healing to relieve his misery.

Still unconvinced, she again expressed reluctance and the psychic said, "God will show you the way. You must lay your hands on his head, but always use a white handkerchief between your hands and the area to be healed."

Somewhat hesitantly, when she arrived home Echo did as she was instructed and says that at the contact of her hands with her father's head, she felt an intensifying heat begin to glow from her hands. "Within a few minutes, my hands cooled off and the headache was gone. I knew then that the psychic had been right and that God had guided me in that first healing. I still feel the presence of God or Jesus during many sessions, but have also received guidance from spirits that range from trained doctors to other psychic healers."

As a case in point of being guided by a wide variety of spiritual resources, Echo began to tell me of another healing – when the phone conversation was abruptly cut off. Neither she nor I had

165

touched our phones and we didn't realize for a moment or two that the telephone connection was broken, since it did not begin the characteristic beeping usually associated with a broken connection. After reestablishing contact with her, we joked about it for a few moments, but agreed that it was an electronic oddity and concurred that if the conversation were severed a second time as she told the story we would consider skipping the tale.

This time, she continued uninterrupted. "After I had gained experience and began working professionally in psychic healing, a woman heard of me and told me that she felt that she was possessed by an unwanted spirit. I agreed to work with her and during our conversation I did perceive that there was something unpleasant connected with her.

"As I began the healing, she fell into a trance or a deep sleep and I continued with my healing. After a few moments, I was surprised to see the spirits of five or six Native Americans appear in the room and tell me what to do. Chanting and dancing, they mixed a concoction that they poured into the woman's mouth. As she recovered, she sat up and told me everything that had happened. For me, it was a reminder that you just never know what may happen during a healing or where your guidance may come from."

In perhaps her strongest experience of the personification of a spiritual presence, Echo says that she was in a healing session with a man and had just lain her hands on him. "Suddenly, I saw the room fill with a brilliant white light and psychically saw Jesus come into our presence and place his hands over mine to guide my healing. Afterward, two women in the room with us and the man all said that they also saw Jesus and the man said he felt healed."

But while her primary focus today is healing and spiritual guidance, one doesn't talk with a psychic for upward of an hour without the conversation turning again and again to hauntings and ghostly presences that stick in their mind.

Of one such haunting at a Twin Cities home that was being sold, Echo recalls encountering an almost unfathomable number of spiritual beings that she took on one by one. Their central theme became clear as she picked her way through the lineup – they were upset that the house was for sale and would be renovated.

"I remember one of the spirits was that of a teenage boy and he told me that the house was close to the scene where he died in a motorcycle accident," Echo says. "He also said that there were kids in the house and he liked being around them. He didn't want the kids to move away."

The inhabitants of the house identified one particularly distressing spirit that they said seemed to continually pace around in the basement of the house.

"When I made contact and confronted the spirit, I learned it was that of Mr. Peterson, who originally built the home and was unhappy that it was being sold and would be renovated. He felt a need to stay there to protect the house the way he had designed and built it."

Echo notes, as did the directors at the Cross River Heritage Center mentioned earlier, that renovation work in buildings often seems to rouse spirits that may not have been apparent prior to the start of remodeling work.

"It just seems to upset them and bring out a need to maintain the building as they have always known it," she says.

When I interviewed her, she was eagerly looking forward to joining four other prominent psychics from across the United States in Los Angeles for 13 weeks of taping a Sci-Fi channel television series called "The Gift."

An interesting side note to those television appearances was that she worked with psychic identical twins who are so in tune with each other that they often experience identical visions and psychic experiences. That observation also lends support to our earlier speculation that clairvoyance is a characteristic that is inherited, an assertion that Echo's family seems to prove. Not only does she make her living in the psychic realm, but her mother, Mae, and brother, Michael, do as well.

Echo is no neophyte personality on television, having been a guest on a wide variety of national shows like "Sally Jesse Raphael," "Sightings" and NBC's "The Other Side." She also hosts her own Twin Cities radio show at FM107.1 on Saturday nights entitled "Intuitive Living with Echo Bodine," a hosting position that was filled by her accomplished psychic acolyte, Bobby Sullivan, who often substitutes when she is otherwise occupied. He is one of a number of Echo's students who have gone on to become psychics and readers in Minnesota and have formed a psychic community around Echo and The Center.[1]

By the fall of 2004, Diana Palm of Stillwater had reached the end of her rope in the apartment she and her daughter lived in. *Pioneer Press* reporter Richard Chin recorded her story and the solution she implemented. It is especially germane here because it reveals a number of the techniques and devices utilized by serious investigators of paranormal activities.

"Night after night, we'd see a man walk past the bedroom door," Diana said, noting that when she jumped up to investigate there was never anyone there.

But the spooky invader was not Diana's only problem. They also heard knocking noises, had the television or lights go on and off by themselves, and heard unexplained voices and sounds of laughing, crying and howling.

Her 10-year-old daughter and a friend once excitedly told her there was an old lady in the bathroom who talked to them. Other renters in the triplex said they saw people walking up and down the building's staircases and Diana's sister said she saw a stream of people walking through the living room when she was visiting.

"It got to the point that I was afraid to go to the bathroom at night. That was especially strange for me, because I'm a real practical person," Diana told Chin.

Involved in the real estate business, Diana began to investigate the history of the place to find reasons for the strange happenings in her home. She discovered that the house had been built on Stillwater's North Hill in 1882 by one of the city's early mayors. Before being developed, the site had been used as an unplatted, informal graveyard.

Taking matters into her own hands, Diana burned sage and prayed in efforts to clean the property of its spirits. "I put out some rosaries and sprinkled holy water. I really wanted to get to the bottom of it."

Nothing she did seemed to be efficacious in ridding the house of its spiritual inhabitants. Then she heard about the Minnesota Paranormal Investigative Group (MNPIG) and contacted them for help. It was their investigation that Chin observed and recorded for the 2004 Halloween ghost story in the newspaper.

Formed in 1997 by co-founders John Savage and Gina Booth, many of MNPIG's members joined the group because they're looking for proof of life after death. Their investigation at Diana's residence occurred in early October 2004 and members of the team included Booth, Deb Sutton, Jon Rehkamp and Phil Hatfield.

At the outset, they told Diana not to reveal what she'd been experiencing until they had a chance to check out the place with a walk-through investigation. Filled with unusual interior details from its Victorian origins and subsequent renovations, the building featured stained glass, elaborate woodwork, pocket doors, skylights, lofts, spiral staircases and unexplained floor panels that added mystery to the MNPIG inspection.

Pointing out an odd storage space, Diana was told by Gina Booth, "They (ghosts/spirits) like to hide in closets. There's no such thing as just a closet (in paranormal circles)."

Once their walk-through was complete, Deb Sutton headed for the basement with the group's video camera to record anything that might deign to reveal itself.

"Entities come in a lot of different forms," Sutton explained as she focused on a gloomy corner. She said that a camera often picks up blurs or orbs of light that indicate energy being given off or absorbed by a spiritual presence.

"I always ask permission before I take a picture. Spirits are people like we are, just not in our form. I hope my intuition is right, so they'll let me take the pictures."

Saying that in her experience the basement was too quiet, Sutton turned to her dowsing rod to try and find answers to questions she had.

The rod moved to the left and she told Chin, "I asked if there is someone here and the rod moving to the left means yes. I'm going to ask if they're male or female."

A moment later, the rod again moved and she interpreted it to mean female.

"Is there more than one person down here?" Again the rod moved to the left, indicating "yes."

"Supposedly, they're telling me there are two females here. They're from the area and died 80 to 90 years ago."

Meanwhile, up in the kitchen, Cathy Olson, a friend of Diana's, exclaimed with a shiver, "Someone just touched me! I thought it was the cat, but there was nothing there."

"There's no doubt there is stuff here," Phil Hatfield stated. His specialty on the investigative team is making psychic contact with spirits.

Olson again exclaimed, "It's touching me again, right now."

"It's mass confusion here," Hatfield stated. "There are more than five of them and they all want to talk at the same time. I'm trying to get to a point where I can communicate with one individual."

He then asked Diana if the place had ever been a doctor's office. She confirmed that it had been.

The batteries of Sutton's video camera suddenly went dead, which she said could be an indication of paranormal energy in the apartment.

Rehkamp, wielding a magnetic field detector, stated, "This whole place is charged, even outside. You normally never get anything outdoors."

In the basement, Hatfield sat down, making notes in his notebook. "It's like the night of the living dead. Where are they all coming from? I'm seeing all these people trying to get out of the ground. They're skeletal, but still have flesh hanging on them. They're coming out hands first, but pulling themselves out."

Estimating the number between 20 and 30, Hatfield said he also sensed something in the bathroom. Rehkamp indicated his detectors didn't pick up anything.

After a few moments of silence, Hatfield said, "A doctor – I'm talking to a doctor now."

Later, he would reveal during the debriefing that the doctor was known as "the grim reaper doctor, because he was the one who chose if they were better off dead or alive."

He also said a female spirit told him that Diana's daughter shouldn't fear her, because she just misses her own daughter, who had drowned.

"Sorry about the books and pictures," he quoted the spirits. Diana noted that she was constantly straightening pictures, but blamed it on the house being old.

Other revelations from the MNPIG investigators was that spirits appeared to be trying to come to the surface in the basement with the ground rotating under them, but the team had no explanation of what it meant. They also found the spirit of a little boy in the house, as well as evidence of a hanging in an upstairs bedroom, someone being pushed down the stairs and a natural death in Diana's bedroom, along with Hatfield's perception of exceptional energy in the upstairs bathroom.

Sutton's videotape showed a speck of light flitting across the room and reminded Diana of a photo she had that showed a whitish orb in the corner that she thought looked like a face.

The investigators also interpreted the parade of people that Diana's sister saw as indicating the living room was a portal for spirits to enter and exit the spirit world.

Despite all of their discoveries, Hatfield reassured Diana, "Nobody is here to hurt you."

Gina Booth concurred, saying, "This is typical. Nothing to be concerned with."

Later, after follow-up examination of their various equipment, the investigators would report that they had also captured a voice on an electronic voice taping that rather plaintively pleaded with the team, "Please don't leave."

For Diana, the MNPIG reports served as validation of what she suspected. "It answers some questions. I feel fine with it, but it's still kind of creepy knowing people died.

"After the MNPIG came out and performed their investigation, we had increased activity at the house," Diana told me in an e-mail follow-up. "I asked the group out a second time, and they recorded many EVPs (ghost voices). I have a copy of one CD that they burned for me afterwards and we were shocked at how many spirits were trying to make contact."[2]

While the investigation was validation and almost comforting to her, Diana and her daughter later moved to another residence, but she confirmed in the November 9, 2005, e-mail just alluded to that everything in the newspaper story is true and accurate.[3]

A sequel to the newspaper story, which was posted without attribution adds a chilling postscript to Diana's story. The anonymous report was posted on July 1, 2005. "I just finished working in this house in the last week of June. While on the stairway, I felt something push me and I almost lost my balance on the steps. I didn't know the story of the house till after this happened, but after reading this report, I have serious chills up my spine."[4]

Those who have come this far with me in this volume will recognize that Brian Leffler of the Northern Minnesota Paranormal Investigators (NMPI) has been a particularly rich source of stories that are told here. He was instrumental in founding the group in 2000 and it numbered 11 experienced investigators when this was being written in late 2005.

During their history, the group has investigated dozens of sites where hauntings are suspected. Using standard tools like a camera and film (Brian emphasizes he doesn't use digital imagery, which he says may enhance or alter images in undesirable ways, nor does he favor other digital equipment for the same reason), electromagnetic field detectors, analog taping equipment to detect electronic voice phenomena and the members' own psychic abilities, NMPI concentrates on what they can detect and learn at each site. Often, there are perfectly rational reasons for things that go bump in the night and they want to rule out such sources before concentrating on the phenomena that can't so easily be explained away.

While investigative equipment is key in physically documenting a haunting, Brian says it's often his own sensibility that tips him off that something psychic is occurring at a site undergoing investigation. "I get a chill that shoots down my back and I can tell that a spirit is around," he explains. "I usually can't tell much more, like whether the spirit is good or evil, but it's almost always a sign that there is something there."

One of the NMPI's first successes in paranormal research after it formed in 2000 occurred at a rental house in Cohasset in 2003, the story of which is told in the Epilogue to this volume. Their "cleaning" of the property ended the strange happenings at the site and there have been no further instances of ghostly activity reported there.

Before that early success, however, Brian had nearly a decade of looking into paranormal occurrences. His first experience of such a phenomenon was at a house he rented in McGregor between the Cuyuna Iron Range and Duluth on Highway 210 in east central Minnesota. After moving in, he was told that it had once been a residence for wayward boys, but that seemed little reason for worry. However, he also learned that it had been the site of a suicide in which a man ended his life with a shotgun to the head and that seemed a bit more problematic. His experience with something unnatural in the house happened one night when he was relaxing in the living room and saw the handle of the kitchen sink faucet rise to allow water to flow.

"That was very strange. No one else was in the downstairs area and everybody else was upstairs sleeping, but that faucet definitely turned on."

While it was his first intimation of something beyond the mortal pale, he didn't really become deeply interested in the paranormal until he moved into an unusually active "spirit house" in Chisholm. He and his girlfriend at that time soon began experiencing unusual things like the sound of voices and seeing a door that was nearly impossible to open suddenly swing wide on its own. He decided that it was time to put his curiosity in the paranormal to more practical use.

"I began to really study the paranormal," Brian says. "It was in the basement of that house that I took a short step backward and felt like half my body was suddenly freezing. I perceived that I had physically backed into a spirit. It didn't really scare me, but it did convince me that these things are real and need to be accepted."

Eventually, he would discern that the house was the scene of seven different spiritual presences. By that time, he was hooked on studying paranormal events and had invested in the gear needed to investigate, first his own home and eventually other haunted sites after forming NMPI.

While adamant in his belief in spirits or ghosts, he is less strident with others, saying it is up to them to believe or not. His wife, Rhonda (who he married in 2003 and who is also psychically gifted and a member of the NMPI team), adds, "I believe everyone has psychic abilities, but we're taught at an early age not to believe it or to avoid it."

Having experienced many hauntings in their years of investigations, Brian and others in NMPI have adopted a sympathetic view of spirits, saying that they are often bound to places, objects or people in much the same way that living people become bonded to places, people or things. It may reveal that something remains undone, that the spirit does not want to leave someone close to them or that the spirit is simply lost between two worlds. The spirits themselves may be good or evil, but Brian states with conviction that there is no recorded instance of an evil spirit taking any life.

"Spirits seem to lack the energy needed for really powerful presences," he says. "They may be able to trip you or give you a poke, but in my experience they aren't usually strong enough to do any serious harm."

While that is his belief, he does admit to adhering to the wishes of those whose property the NMPI may investigate. If the owner wishes the group to clean the property of the spirits, Brian and the team will lay the groundwork by lighting sage and threatening or insulting the unwanted spirits.

"You have to show you're boss – sort of be a threat like an M-16 would be for you and me,'" he explains. "You have to coerce them out and sometimes it takes more than one cleaning."

Where the spirits may go is a question, but Brian's belief is that they return to their own plane of existence. Other spiritualists choose to believe that the spirits simply dissipate into the "light" or some other plane.

Having subsequently moved from the unusually spirited Chisholm house to a home in Keewatin, the Lefflers maintain their high interest in paranormal activity. Significant investigations by NMPI have uncovered evidence of orbs and ectoplasmic mist at Capaletti Farm near Grand Rapids, as well as at a number of Iron Range cemeteries. In their experience, one of the most haunted in the latter category of site is the Lakeview Cemetery in Buhl. They also cleaned an Eveleth apartment of unwanted spirits that were reported to extinguish candles, speak in tongues and leave residents with bite and bruise marks.

A particularly vivid videotape taken during an investigation in Mountain Iron also appears to show quite a clear image of something filmy and semitransparent passing in front of the camera. The impression was particularly important because two investigators both saw it on the camera's viewfinder as it passed.

"That's really the most concrete evidence we've gathered so far that something from another dimension may have continued at the site," Brian states. "It is very visible and realistic on the tape, which was new and had never been used before or since."

While always happy to learn of new sites to investigate, a rash of 2005 Halloween newspaper stories about the group resulted in a backlog of a dozen or more potential investigations at the end of the year and into 2006.[5]

It may seem odd in searching for evidence of hauntings or psychic activity to turn to a forensic pathologist and practicing coroner for several Minnesota and western Wisconsin counties. Usually, our TV-inspired image of that profession would show a gowned, masked, gloved and intensely scientific searcher for the underlying truth of a death, laying aside any assumptions that they might have in an all-out effort to "gather information, document the scene, follow the guidelines and trust that you will arrive at the truth," as Dr. Janis Amatuzio explains as a prelude to her book, *Forever Ours: Real Stories of Immortality and Living From a Forensic Pathologist.*

"Occasionally, something unexpected happens during an investigation for which I was not professionally prepared.... These experiences always baffle me, partly because as a scientist, I seek to reach a reasonable degree of medical certainty, a rational explanation. But I have come to realize that for some experiences there are no explanations, just a deep knowing that I have encountered the divine."

Because I found the stories that are paraphrased here at different Websites, I footnote those sources, but strongly recommend going directly to her Website at www.foreverours.com for information about the book.

Her earliest encounter with something unusual seems to have been as an intern in internal medicine in 1978 at University of Minnesota medical school and rotating on the cardiology service at Heart Hospital, when a patient was admitted for atypical chest pain. No cause for his pain showed up during extensive work-ups, so a coronary artery angiogram was ordered to look more closely into his symptoms. It was during this examination that an unusual episode first caught Dr. Amatuzio's attention.

The procedure involves threading a thin tube called a catheter through the arterial system to look at the coronary arteries. During the procedure, opaque dye is injected into the arteries to "light up" the many branches of the heart's otherwise somewhat vaguely pictured life support system.

After first examining the left coronary arterial labyrinth, the catheter was advanced into the right coronary artery, where a sudden, abnormal "blush" appeared on the monitor near the tip of the catheter as the dye was injected. The senior cardiologist repeated the dye injection and the abnormal blush became much brighter outside the artery.

The cardiologist ordered, "I want the attending physician in here STAT!"

Holding her patient's hands to comfort him during the procedure, which he had chosen to undergo while fully awake, Dr. Amatuzio felt sweat begin to accumulate in the palms and heard the anesthesiologist state, "Pulse rate rapid at 90 to 95 beats a minute."

"We have a perforation, the vessel is torn," the cardiologist stated with a rising inflection in his voice.

At that moment, the staff doctor entered the examination room, donning a gown and gloves. Her patient's grip on her hand tightened as he asked what was happening.

The cardiologist explained there appeared to be a tear in the main artery near the point where the catheter entered it.

The primary physician ordered the patient placed on a bypass machine, while demanding that an operating room be cleared for immediate use. He also noted the need for the cardiac staff surgeon immediately.

Holding on to "Andy's" hand, Dr. Amatuzio reassured him as best she could, given the gravity of the situation. "I promise, I won't leave your side," she added.

Her patient paused, looking at her. "I'm scared, but I'm going to get through this," he told her.

She agreed and he said, "One more thing, Doc. Do me a favor?"

She agreed and he whispered, "Tell my wife that I love her with all my heart."

She promised and his grip loosened as high-powered anesthetics began working to relax and prepare him for cardiac surgery.

A few minutes passed as the team prepared to transfer the patient to the bypass machine, which would take over cardiac function and possibly reduce stress at the damaged site.

The beeping of the heart monitor suddenly changed to an arrhythmic beat that indicated ventricular defibrillation, a life-threatening situation that could possibly be corrected by shocking the heart. The paddles were applied and the charge surged through the chest without effect. A second charge was administered and normal rhythm was reestablished as the staff crowded the scene with renewed intensity as they prepared to transfer his cardiac function to the bypass pump.

Amidst the activity, Dr. Amatuzio was pushed to the edge of the room. Silently, she assured Andy, "I'm right here. I'm not leaving," while also whispering a prayer.

At that moment, she says, "All of a sudden, something happened. I saw, or more accurately, felt a shimmer of light in the corner of the room above the foot of the table. I quickly looked to see if the pump team was using a lighting device that perhaps reflected off the wall – nothing. I looked again, somewhat puzzled, and had the profound sense of a deep, calm presence in contrast to the frantic activity in the room. As I stared at the glimmer in the corner, an odd thought formed in my mind. 'He's watching and he's fine!'"

But the strong presence made her wonder as she again sensed the specter. "Can't anyone else see that? Am I losing my mind?"

At that moment, the anesthesiologist announced that Andy's pulse and blood pressure were gone. "We've lost him," he stated.

Cardiopulmonary resuscitation was ordered and a moment later the bypass pump began to substitute for his cardiac function. As the frantic team prepared to move the patient to the operating room, the chief physician ordered Dr. Amatuzio, the smallest

person in the room, to ride on the cart and administer one chest compression per minute during the interim.

Once in the operating room, they began repair surgery, but it was too late for Andy. The sac around the heart had filled with the leaking blood, damaging the muscle beyond repair. He slipped away from the team of skilled medical people there on the table.

It now fell to the doctors to meet with the widow to offer what comfort they could and answer any questions she might have. The cardiac surgeon went first, explaining that everything that could have been done was tried, but that the surgical team had been unable to save her husband. The widow began weeping and Dr. Amatuzio sat down beside her. The surgeon asked if she had any questions and she replied that she couldn't think of anything.

Assuring the surgeon that she would stay with Mrs. Nelson, Dr. Amatuzio turned to her after the other doctor left, asking, "Do you have anyone to be with you?"

"Yes. My sister is on her way," a weeping Mrs. Nelson responded, hesitantly adding, "Were you with him?"

"Yes. I never left his side," Dr. Amatuzio stated, adding that she had held his hands, performed CPR on the ride to the operating room and was part of the crew that worked frantically to save him.

Looking back at the events prior to Andy's death, Dr. Amatuzio said, "Before we went into surgery, when we knew something had gone wrong, he asked me to tell you something."

Expectantly, the young widow said, "Yes?"

"Your husband asked me to tell you that he loves you with all his heart."

"When did he say that?"

"Just before they put him under for the surgery."

"I'm still so shocked," the widow said. "He was so smart and so sure that this would go well. He told me not to worry, because he would be watching and would be fine."

Dr. Amatuzio says in her remembrance of the events, "Two things happened simultaneously. I felt a shiver go down my back as I remembered my experience of his peaceful presence in the catheter lab. Then the door to the waiting room suddenly burst open as her sister and family arrived."

As she walked away, Dr. Amatuzio recalls thinking, "Maybe he really was watching. Maybe that was the calm, peaceful presence I sensed before we took him into surgery."[6]

It would be years and numerous incidents involving the mystery of death and near death before this rational person of science could make sense of the flash of insight she experienced that afternoon.

Years later, during the winter of 1994, she encountered another psychic event that she was unable to explain at the time, but which she viewed as pivotal in her acceptance of the unknown.

Police officers in Coon Rapids discovered the tracks of a car leading off the roadway and into a frozen creek bed. The car was overturned with the engine running and the driver was slumped over with head injuries. It was 4:45 a.m. and the police call for an ambulance was answered shortly, with the injured driver being rushed to the hospital, where the 26-year-old victim was diagnosed with massive head trauma.

Despite the best of treatment, the young driver was declared brain dead after a couple of hours and his recent bride was notified. Since the death was due to trauma, a coroner's investigation was indicated and Dr. Amatuzio was notified.

In conferring with the attending physician, she was told that the family wanted to donate the victim's organs for transplants. Dr. Amatuzio told the doctor she would approve organ removal, so long as it did not interfere with her investigation.

"Do you see any evidence of injury to the chest or abdomen?" she asked the attending doctor.

"It appears to be all head injury," he responded. "The chest and abdominal scans read as clear with no sign of internal injury."

Nodding, Dr. Amatuzio agreed to approve donation of the organs before proceeding with her postmortem examination.

Later that afternoon, after finishing her hospital duties, she was hurrying through an underground tunnel to reach her office when the hospital chaplain stopped her. Looking concerned, he exclaimed, "I have to talk with your about the fatality in the emergency room."

She assured him, "I spoke with the attending physician and okayed the tissue and organ donation prior to the autopsy."

"That's not what I wanted to talk with you about," the chaplain said. "You're not going to believe this."

Unlocking her office door, she escorted him into her cubicle as he asked, "Do you know how the body was found?"

"Yes, by the police department in a frozen creek bed at about 4:45 a.m."

"No," he responded. "Do you know how they really found him?"

She waited as he carefully chose his words before continuing. "I spoke with his wife and she said something that really stopped me."

Pausing, he assured himself that he had her full attention, then stated, "She told me that at about 4:20 a.m. she had a dream, a profound dream in which her husband was standing by her bedside apologizing and telling her that he loved her. He said that he had been in an accident and his vehicle was in a ditch where it couldn't be seen from the road. She abruptly awoke, called the Coon Rapids Police and with certainty told them her husband was in an accident not far from their home and that his car was in a ravine where he could not be seen from the road. His body was discovered by the officers less than 20 minutes later."

Saying she felt a chill run down her spine, Dr. Amatuzio said, "Let me call the police," dialing the number. The desk sergeant confirmed with his dispatcher the time of the wife's call and the content of it.

After hanging up and turning back to the chaplain, Dr. Amatuzio pronounced, "Amazing. Did she say anything else?"

"Yes, she told me that it didn't really seem like a dream – he was really standing there next to the bed."[7]

Recognizing that the wife's statement rang so true that it created nearly an epiphany for her, Dr. Amatuzio credits the incident with spurring a new awareness of the great mysteries that are associated with death and the afterlife.

Concluding her thoughts on the subject, Dr. Amatuzio says, "Although I still document the 'body of evidence,' I have become fascinated with the essence of what has left. For a scientist and physician, the problem is that this area of study isn't precise. It can't be measured or photographed, and people's experiences around death can't be proven beyond a reasonable degree of medical certainty. Studying death has required me to take a leap – a huge leap professionally – from my mind to my heart. And in doing so, I've remembered that what is most meaningful often cannot be measured, and that everything that counts cannot be counted.

"The search has led me on an unexpected journey, and I have encountered some treasures along the way. I have grown much more aware of the Divine Presence in the universe than I ever imagined I would be. I remember more often to see magic unfolding in my life. I have begun to trust that I am never alone. I have come to believe that our loved ones are truly forever ours."

Thus, while she began documenting the stories she had collected as a benefit or comfort to others, her effort led to a much deeper understanding of her own mortality – and that of all mankind.

And if we ponder for a moment, perhaps that inner knowledge and serenity is what others who are involved in paranormal, psychic or mystical studies are also seeking and come to accept in their activities.

Epilogue

Having arrived at the end of this volume of paranormal activities in the Land of Sky Blue Waters, I fully understand that most folks spending their hard-earned money on a book of ghost stories wouldn't be particularly happy to find the end of the book outlining spirits of a decidedly kindly nature, so I've reserved one final story of a particularly unsavory spirit that Brian Leffler and the Northern Minnesota Paranormal Investigators group recently discovered while investigating a haunting of a rental home in Cohasset, just west of Grand Rapids in north central Minnesota.

As Brian tells the story, "A young couple lived in the house with what we discovered to be five different spirits and we also learned that it was the site of tragedy at some point in the past. We believe that a mother and her two children were brutally murdered in the basement of the house."

Saying that, as the investigators sifted through the evidence that they collected at the house, they came to believe that one of the spirits was extremely sinister and had been the mother's uncle. It was he who killed her, her 12-year-old son and 8-year-old daughter with an axe, possibly abetted by his brother, who accompanied him at the scene.

Using a variety of paranormal research devices, including Electronic Voice Phenomenon (EVP) equipment that proved to be especially valuable in this investigation, the team managed to collect a number of recordings of both the murderer's brother and the victims. They also managed to get a few spectral pictures.

Brian indicates that while communicating with the murderer's brother, he told the spirits that they will be forever "bound" to the property because of the ghastly nature of their activities there. Reportedly, the brother replied on the recording, "We are bound. We are not going anywhere."

Despite his apparent willingness to communicate with the investigators, the brother regrettably did not divulge a motive for the murder of the woman and her children.

The emotional aspect of paranormal investigations that his title alludes to was found by Brian in the EVP recordings of the victims. In one EVP obtained in the dining room, Brian says that the little girl plaintively asked, "Mother, can we eat?" In another they obtained on a later trip to the property, they recorded the girl saying, "Hey, I feel like playing."

Brian says such evidence always gives him pause, nagging because it reminds him that the spirit was once a real person with real emotions and needs. One cannot but wonder what the person's life was like, he intimates.

Getting back to this Cohasset haunting, Brian writes that the murderous uncle would not enter the house, likely the result of severe guilt, perhaps even a feeling of remorse over the murderous activity he indulged in there. He also did not provide any EVP evidence that they identified, despite his brother being quite communicative and vocal. After their initial investigation inside the house, the investigators reported encountering an increasing sense of dread as they moved outside into the province of the uncle, while also experiencing a sense that he hovered about them, "constantly on top of us while we were there."

Saying their first trip produced the most telling evidence, Brian states that the couple inhabiting the house chose not to have his team attempt a "cleaning" of the three innocent spirits from the home. The team did reveal to the couple all that they had come to know of the haunting and the several spirits on the property.

"Later, I think they became emotional about the children and mother and they finally agreed with my thought that the mother and children should move on to the other side and leave the scene of this horrible tragedy."

Upon the couple's request for a "cleaning," the Northern Minnesota Paranormal Investigators returned to Cohasset, collecting more evidence before beginning their cleaning ritual. This was when the EVP of the girl wanting to play was collected and the team also gathered a recording that was particularly compelling and striking to Brian.

As he tells it, "When the cleaning ritual started, we still kept the tape recorder going and collected the mother telling her son, 'David, go into the light.' It was strange to hear that for the first time in my experience. Not only does it confirm that there is some kind of light involved in crossing over to the other side, but there must be a comfort in it also. I can't imagine that a mother would calmly tell her son to go into the light unless she was confident that it was a good thing to accomplish."

Brian concludes this story by stressing that the emotions of investigators at the scene of a paranormal occurrence are often intense, but ought to allow for the same compassion, perhaps even reverence, for the spirits as one would elicit for the person while they were living.[1]

He does not intimate what the reaction should be to spirits like the murderous uncle and his apparently complicit brother, who in any case are reportedly condemned to spend eternity on the scene of their villainous activity. Certainly, such sinister spirits must be a source of revilement for spiritual investigators, yet are also obviously a concern to them, since they reported an increasing sense of dread as they entered the outdoor realm inhabited by the spirit of the uncle.

Does the fact that the sinister spirit did not create mayhem for the investigators mean that he lacked the power to have any influence over their activities? Might his murderous inclinations have been blunted by some higher power before his spirit was condemned to its perdition?

We are given no clues to help answer our questions, and the nature of hauntings and paranormal incidents is such that they more often raise questions than answer them.

Perhaps that is the reason that so many ghostly stories exist and pass down from generation to generation. We can, perhaps, experience the supernatural, while failing to gain an understanding or final resolution of such events.

Thus, books of this nature will continue to be published and will continue to find readers who seek answers about the supernatural or paranormal realm.

Hope you've enjoyed this read and – brrrr. That really was an unbearably cold spot that just passed by!

Endnotes

INTRODUCTION

[1]Bill Buzenberg, "Mr. Foshay's Tower," Minnesota Public Radio, February 1, 2000, as found at www.news.minnesota.publicradio.org/features/200001.31.

CHAPTER 1

[1]Johann Georg Kohl, *Kitchi-Gami: Life Among the Lake Superior Ojibway*, Minnesota Historical Society Press, St. Paul, Minnesota, 1885, (1985 reprint), pp. 356-365.

[2]*History of Stearns County*, St. Cloud, Minnesota, 1915, Volume 1 Chapter 32, as quoted at www.stcloudlinks.com/StCloudCyclone.htm.

[3]"Famous Minnesota Winter Storms," Climatology Working Group, December 10, 2001, climate.umn.edu/doc/historical/winter_storms.htm.

[4]Ruth D. Hein, *More Ghostly Tales from Minnesota*, North Star Press of St. Cloud Inc., St. Cloud, Minnesota, 1999, pp. 92-94, but first reported by A.P. Miller in the *Worthington Advance* newspaper of January 13, 1881.

[5]Gina Teel, *Ghost Stories of Minnesota*, Ghost House Books, Edmonton, Alberta, 2001, pp. 189-190.

CHAPTER 2

[1]Ruth D. Hein, *More Ghostly Tales from Minnesota*, North Star Press of St. Cloud Inc., St. Cloud, Minnesota, 1999, pp. 42-44.

[2]Troy Taylor, "Ghosts of the Prairie, The Guthrie Theater," 1998. The tale of the Guthrie Theater ghost can be found on virtually every Website dealing with Minnesota ghosts, but I credit Troy Taylor's www.prairieghosts.com/guthrie.html here because I have found this writer to be very reliable in past research projects.

[3]Gina Teel, *Ghost Stories of Minnesota*, Ghost House Books, Edmonton, Alberta, 2001, pp. 63-64.

[4]Northern Minnesota Paranormal Investigators, www.nmpi-scary.com.

[5]Kelly Grinsteinner, "Students meet to remember fallen classmate," *Hibbing Daily Tribune*, Jan. 25, 2005.

[6]www.kstp.com/article/stories/s3571.html.

[7]*Ibid.*

[8]Hugh E. Bishop, *Haunted Lake Superior*, Lake Superior Port Cities Inc., 2003, pp. 145-146. For incisive documentation of the Glensheen murders, trials and subsequent events, see Sharon Darby Hendry's *Glensheen's Daughter*, Cable Publishing, Bloomington, Minnesota, 1999, and *Will to Murder*, X-Communications, Duluth, Minnesota, 2004, by Gail Feichtinger in collaboration with prosecutor John Desanto and chief investigator Gary Waller.

[9]Bishop, *Haunted Lake Superior*, pp. 81-85.

[10]Thayer's Historic Bed-and-Breakfast Inn, www.thayers.net.

[11]www.kstp.com/article/stories/s3571.html.

[12]Taylor, "Ghosts of the Prairie, Forepaugh's Restaurant," 1998, found at www.prairieghosts.com/forep.html.

[13]"The History of Forepaugh's," www.forepaughs.com/history.html.

[14]Gina Teel, "Benchwarmer Bob's," *Ghost Stories of Minnesota*, Ghost House Books, Edmonton, Alberta, 2001, pp. 84-85.

[15]Hein, *More Ghostly Tales from Minnesota*, pp. 92-94.

[16]Don Boxmeyer, "Gangster still haunts St. Paul," *St. Paul Pioneer Press*, August 15, 2001, but Hamm family history synopsized from www.mbaa.com/Districts/StPaulMpls/pdfs/DistrictHistory.pdf.

[17]Minnesota Paranormal Investigators, "Investigation: Haunted Minnesota," www.minnesotaparanormalinvestigators.com/hauntedmn1.htm.

[18]Jake Erickson, "'Ghost File' documents unexplained phenomena on campus," *St. Olaf News*, October 21, 2003.

[19]Bishop, *Haunted Lake Superior*, pp.158-159, with 2005 update from author interview with Marie Mueller, director of Cross River Heritage Center.

[20]Hein, *More Ghostly Tales from Minnesota*, pp. 1-4.

[21]Author telephone interview with John Savage of Minnesota Paranormal Investigators Group, July 21, 2005.

[22]"The Ghost of Heffron Hall." This story appears in nearly all books on ghosts as well as on virtually every Website dealing with the supernatural, however the most journalistically complete and objective reports are by Patrick Marek of the *Winona Post*, and can be found at www.winonapost.com/stock/functions/VDG_Pub/display.php?CatNavClicked=71&expand=minus.

[23]Don Boxmeyer, "Glancey's Gym, St. Paul, MN," *St. Paul Pioneer Press*, May 14, 1996, as found www.ghosts.org/glanceysgym.html.

[24]Mike Mosedale, "The Ghost of Clyde Mudgett," *City Pages*, October 25, 2000, as found at www.citypages.com/databank/21/1038/article9082.asp.

[25]Author personal interview with Brian Leffler, November 21, 2005.

[26]Teel, *Ghost Stories of Minnesota*, pp.101-105. Hauntings of the Wabasha Caves are also widely reported at numerous Website listings.

[27]Janisch, Kris, "An overpopulated ghost town: Stillwater continues to preserve its paranormal stories," *Stillwater Gazette*, October 14, 2005.

[28]Erin Adler and Keri Carlson, "School spirits," *Minnesota Daily*, Minneapolis, Minnesota, October 27, 2005.

[29]Judge Bert Feeler, "Reminiscences of Col. Colvill," as found at www.gdg.org/Research/OOB/Union/July1-3/wcolvill.html.

[30]Logan family oral history, but confirmed by searching "Logan, John D." at FirstMN.phpwebhosting.com.

[1] Taylor, "Ghosts of the Prairie, St. John's University," 1998, found at www.prairieghosts.com/stjohn.html.

[2] Rurik Hover, "Ghosts in the Granite City," *Graffitos*, St. Cloud, Minnesota, October 31, 1991, p. 4, Feature Section.

[3] Connie Nelson, Home and Garden Section, Minneapolis *Star Tribune*, October 31, 2002.

[4] Celia Tarnowski, "Haunted Homes with History," *The Reader of Duluth/Superior*, October 1997, p. 18.

[5] The bulk of material in the Griggs Mansion story comes from the Minnesota Paranormal Investigative Group's report as found at www.geocities.com/area51/rampart/9114/griggs.html, but this story is ubiquitous on Websites devoted to paranormal events.

[6] Taylor, "Ghosts of the Prairie, The Jensen House," 1999, found at www.prairieghosts.com/jensen.html.

[7] Hugh E. Bishop, *Haunted Lake Superior*, Lake Superior Port Cities Inc., 2003, pp. 132-134.

[8] The fragmentary reports in the previous several paragraphs come from various locations after searching "Haunted Minnesota colleges" on the Web. Some are also recorded in Ruth D. Hein's *Ghostly Tales of Minnesota* and *More Ghostly Tales from Minnesota*, as well as Gina Teel's *Ghost Stories of Minnesota*.

[9] Eugene Tucker, "Is South Campus Haunted?," *The Aquin* newspaper, November 1, 2002, p. 11.

[10] Taylor, "Ghosts of the Prairie, The William Hamm House," 1999, found at www.prairieghosts.com/hamm.html.

[11] Laurie Hertzel, "Ghost Stories People Believe," *Duluth News Tribune*, October 29, 1989, Section E.

[12] Ruth D. Hein, *Ghostly Tales of Minnesota*, 1992, Adventure Publications Inc., Cambridge, Minnesota, pp. 107-113.

[13] Bishop, *Haunted Lake Superior*, pp. 144-145.

[14] Reports of the Northern Minnesota Paranormal Investigators, as found at www.ghostvillage.com archives. Photographic images of some phenomena can also be found at www.nmpi-scary.com, the homepage of the organization. In the introduction to this book, I warn of placing too much trust in Website information, but I find the Ghost Village site particularly interesting because the reports are all in the first person, often identify the reporter, are dated and every sign is that the reporters sincerely believe their stories.

[15] Hein, *More Ghostly Tales from Minnesota*, pp. 148-149.

[16] Author conversation with anonymous sources, September 21, 2005.

[17] Anonymous, "Knocks, Shadows and Apparitions," GhostVillage.com, September 5, 2005, at www.ghostvillage.com/encounters/2005/09052005.shtml.

[18] Author telephone interview with anonymous source, September 30, 2005.

[19] Ellen Tomson, "Home eek! Home: a local ghost story," *Pioneer Press*, St. Paul, Minnesota, October 30, 2005. Also see Annie Wilder's personal account, "Ghost House Stories," October 10, 2005, at www.llewellynjournal.com/article/949.

[20] Mikki Eken, "Ghosts haunt campus: Dolly, the ghost of Fjelstad Hall," *The Concordian*, October 29, 2004, found at www.cord.edu/dept/concord/issues/2004-10-29/features.html.

[21] *Ibid.*, subheads "Hoyum and Brown Halls" and "Old Main."

[22] Bishop, *Haunted Lake Superior*, pp. 135-136, originally noted as "Author interview with anonymous source, spring 2002."

[23] *Ibid.*, pp. 136-137.

CHAPTER 4

[1]Hugh E. Bishop, *Haunted Lake Superior*, Lake Superior Port Cities Inc., 2003, pp. 131-132.

[2]*Ibid.*, pp. 134-135.

[3]Gina Teel, *Ghost Stories of Minnesota*, Ghost House Books, Edmonton, Alberta, 2001, pp. 199-204, but also found on a number of Websites, notably Troy Taylor, "Annie Mary's Grave," 1998, at www.prairieghosts.com/annie.html.

[4]Hertzel, "Ghost Stories People Believe," *Duluth News Tribune*, October 29, 1989, Section E.

[5]Ruth D. Hein, *Ghostly Tales of Minnesota*, 1992, Adventure Publications Inc., Cambridge, Minnesota, pp. 19-22.

[6]Taylor, "Deadman's Hill," 1998, as found at www.prairieghosts.com/deadman.html.

[7]Frederick Stonehouse, *Haunted Lakes*, Lake Superior Port Cities Inc., Duluth, Minnesota, 1997, pp. 74-75.

[8]Julius F. Wolff Jr., *Lake Superior Shipwrecks*, Lake Superior Port Cities Inc., Duluth, Minnesota, 1990, p. 98.

[9]Bishop, *Haunted Lake Superior*, pp. 54-55.

[10]Dixie Franklin, "Captain Jimmy Hobaugh – A Profile", *Lake Superior Magazine*, Duluth, Minnesota, June/July 1998, pp. 38-42.

[11]*Op. cit.*, Stonehouse, *Haunted Lakes*, p. 110, and *Haunted Lakes II* p. 60.

[12]Bishop, *Haunted Lake Superior*, pp. 61-62.

[13]Bishop, personal conversation with *Blough* crewman, July 2003.

[14]The story of the Milford Mine disaster is almost ubiquitous, being found on numerous Websites (for the best of them check Troy Taylor's www.prairieghosts.com/mine.html or www.brainerdham.org/2003/12-6-03-special-event.html). Gina Teel's *Ghost Stories of Minnesota* also has a good account of the disaster and the ghost of Clinton Harris.

[15]This story is also found at a number of Websites and is recorded as "Soldier Spirits" in Teel's book, p. 105.

[16]Author conversation with John Savage of the Minnesota Paranormal Investigative Group (MNPIG), July 21, 2005.

[17]Author interview with Bill Meierhoff, December 21, 2005, and personal stories by employees of Lake Superior Port Cities Inc.

[18]Interview with Bill Meierhoff, January 2006.

CHAPTER 5

[1]Hugh E. Bishop, *Haunted Lake Superior*, Lake Superior Port Cities Inc., 2003, pp.10-11.

[2]A.J. Davis (editor), *History of Clarion County, Pennsylvania*, 1887, p. 57.

[3]As noted in text, *St. Paul Pioneer Press* of June 29, 1888, tells of Clearwater discovery and *St. Paul Globe* of August 12, 1896, revealed the Paynesville skeleton. See also the Paynesville Area Historical Society account at www.paynesvillearea.com/community/histsociety/mounds071702.html.

[4]As noted in text, this report is found in the *St. Paul Globe* of May 23, 1883, but is also nearly ubiquitous on the Internet.

[5]Johann Georg Kohl, *Kitchi-Gami: Life Among the Lake Superior Ojibway*, Minnesota Historical Society Press, St. Paul, Minnesota, 1885, (1985 reprint), pp. 356-365.

[6]Taylor, "Ghosts of the Prairie, The Wendigo," 2002, found at www.prairieghosts.com/wendigo.html.

[7]Gayle Highpine, "Traditional Attitudes Toward Bigfoot in Many North American Cultures," *The Track Record*, #18, July 1992, as found at www.bfro.net/legends.

[8]The previous four reports of Bigfoot encounters can be found at the Bigfoot Field Researchers Organization site at www.bfro.net by clicking United States on the map and following the Minnesota link.

[9]Keith McCafferty, "Bigfoot May Exist," *Field and Stream Magazine*, January 2000.

[10]Stefan Lovgren, "Forensic Expert Says Bigfoot is Real," *National Geographic News,* October 23, 2003.

[11]Minnesota Historical Society site under Minnesota Forest History Center, but also found on many sites by searching the Internet for "Agropelter."

[12]"Creature sighted twice by three men while camping in northern Minn.," Bigfoot Field Researchers Organization, October 19, 2001, at www.bfro.net/GDB/show_report.asp?id=3227.

[13]The Virtually Strange Network, UFO Updates. Found at www.virtuallystrange.net/ufo/updates/2005/mar/m23.008.shtml.

[14]Bishop, *Haunted Lake Superior*, pp. 102-105.

[15]*Ibid.*, pp. 100-102, but also ubiquitous on the Internet by searching Sanderson, *Argosy*, Iceman.

[16]D. Parvaz, "For Sasquatch Believers There's No Turning Back," *Seattle Post-Intelligencier,* September 28, 1999, found at www.geocities.com/area51/shadowlands/6583/cattle042.html.

CHAPTER 6

[1]Chuck Frederick, "Visitors from the Beyond," *Duluth News Tribune*, Duluth, Minnesota, July 31, 2002.

[2]"The Bluebook 'Unknowns,'" National Investigations Committee on Aerial Phenomena, November 24, 1951, found at www.nicap.org/bluebook/unknowns.htm. Also ubiquitous on the Web.

[3]Jay Rath, "Land of 10,000 Flying Saucers," *The M-Files: True Reports of Minnesota's Unexplained Phenomena*, Wisconsin Tales and Trails, Madison, Wisconsin, pp. 34-51.

[4]Chris Rutkowski, *The Swamp Gas Journal,* April 1980, found at www.geocities.com/Athens/Delphi/7998/sgj1no7.txt.

[5]Ruth D. Hein, *Ghostly Tales of Minnesota*, 1992, Adventure Publications Inc., Cambridge, Minnesota, pp. 73-74.

[6]Hugh E. Bishop, *Haunted Lake Superior*, Lake Superior Port Cities Inc., 2003, pp. 109-112.

[7]Author personal telephone interview with anonymous caller, approximately July/August 2003.

[8]The stories in the above section were all found at www.bobpratt.org. Bob passed away November 21, 2005, and the Website is no longer in operation. Some files are at www.mnmufon.com/bobpratt_frame.htm.

[9]Bishop, *Haunted Lake Superior*, pp. 112-113.

[10]Rath, *The M-Files: True Reports of Minnesota's Unexplained Phenomena,* pp. 52-54.

[11]*Ibid.* pp. 55-58.

[12]*Ibid.*, p. 46.

[13]Mark Rodeghier, "UFO Reports Involving Vehicle Interference, A Catalogue and Data Analysis," Center for UFO Studies, 1981. Most easily accessed at www.scientificexploration.org/jse/articles/ufo_reports/rodeghier/2.html.

[14]The bulk of this report comes from www.zetatalk.com/the word, with additional material from several other of the more credible Websites.

[15]The two crop circle reports are found at www.mnmufon.org/cc1.htm. The Website of the Minnesota Mutual UFO Network *Journal*, from which these stories are taken is

www.mnmufon.org, but is somewhat dated. Those who are more than casually interested in UFOs may also want to log on to www.mnmufon.org/mmjpdf.htm for a complete electronic file of the organization's newsletter going back to 1999, which includes some investigative reports on the incidents cited.

[16]Greg Moynaugh, "Crop circles attract attention," *South Washington County Bulletin*, Cottage Grove, Minnesota, August 9, 2004.

[16]The previous two reports of investigations of abductions is found at www.mnmufon.org/abdinv.htm#smp.

CHAPTER 7

[1]Hugh E. Bishop, *Haunted Lake Superior*, Lake Superior Port Cities Inc., 2003, pp. 147-150.

[2]*Ibid.*, pp. 152-156.

[3]Ruth D. Hein, *More Ghostly Tales from Minnesota*, North Star Press of St. Cloud Inc., St. Cloud, Minnesota, 1999, pp. 85-87.

[4]Siiri Branstrom, December 2005, e-mail account to author.

[5]Hein, *More Ghostly Tales from Minnesota*, pp. 85-87.

[6]Mary, "Spirits Magnet," GhostVillage.com, November 4, 2003, found at www.ghostvillage.com/encounters/2003/11042003.shtml.

[7]M.J. Downs, "Mom's Visit and the Smell of Gardenias," Ghost,Village,com, May 11, 2003, found at www.ghostvillage.com/encounters/2003/10172003.shtml

[8]Dan Gunderson, Tom Robertson, "The spirits spoke to him," Minnesota Public Radio, August 20, 2003.

[9]Hein, *Ghostly Tales of Minnesota*, pp. 55-57.

[10]*Ibid.*, pp. 157.

[11]Reverend Linda C. Loving, "Angels we have heard," December 12, 2004, in her final sermon preached as pastor at House of Hope Presbyterian Church, St. Paul, Minnesota, found at www.hohchurch.org/pdf/2004/sermon_121204.pdf.

[12]Bodine, Echo, "Introduction," *Echoes of the Soul*, New World Library, Novato, California, 1999.

[13]Personal interview with anonymous source, March 2002.

[14]The story of Father Francis Pierz's momentous cross can be found at the Diocese of Crookston Website, www.crookston.org/redlake/missionbeginnings.htm.

CHAPTER 8

[1]Author interview with Echo Bodine, August 31, 2005.

[2]Richard Chin, "The Ghost Hunters in Stillwater," *Pioneer Press*, St. Paul, Minnesota, October 31, 2004.

[3]Author communication with Echo Bodine, November 9, 2005.

[4]"Ghost Hunters in Stillwater," Chris Toney Website, found at www.christoney.org/blog/2004/10/ghost-hunters-in-stillwater#comments.

[5]Author interview with Brian Leffler, November 21, 2005.

[6]Janis Amatuzio M.D., "With All My Heart," *Forever Ours: Real Stories of Immortality and Living from a Forensic Pathologist*, New World Library, Novato, California, 2003.

[7]*Ibid.*, "What Really Happened."

EPILOGUE

[1]Brian Leffler, "Emotions of the Paranormal," GhostVillage.com, March, 16, 2005, as found at www.ghostvillage.com/resources/2005/resources_05132005.shtml.

Bibliography

BOOKS

History of Stearns County. St. Cloud, Minnesota: 1915.

Bishop, Hugh E. *Haunted Lake Superior*. Duluth, Minnesota: Lake Superior Port Cities Inc., 2003.

Bishop, Hugh E. *The Night the Fitz Went Down*. Duluth, Minnesota: Lake Superior Port Cities Inc., 2000.

Bodine, Echo. *Echoes of the Soul*. Novato, California: New World Library, 1999.

Davis, A.J. (editor). *History of Clarion County, Pennsylvania*. Syracuse, New York: D. Mason & Co. 1887.

Eastman, Charles A. *Soul of the Indian*. Lincoln, Nebraska: University of Nebraska Press, 1980 (reprint).

Hein, Ruth D. *Ghostly Tales of Minnesota* Cambridge, Minnesota: Adventure Publications Inc., 1992.

Hein, Ruth D. *More Ghostly Tales from Minnesota* St. Cloud, Minnesota: North Star Press of St. Cloud Inc., 1999.

Kohl, Johann Georg *Kitchi-Gami: Life Among the Lake Superior Ojibway*. St. Paul, Minnesota: Minnesota Historical Society Press, 1885, 1985 (reprint).

Miller, David Reed. *Encyclopedia of North American Indians*. New York, New York: Houghton Mifflin Company, 1996.

Rath, Jay. *The M-Files: True Reports of Minnesota's Unexplained Phenomena*, Madison, Wisconsin: Wisconsin Tales and Trails, 1998.

Stonehouse, Frederick. *Haunted Lakes*. Duluth, Minnesota: Lake Superior Port Cities Inc., 1997.

Teel, Gina. *Ghost Stories of Minnesota* Edmonton, Alberta: Ghost House Books, 2001.

Wolff Jr., Julius F. *Lake Superior Shipwrecks*. Duluth, Minnesota: Lake Superior Port Cities Inc., Duluth, Minnesota, 1990.

PERIODICALS AND OTHER ARTICLES

Adler, Erin, and Carlson, Keri. "School spirits." *Minnesota Daily*, October 27, 2005.

Boxmeyer, Don. "Gangster still haunts St. Paul." *St. Paul Pioneer Press*, August 15, 2001.

Boxmeyer, Don. "Glancey's Gym, St. Paul, MN." *St. Paul Pioneer Press*, May 14, 1996.

Chin, Richard. "The Ghost Hunters in Stillwater." *Pioneer Press*, October 31, 2004.

Clearwater giant humanoid discovery. *St. Paul Pioneer Press*, June 29, 1888.

Eken, Mikki. "Ghosts Haunt Campus/Dolly, the ghost of Fjelstad Hall." *The Concordian*, October 29, 2004.

Erickson, Jake. "'Ghost File' documents unexplained phenomena on campus." *St. Olaf News,* October 21, 2003.

Frederick, Chuck. "Visitors from the Beyond." *Duluth News Tribune*, July 31, 2002.

Grinsteinner, Kelly. "Students meet to remember fallen classmate." *Hibbing Daily Tribune*, Jan. 25, 2005.

Hertzel, Laurie. "Ghost Stories People Believe." *Duluth News Tribune*, October 29, 1989.

Janisch, Kris. "An overpopulated ghost town: Stillwater continues to preserve its paranormal stories." *Stillwater Gazette*, October 14, 2005.

Johnson, Lois E. "Commemorating the 80th Anniversary of the Fires of 1918." *Minnesota History Interpreter*, Minnesota Historical Society, June 1998.

"July 4 Storm Hits Area." *Cook County News-Herald*, July 12, 1999.

Lovgren, Stefan. "Forensic Expert Says Bigfoot is Real." *National Geographic News,* October 23, 2003, Washington, D.C.

Marek, Patrick. "The Ghost of Heffron Hall." *Winona Post*, 2002.

McCafferty, Keith. "Bigfoot May Exist." *Field and Stream Magazine*, January 2000.

Mosedale, Mike. "The Ghost of Clyde Mudgett." *City Pages*, October 25, 2000.

Moynaugh, Greg. "Crop circles attract attention." *South Washington County Bulletin*, August 9, 2004.

Nelson, Connie. Home and Garden Section. Minneapolis *Star Tribune*, October 31, 2002.

Paynesville giant humanoid skeleton. *St. Paul Globe,* August 12, 1896.

Tarnowski, Celia. "Haunted Homes with History." *The Reader of Duluth/Superior*, October 1997.

Tomson, Ellen. "Home eek! Home: a local ghost story." *Pioneer Press*, October 30, 2005.

Warren, Minnesota, report of burial mound containing 10 giant skeletons. *St. Paul Globe,* May 23, 1883.

PUBLIC DOCUMENTS, COLLECTIONS & WEB SEARCHES

"1997 Record Spring Floods." Minnesota Department of Natural Resources.

"Agropelter," the lumberjack Bigfoot. Minnesota Historical Society under Minnesota Forest History Center (www.mnhs.com), but also many other sites.

Amatuzio, Janis, M.D. "With All My Heart." "What Really Happened." *Forever Ours: Real Stories of Immortality and Living from a Forensic Pathologist*. Novato, California: New World Library, 2003.

Buzenberg, Bill. "Mr. Foshay's Tower." Minnesota Public Radio, February 1, 2000.

Cattle mutilation reports found at www.zetatalk.com/the word and other sites.

"A Dakota Legend of Creation." Marvin, South Dakota: American Indian Culture Research Center, Blue Cloud Benedictine Abbey.

"Famous Minnesota Winter Storms." Climatology Working Group, University of Minnesota.

Feeler, Judge Bert. "Reminiscences of Col. Colvill." Gettysburg Discussion Group.

"Fire in the Forest." National Park Service.

Gunderson, Dan, Robertson,Tom, "The spirits spoke to him." Minnesota Public Radio, 2003.

Highpine, Gayle. "Traditional Attitudes Toward Bigfoot in Many North American Cultures." Bigfoot Field Researchers Organization, June 18, 2000.

"Ho-Chunk Nation, A Brief History." Ho-chunknation.com.

"Knocks, Shadows and Apparitions." Ghostvillage.com, September 5, 2005.

Leffler, Brian. "Emotions of the Paranormal." Ghostvillage.com, March 16, 2005.

Logan family oral history. First Minnesota Volunteer Infantry Regiment Website.

Loving, Reverend Linda C. "Angels we have heard." Sermon, December 12, 2004.

Milford Mine disaster. Ubiquitous, being found on numerous Websites.

Miller, David Reed. "Eastman, Charles (Ohiyesa)." *Encyclopedia of North American Indians*, Houghton Mifflin Company, 1996.

Minnesota UFO Network Website.

Northern Minnesota Paranormal Investigators reports. Ghostvillage.com.

Pafko, Wayne. "History of James Root." Minnesota Heroes Website.

Parker, Mrs. Z.A. "The Ghost Dance among the Lakota." Public Broadcasting Services Website.

Pierz, Father Francis. Narration of seeing a miraculous cross of light. Diocese of Crookston Website.

Rodeghier, Mark. "UFO Reports Involving Vehicle Interference, A Catalogue and Data Analysis." Center for UFO Studies, 1981.

"Sioux Religion." St. Martin's College, Division of Religion and Philosophy.

"Some Noted Tornados from Minnesota History." Climatology Working Group, University of Minnesota.

"Wakan." Sword (a Sioux wise man), translated by Burt Means. sacred-texts.com.

Taylor, Troy. "The Guthrie Theater." Ghosts of the Prairie, 1998.

Thayer's Inn haunting tales are found at www.thayers.net.

Pratt, Bob. A sizable collection of UFO stories, collected over more than 20 years at www.bobpratt.org.

"White Buffalo." *Share International Magazine*, September 1996.

Wilder, Annie. "Ghost House Stories." The Llewellyn Journal, October 10, 2005.

Wovoka and the Ghost Dance. Discussion of the religion and the state of the Sioux people in 1890. Public Broadcasting Service Website.

Zapf, Charles. Untitled manuscript on burial mounds. Paynesville Area Historical Society Website.

Index

193

About the Author

HUGH E. BISHOP

Making his home in Two Harbors, Minnesota, and maintaining an interest in almost everything having to do with the North American mid-continent, Hugh Bishop has been poking stories about the Lake Superior and Minnesota into the back of his mind since 1975. He first encountered the big lake that year as an employee of Erie Mining Company, which

Hugh E. Bishop

had its docks at Taconite Harbor on Minnesota's north shore. Moving to Two Harbors in 1983 gave him much easier access to the stories and the storytellers of the big lake.

Bishop, as senior writer at Lake Superior Port Cities Inc., publisher of the bimonthly *Lake Superior Magazine,* wrote five books, including this current volume. After more than a decade of writing for *Lake Superior Magazine* and being closely associated with producing the annual *Lake Superior Travel Guide,* Bishop retired in 2006. He plans to continue his writing career.

Also from Lake Superior Port Cities Inc